REGIONALISM AND BEYOND

Randall Stewart in 1964, photographed in front of Old Central at Vanderbilt University. Photograph by Hanson Carroll.

REGIONALISM
AND BEYOND ❦

ESSAYS OF RANDALL STEWART

EDITED BY GEORGE CORE

FOREWORD BY NORMAN HOLMES PEARSON

VANDERBILT UNIVERSITY PRESS ∿ *Nashville: 1968*

Printed in the United States of America
by The Parthenon Press, Nashville, Tennessee
Library of Congress Catalogue Card Number 67-20426

RANDALL STEWART: A CHRONOLOGY

1896.	Born in Fayetteville, Tennessee, July 25.
1898.	His family moved to Nashville where he grew up and was educated.
1917.	Was graduated from Vanderbilt University as Founder's Medalist.
1917–1920.	Instructor of English at the University of Oklahoma.
1918.	Served briefly in the armed forces.
1920.	Married Cleone Odell in Oklahoma City.
1921.	Awarded master of arts degree by Harvard University.
1921–1922.	Instructor, U. S. Naval Academy.
1922–1925.	Assistant Professor, University of Idaho.
1927–1931.	Instructor, Yale University.
1930.	Awarded doctor of philosophy degree by Yale.
1931–1934.	Assistant Professor, Yale.
1932–1939.	Associate Editor, *New England Quarterly*.
1934–1937.	Professor, Vanderbilt.
1937–1955.	Professor, Brown University.
1943.	Guggenheim Fellow.
1947–1948.	Visiting Professor, Yale University.
1949–1950.	Chairman, Department of English, Brown.
1949–1950.	Visiting Professor, Connecticut College.
1951.	Chairman, American Literature Group, Modern Language Association.
1955–1963.	Professor of English and Chairman, Department of English, Vanderbilt University.
1956.	Fugitive Reunion.
1958.	Mrs. Harold S. Vanderbilt Literary Symposium established.
1963–1964.	Professor, Vanderbilt.
1964.	Died June 17.

TABLE OF CONTENTS

PART III: SOUTHERN LITERATURE
IN OUTLINE AND PERSPECTIVE

ACKNOWLEDGEMENTS

SPECIAL acknowledgement is made to the following who have granted permission for the reprinting of copyrighted material from the periodicals and books that are listed below:

"Editing *The American Notebooks*" appeared in the Essex Institute *Historical Collections* (July 1958). Reprinted by permission of the Essex Institute.

"The Development of Character Types in Hawthorne's Fiction" and "Recurrent Themes in Hawthorne's Fiction" are Chapters III and IV of the Introduction to Randall Stewart's *The American Notebooks by Nathaniel Hawthorne* (New Haven: Yale University Press, 1932). Reprinted by permission of the Ohio State University Press.

"Hawthorne and *The Faerie Queene*" appeared in the *Philological Quarterly* (April 1933). Reprinted by permission of the Department of Publications, State University of Iowa.

"Hawthorne and the Civil War" appeared in *Studies in Philology* (January 1937). Reprinted by permission of the University of North Carolina Press.

"Melville and Hawthorne" and "The Social School of American Criticism" appeared in the *South Atlantic Quarterly* (July 1952 and January 1944). Reprinted by permission of the Duke University Press.

"Hawthorne and Faulkner," "Regional Characteristics in the Literature of New England," and "Three Views of the Individual as Reflected in American Literature" appeared in *College English* (February 1956, November 1941, and March 1944). Reprinted by permission of the National Council of Teachers of English.

"The Golden Age of Hawthorne Criticism" and "The Moral Aspect of Henry James's 'International Situation' " appeared in *The University Review* (October 1955 and Winter 1943). Reprinted by permission of *The University Review*.

"Moral Crisis as Structural Principle in Fiction: A Few American Examples" appeared in *The Christian Scholar* (December 1959). Reprinted by permission of *The Christian Scholar*.

"The Old Cost of the Human Redemption" is Chapter VI of *American Literature and Christian Doctrine* by Randall Stewart. Copyright 1958 by the Louisiana State University Press. Reprinted by permission of the publisher.

"Tidewater and Frontier" appeared in the *Georgia Review* (Fall 1959). Reprinted by permission of the *Georgia Review*.

"The Relation between Fugitives and Agrarians" appeared in the *Mississippi Quarterly* (Spring 1960). Reprinted by permission of the *Mississippi Quarterly*.

"Donald Davidson" is an essay in *South: Modern Southern Literature in Its Cultural Setting*, edited by Louis D. Rubin, Jr., and Robert D. Jacobs. Copyright © 1961 by Louis D. Rubin, Jr., and Robert D. Jacobs. Reprinted by permission of Doubleday & Company, Inc.

"Outlook for Southern Writing: Diagnosis and Prognosis" appeared in the *Virginia Quarterly Review* (Spring 1955). Reprinted by permission of the *Virginia Quarterly Review*.

After the Lost Generation by John W. Aldridge. Copyright 1951 by McGraw-Hill Book Company. Reprinted by permission of the publisher.

A Progress to the Mines from *The Prose Works of William Byrd of Westover*, edited by Louis B. Wright. Copyright 1966 by the President and Fellows of Harvard College. Reprinted by permission of the Harvard University Press.

Death Comes for the Archbishop by Willa Cather. Copyright 1929 by Willa Cather. Renewed 1956 by Edith Lewis and the City Bank Farmers Trust Co. Reprinted by permission of Alfred A. Knopf, Inc.

"Two Old Wests" from *Attack on Leviathan* by Donald Davidson. Reprinted by permission of the author.

"Lee in the Mountains," "The Sod of the Battle-Fields," "Gradual of the Northern Summer," "Lines Written for Allen Tate on His Sixtieth Anniversary," "The Breaking Mould," "Fire on Belmont Street," and "Epithalamion" from *Poems: 1922–1961* by Donald Davidson. Copyright 1966 by Donald Davidson. Reprinted by permission of the author and the University of Minnesota Press.

"The Deserter: A Christmas Eclogue" and "The Running of Streight" from *Lee in the Mountains and Other Poems Including The*

ACKNOWLEDGEMENTS xi

Tall Men by Donald Davidson. Copyright 1938 by Donald Davidson. Reprinted by permission of the author.

"Why the Modern South Has a Great Literature" from *Still Rebels, Still Yankees and Other Essays* by Donald Davidson. Copyright 1957 by the Louisiana State University Press. Reprinted by permission of the publisher.

"There is no Frigate like a Book," "He ate and drank the precious Words," "Some Keep the Sabbath Going to Church," and "The Robin's my Criterion for Tune" from *The Poems of Emily Dickinson*, edited by Thomas H. Johnson. Copyright 1951, 1955, by the President and Fellows of Harvard College. Reprinted by permission of the Harvard University Press and the Trustees of Amherst College.

After Strange Gods by T. S. Eliot. Copyright 1934 by Harcourt, Brace & World, Inc. Reprinted by permission of Harcourt, Brace & World, Inc. and Faber and Faber, Ltd.

The Waste Land and *Ash Wednesday* from *Collected Poems 1909–1962* by T. S. Eliot. Copyright 1936 by Harcourt, Brace & World, Inc.; copyright © 1963, 1964, by T. S. Eliot. Reprinted by permission of Harcourt, Brace & World, Inc. and Faber and Faber, Ltd.

The Sound and the Fury by William Faulkner. Copyright 1929, 1956, by William Faulkner. "The Bear" from *Go Down, Moses* by William Faulkner. Copyright 1942 by William Faulkner. *Intruder in the Dust* by William Faulkner. Copyright 1948 by William Faulkner. All reprinted by permission of Random House, Inc.

"Good-By and Keep Cold" from *Complete Poems of Robert Frost.* Copyright 1923 by Holt, Rinehart and Winston, Inc. Copyright 1951 by Robert Frost. Reprinted by permission of the publisher.

The Fall of the City by Archibald MacLeish. Copyright 1937, 1964, by Archibald MacLeish. Reprinted by permission of the author.

American Renaissance by F. O. Matthiessen. Copyright 1941 by the Oxford University Press. Reprinted by permission of the publisher.

The Puritans, edited by Perry Miller and Thomas H. Johnson. Copyright 1938, 1963 by Perry Miller and Thomas H. Johnson. Reprinted by permission of Thomas H. Johnson and Harper and Row, Publishers.

"The Joy of Church Fellowship rightly Attended" from *The Poetical Works of Edward Taylor*, edited by Thomas H. Johnson. Copyright © 1939 by Rocklands Editions. Copyright © 1943 by Princeton University Press. Reprinted by permission of Princeton University Press.

There remains the more pleasant duty of thanking the many people who have helped me in various ways in the editing of the collection. Virtually every query I have addressed to several dozen persons has been answered—always with politeness and nearly as often with astonishing alacrity and fullness. First and foremost, I wish to express my deep gratitude to Mrs. Randall Stewart for giving me her permission to edit the book and for making Mr. Stewart's papers and books available to me. Next I want to acknowledge some of my many debts to friends, colleagues, and students of Mr. Stewart and to my own friends and teachers. I thank Theodore Hornberger, University of Pennsylvania; Hyatt H. Waggoner and Edward A. Bloom, Brown University; Dorothy Bethurum, Connecticut College; C. Carroll Hollis and Louis D. Rubin, Jr., University of North Carolina; Donald Davidson and Walter Sullivan, Vanderbilt University; Charles W. Crosby, Providence Public Library; and William Gobble, Scott, Foresman and Company. I want to record my especial appreciation to Edgar Hill Duncan, Vanderbilt University; C. Hugh Holman, University of North Carolina; M. E. Bradford, University of Dallas; and Norman Holmes Pearson, Yale University. Finally, I am even more indebted to H. K. Russell, University of North Carolina, for his unfailing interest and sympathetic counsel and to my wife Susan for her help and continuing encouragement.

George Core

FOREWORD

"FOR auld lang syne," Randall Stewart wrote on the flyleaf of the copy of *American Literature and Christian Doctrine* he sent me in 1958. In the spring of 1931 I first climbed to his third-story office at Yale. When Stanley Williams mentioned offhand in an undergraduate lecture that little was known about Hawthorne's college years, I decided to find out. Professor Williams sent me to Stewart, who had just received his doctorate for editing Hawthorne's American Notebooks. "Maybe I should publish them," he murmured, as though the idea had just struck him; "I really ought to get at it." Not every student of Hawthorne could delight in that smiling lift of the head and laughter of the eyes when Randall welcomed you, or the easy relaxed manner with which he shared his scholarship and his humanity. But after his edition of the Notebooks appeared no one, anywhere, could ever again work on Hawthorne without becoming his debtor. His many articles on Hawthorne, his subsequent edition of the English Notebooks, and his meticulous biography only increased the debt.

The failure of publishers to keep the *American Notebooks* in print, or reprint them, cut a younger generation of students off not only from a unique document in American literature but from direct contact with Stewart's introductory chapters. Their influence was immense but diffused beyond identification. Stewart, however, taught the ropes. His classification of character types has scarcely been altered. The scholar-idealist and the villains and reformers remain as named; the wholesome, the frail, and the exotic women of Hawthorne's fictions are still recognizable. So are the detached observers, acting within the

tales much like Stewart from outside. In discussing these types
and repeated themes, Stewart often gives in a series of sentences
what a series of articles could have been devoted to, what indeed
the dissertations and exegeses of others have later consisted of.
Stewart was a pioneer.

His article on "Hawthorne and *The Faerie Queene*" is an
example of the scholarly precision of his thought and its extension in the directions which an academic career then encouraged.
His span of reference within Hawthorne's work is impressive;
he knew the plains as well as the peaks. Even *Doctor Grimshawe's
Secret* was linked to Spenser, as was a contribution to *The
American Magazine of Useful and Entertaining Knowledge.*
Stewart's style had become more fluent than in the introductory
chapters to the *American Notebooks,* but his approach was still
Germanic and doctoral. One wished from him, even expected,
similar articles on the influence of Milton, of Bunyan, and, less
predictably, of Shakespeare. But in essays like "Melville and
Hawthorne" and "Hawthorne and Faulkner" he began the rejection of his earlier scholarly stance. Not much, for example, he
said, has been done with the influence of Hawthorne on Melville.
But: "I have no intention of attempting to make good this deficiency in the present paper. The subject would require long
and patient study. The results would doubtless be interesting,
but more effort would be required than anyone is likely to be
willing to give today to an 'influence' subject. If the late Professor Lowes had heard of this subject thirty years ago, and if the
authors concerned had been as respectable then as they are now,
we should have had long since a Harvard monograph, solid,
weighty, and buttressed with parallel passages." Stewart himself
had published "Hawthorne and *The Faerie Queene*" nineteen
years before.

In 1955, by the time of "The Golden Age of Hawthorne
Criticism," Stewart had cast off from his early work. "The
marked interest in Hawthorne is one of the more striking
phenomena of our time," he wrote in beginning his survey. "The

interest of which I speak is hardly at all biographical; readers of
Hawthorne today are not interested in the facts of Hawthorne's
life, nor do they read the works to discover 'autobiographical'
passages, or glimpses of the personality of the author, or characters who may be taken as 'spokesmen' for the author, or
traces of the author's use of this or that 'source.' " Even a hasty
look at Stewart's bibliography, prepared so ably by Mr. Core,
shows how much of his own honorable accomplishment he now
put aside. Such a shift in the climate of the schools as well as in
himself he perhaps felt in writing his biography of Hawthorne.
His heart was no longer in the sort of scholarship it depended on.
The book was an obligation, however. The facts had to be put
in order. He knew them as perhaps no one else will. He was
deferent to his subject but he remained detached from Hawthorne's spirit; the book is aloof from Hawthorne as a writer.
The biography was strictly conceived and carried out. He may
have lost some of his enthusiasm but none of his established
ability was wasted.

The change in attitude brought an accompanying change in
plans. Together we were to have edited Hawthorne's letters, first
with the help of Stanley Williams and Manning Hawthorne,
then, increasingly, just the two of us. The amount of preliminary
work which he and his wife, Cleone, put into the checking of
transcripts and the deciphering of obliterated passages was immense. He made good use of them in his biography, but suddenly in 1948, the life of Hawthorne published, he wrote to
thank me, as he put it, for "the accumulated richness of the
years" and to say he could no longer continue as an editor. "It
is clearly a necessary decision for me," he wrote. "It has been
building up ever since I resumed the editorial labor last summer.
I have reached the end of the Hawthorne rope. I have done three
books in 20 years. Let them stand on the shelves, with all their
imperfections, downright errors, limitations or what have you.
I am drained of any desire to do more with Hawthorne, to look
up another reference, or write another footnote. I must take

another tack in the years that remain. Just what, I don't know, but I can at least begin to read a few things I've wanted to read, and mend my growing illiteracy a bit."

Stewart had already begun to tack. The essays grouped as "Aspects of American Literature" chart his new course. "Regional Characteristics in the Literature of New England" (1941) had been written about adopted parents. "It would appear, then," he concluded, "that the best New England writers have stayed at home and that their knowledge of the cultures of other lands and ages has been of value to them chiefly as it has helped them to understand their own inheritance and has sharpened their perceptions of the home-bred virtues and the home-felt scenes. The paradox of such a provincialism is that it achieves, without deliberately setting out to do so, the real thing in universality." In choosing examples to illustrate "Three Views of the Individual" (1944) he kept to the writers of the North, but he had begun to examine them in terms of their universal ethical and social implications. It was a stretching out of his earlier concerns with literature. His views became more positive. In discussing, in the same year, the social approach to literature exemplified by Parrington, among others, he stated firmly, "I am unwilling to accept the disparagement of literary art as such, the rejection of conservative values in literature, the restriction of literature to social phenomena, and the establishment of scientific materialism as an 'over-all' philosophy. I am unwilling, moreover, to believe that the health and prosperity of democracy are contingent upon this body of doctrine, for such a belief excludes from a democratic society art and religion, traditions and manners, and a proper respect for the individual life." The ethical criticism that dominated the tone of the thirties was making itself felt in Stewart but on his own terms. Writing of Henry James in 1943, he was one of the early ones to argue the idea that Jamesian Americans might be culturally inferior but were morally superior to Europeans. The important issue to Stewart was not patriotism but morality.

He came to put a still higher value on Christian theology. In his later essay on "The Golden Age of Hawthorne Criticism," he spoke out with increased religious conviction. "The re-emergence of some of the basic tenets of Christian theology I regard as one of the more hopeful signs of our times. This radical ideological shift is finding important support (in imaginative American literature) not only in the work of contemporaries like Faulkner and Warren, but in perceptive re-readings of Melville and Hawthorne. If the critic actually thinks the ideological shift is a good thing, it is making a fetish of critical disinterestedness to insist that he refrain from saying so." The disavowal of critical detachment had all the enthusiasm of speakers at a Writers Congress in the thirties. Stewart's own doctrine, however, was far different from theirs. Increasingly he was aware that he was a Southerner, the son of a minister, and a conservative.

When he wrote "Hawthorne and Faulkner" in 1956, linking a first love with a new, he had come back to Vanderbilt. He had not forgotten New England but he had rediscovered the South. Hawthorne and Melville were now allied with Faulkner and Warren, whose works must have been among the "few things I've wanted to read." Roy Blount, in a tribute to Stewart, tells how Randall liked to quote someone's appreciation of Hester Prynne as "a damned fine woman." Stewart would have smiled to hear it said that he reconciled his literary favorites as "brothers under the Sin." "Perhaps I should say that I am not concerned with 'influences'," he reiterated early in "Hawthorne and Faulkner," as though "Hawthorne and *The Faerie Queene*" still haunted him. "I have made no attempt to ascertain whether Faulkner likes Hawthorne, or has read him much, or little, or not at all. . . . For the purposes of this paper, the extent of his acquaintance with Hawthorne is of no great consequence, for we are concerned not so much with actual influence as with a common view of the human condition."

" 'Poetically the Most Accurate Man Alive' " (1961) was, for

Faulkner, Stewart's parallel to "The Golden Age of Hawthorne Criticism." "Faulkner," Stewart wrote, "is describing the human condition, he is reporting on original sin in its many fascinating manifestations, and original sin is . . . 'in widest commonality spread.' " "Faulkner draws upon the South just as Hawthorne drew upon New England. It is the subject matter which he knows, and his knowledge of it is inherited and instinctive—the best kind of knowledge for an imaginative writer." Hawthorne and Faulkner could stand together because each wrote about the human condition and because each, by Stewart's definition, believed in original sin. Speaking of Faulkner criticism, Stewart ventured that "most of the good criticism for some time is likely to come from Southern critics for the simple reason that the non-Southerner who understands the South is hardly in a position to understand a writer so completely immersed in the South as Faulkner is." Still, it was the human condition that Faulkner was writing about, and what he achieved was what Stewart praised in New Englanders: "the real thing in universality"—that which the best literature embodies and good readers understand anywhere.

Southern writing in Stewart's time did achieve universality, and good readers. "The most striking aspect of the contemporary literary scene in the United States, it now goes without saying," Stewart said, "is the Southern renascence." This was in 1955, the decade when most of Stewart's essays on Southern writing and writers were published. It could be said now of him, as "a Southern exile" who "returns," what he said of New Englanders who stayed at home—"that their knowledge of the culture of other lands and ages has been of value to them chiefly as it has helped them to understand their own inheritance and has sharpened their perceptions of the home-bred virtues and the home-felt scenes." This gets to the heart of what Stewart was working toward—the acceptance of intense regionalism and the reconciliation of regionalisms—the definition of great individual literary artists and the community they make. Nothing else is so central. Consequently, he was in a position to make the most of the South.

Stewart's most ambitious work was his volume on *American Literature and Christian Doctrine* (1958). "The Old Cost of the Human Redemption" is the chapter Mr. Core has chosen from it for this volume we now so gratefully have. It is a good choice. When it is read against "The Social School of American Criticism," the book can be seen as Stewart's answer to Parrington. All of Stewart's breadth of experience, all of his special studies, and his particular concerns and convictions were embraced as he examined the human condition of the American as our writers have set it forth. "Man is moral agent and a tragic figure," Stewart concluded. "For man is an imperfect, nonperfectible being. He cannot be improved by technology. He is not a machine, but a very fallible human. Poor wayward creature, he appears even now to be plotting, with all ingenuity and speed, his own destruction. But his state, unless by his own perverse wilfulness, is not beyond the reach of God's redeeming grace. This is the essence of the human condition, and the Christian hope. And this is the meaning of the dramatizations of human experience by the greatest American writers."

This was more than history; it was Randall Stewart's statement to the world. He had found the literary counters he needed. And he was able to accept them and to use them within a common tradition that reconciled too the regions from whence they sprang. He had found the tack.

—Norman   Holmes Pearson

New Haven, Connecticut
September 1967

INTRODUCTION

RANDALL STEWART was a modest, unassuming man who was profoundly committed to the humanities in a way that extended far beyond the strictly academic. Marking the length of his active contribution to learning—nearly a half-century—and calling the roll of universities where he taught during those years does little, truly, to indicate the great contribution he made to American literature. In the same manner this volume of essays is only a partial record of the range and depth of his achievement. Mr. Stewart's scholarship revealed itself in many forms, and these essays are work which largely resulted from the preoccupations of teaching and from wrestling with particular problems; yet they are also part and parcel of his devotion to the humanities—even as they are a meaningful fact of his life. It is only natural there is some duplication here and there because Stewart frequently returned to concepts which he believed important, especially when he wanted to give an idea as much currency as possible. He doubtless had no intention of collecting his miscellaneous essays, and had he done so, it is likely he would have made a good many revisions. And so one apologizes for a job which is necessarily incomplete, but which is nonetheless impressive insofar as Stewart's own writing is concerned.

Stewart's work as a teacher of American literature and as an editor is far more significant than a chronology or a bibliography or an essay can convey. He was one of the early settlers in the field of American literature, following hard on the heels of pioneers like his friend and teacher, Stanley Williams. And as Norman Holmes Pearson has shown in his Foreword, Stewart was a pioneer himself in many ways. He did much to make

American literature a respectable subject—not by apologizing for it or by pleading a special case, but by showing over and again by precept and principle its inherent greatness and its enduring qualities. Stewart believed in the importance of literature as such, and he staunchly resisted attempts to diminish its stature and subordinate it to other disciplines. He saw the humane tradition of the western world as solidly rooted in its literature, and he rightly believed that American letters, especially since 1830, represent at once a continuance of that tradition and a distinctive development. The tradition as he saw it is primarily regional—that is, in the words of Allen Tate, it embodies "locality in the sense of local continuity in tradition and belief"; it is fundamentally moral in that its great moments and controlling themes deal with the conflict of good and evil as the recurring, inescapable dilemma of mortal man in his imperfection; and in the same manner it is religious—and, more specifically, Christian—in its final import.

Stewart's search for a usable, vital critical strategy is an arresting, central aspect of his career, and it demonstrates the degree of his involvement in art and life. In his published work the search began with the concluding chapters of the Introduction to *The American Notebooks;* it ended about 1959 with two fine essays which represent different, yet complementary, methods—"Tidewater and Frontier," a scholarly article showing historical developments and parallels in the making of Southern literature, and "Moral Crisis as Structural Principle in Fiction: A Few American Examples," a perceptive work with a new critical direction as well as a firm moral dimension. These essays round off Stewart's major published work in terms of its main development and essential nature, although some fine articles followed, notably "Donald Davidson" and " 'Poetically the Most Accurate Man Alive.' " As Mr. Pearson has cogently argued, Stewart moved from the historical method of "Hawthorne and *The Faerie Queene*" and "Hawthorne and the Civil War" to a kind of moral new criticism in the course of his career. The

journey has a clearly definable progress and a remarkable sense
of the ending, even though the traveler did not have a precise
goal in mind at the outset. One can see that Mr. Stewart started
to write under the direct influence of scholars like Kittredge and
Lowes, although he was probably influenced in part by critics
like Matthew Arnold and the new humanists—Babbitt, More,
and, more particularly, Foerster. He saturated himself in English
literature in those early days of teaching (so much so that
Chauncey Brewster Tinker told him that his performance on
the general oral examination at Yale was the best he had ever
witnessed). His field in those days was the English renaissance,
and among other things he taught sixteenth- and seventeenth-
century poetry and drama, with individual courses in Spenser
and Shakespeare. His interest in this renaissance led him to study
the two great "rebirths" in American literature—the New
England flowering of the nineteenth century, and the Southern
renascence of the twentieth which occurred almost precisely one
hundred years later. As time went on, Stewart became less historical and more critical in his interpretation of literature, responding in large part to the criticism of Eliot, Brooks, Warren,
Ransom, and Winters. The greatest influence was probably the
criticism of Allen Tate, but he was always attracted to the work
of such scholars as Perry Miller and F. O. Matthiessen.

It all began with Hawthorne. When Randall Stewart "discovered" Hawthorne, in the late 1920s, he was partly responsible
for starting a revaluation which was not limited to Hawthorne.
Stewart's edition of the American Notebooks is a landmark in
the reassessment of American literature in this century because
its appearance made it dramatically evident that sound texts
were needed for the study of American letters. The Notebooks
also made it clear how subtle and complex and rich is the background of Hawthorne's fiction whose ultimate source might
justifiably be called the New England mind. And when Hawthorne assumed his rightful place, the previously existing order
of American literature was radically altered. This modification

led to the accelerated rise of Melville's reputation, and, more importantly (to continue using Eliot's language in "Tradition and the Individual Talent"), the overall reassessment of American literature caused a slight alteration in the *whole* existing order of literature. This readjustment made it possible for a thoroughgoing critical and historical revaluation of American literature—and pointed the way toward its central development.

Stewart recognized the indigenous, yet universal, character of Hawthorne's fiction; he also perceived that the allegorical and symbolic elements have moral and religious significance—that Hawthorne, like Henry James, Emily Dickinson, and T. S. Eliot, is a Puritan in the largest and best sense by virtue of his asceticism, restraint, and discipline. He perceived, too, especially through his study of the American Notebooks, that Hawthorne, like most great writers, had a strong grasp of the palpable and the real, despite the fact that his fictions are often romance. And he remarked in Hawthorne's notebook prose the beginnings of a truly American idiom and style. In arriving at these conclusions, through reading and re-reading early New England literature, Stewart came to see the application of many of these same principles to other American writers, especially Melville, James, Eliot, and Faulkner.

And so by the early 1940s Stewart had decided on what for him is the principal tradition in American literature. He steadily moved toward his own way of anatomizing that tradition in such essays as "Regional Characteristics in the Literature of New England" and "Three Views of the Individual as Reflected in American Literature." In the middle forties he wrote one of his finest essays in "The Moral Aspect of Henry James's 'International Situation,'" a piece remarkable for its insight and comprehensiveness. (This comprehensiveness is one of the distinctive qualities of Stewart's criticism, particularly of his interchapters in *The Literature of the United States*.) In this essay Stewart conveys his profound understanding of what James means in the Preface to *The Portrait of a Lady*: "There is, I think, no more nutritive or suggestive truth . . . than that of the perfect dependence of the 'moral' sense of a work of art on the amount of felt life producing it." (This passage can stand as an epigraph for Stewart's criticism as a whole.) Stewart illuminates the fusion of the moral element in James's international novels with the enveloping action which flows out of the tension between the societies of the old world and the new. This cultural tension and the moral vibrations it produces are central in nineteenth-century American literature: it prominently appears in different forms in the Leatherstocking tales, in Hawthorne's fiction, and in Melville's novels.

About the same time Stewart's attitudes toward the pragmatic approach to literature crystallized in the hard precipitate of his "The Social School of American Criticism." At an early date he recognized the fraudulent and impermanent aspect of a criticism founded in the topical, the temporal—the shifting political currents of the times; and he spoke out when Marxist criticism still had a firm hold in American letters. He always objected to using literature as a text for narrowly political interpretations of art and history; to the contrary, he believed that literature should be read for itself and for what it depicts which is unchanging and forever true about the human condition. For Stewart great poetry was art first and foremost—propaganda afterwards, if at all.

Randall Stewart was committed to a criticism which goes beyond dispassionate analysis and strict formalism. He always seemed aware of the divine guide whom John Crowe Ransom describes in "Why Critics Don't Go Mad": "the Great Scholar, so modest that he is anonymous . . . perfect in his attainments; possessing of the sense of art as wholly as he possesses the text, in beautiful proportion and justice, yet intuitively, without an effort; it is precisely because he has been a faithful scholar that this grace has been added unto him." Mr. Stewart is not the Great Scholar, who is an ideal abstraction, as Ransom would be the first to admit; but Stewart has many of his virtues, and he is a very good scholar, so good indeed that his *The English Note-books by Nathaniel Hawthorne* (1941) will not need to be included in the Ohio State Centenary Edition of Hawthorne's works since it was prepared with such great thoroughness and accuracy.

In 1948 Stewart finished his principal work on Hawthorne with a biography that is still the standard one after two decades, presenting in the concluding chapter a short but far-ranging critical reading of Hawthorne's fiction. It is a coda for Stewart's Hawthorne criticism. Stewart described his biography as "severely objective" in a letter to a friend, and this is a large part of its strength: the facts are there, with as great an accuracy and economy as one can expect. No lawyer ever handled his evidence more skillfully or presented his case more surely than Stewart does in *Nathaniel Hawthorne: A Biography*.

The early 1950s were an extremely productive period for Randall Stewart. In 1951 he and Stanley Williams initiated the plan which would result in *Eight American Authors: A Review of Research and Criticism,* a major critical bibliography which has led directly to the invaluable *American Literary Scholarship: An Annual.* The following year Stewart presented many of the essential documents necessary for an assessment of the Southern literary renascence in an anthology of Southern literature. In the Foreword to *The Literature of the South* he said that "Southern literature is more than a provincial record," and in "Outlook for Southern Writing" he proved why the best of that literature is timeless and universal. He then turned his efforts largely toward the formulation of a Christian approach to American literature, and his Faculty Paper, "American Literature and the Christian Tradition" (1955) shows that his ideas and methods were taking shape in a highly usable strategy which would issue forth in *American Literature and Christian Doctrine* three years later, a book which Richard Weaver praised for being very brave and for its "principle of interpretation which enables us to see the reason behind greatness." Weaver went on to point out the book's controlling theme and its vital focus: "The thesis will have to be interpreted as saying not that Christianity is the necessary cause of a great literature, but that something like it is the necessary condition . . . that being a great writer does entail having the Christian-like view of man, which sees him as a dual creature, possessing the capacity for glory and damnation." This statement is a remarkable complement to the concluding sentence of Stewart's *Hawthorne*: ". . . no one is likely to impugn Hawthorne's central moral—the importance of understanding mankind in whole, and the need of man's sympathy with man based upon the honest recognition of good and evil in our common nature." Thus Stewart himself played an important role in the "re-emergence of some of the basic tenets of Christian theology" (to use his own words) as they apply to literature. It is a matter of some interest that this study continues today with steadily increasing vigor.

American Literature and Christian Doctrine is only one part of Randall Stewart's commitment to the humane tradition, a commitment perfectly described by Frederick Pottle: "A Christian teacher makes his great apologetic effect by indicating his own commitment, and by treating Christianity as intellectually respectable." Indeed Stewart was a Christian and a gentleman, a man who respected and practiced the old virtues in a natural and unpretentious way; it was therefore only logical that he join his religion to his traditional and historical apprehension of literature—both in his published work and in his teaching.

To those who had the pleasure of knowing Randall Stewart—most especially his students—one would think that his most striking quality was a definite style, one that was truly felicitous and memorable. There was his physical appearance for one thing —the trim and almost jaunty figure, the strong facial features, the neatly combed white hair. There was his dress for another. At Vanderbilt Mr. Stewart invariably wore a blue oxford cloth shirt and a challis bow tie to class, with a cord coat in summer, a tweed one in winter. He wore his clothes as naturally as he carried himself—with ease and grace. His ready and ebullient smile was perhaps the most representative outward sign of his old-fashioned courtliness, his ease of manner, his unaffected grace. Mr. Stewart was quite simply a very charming man.

Randall Stewart was at his best and in his true glory teaching Hawthorne or Faulkner before a large class of undergraduates, and he conducted his courses with a zest and verve which convinced his students that literature was not only important but great fun as well. It was amazing to watch Stewart teach a class of one hundred students and more as if it were a group of fifteen or twenty. He never preached, nor did he become shrill; his point of view was clear, but he was willing to listen to another, even to seek it out. He taught by suggestion, and his lectures had an allusive, nagging quality that drove his students to think out the meaning and value of literature for themselves. He liked to ask questions, not answer them in the final pedagogical sense. Mr. Stewart's questions were deceptively simple at first glance; a later inspection revealed their subtlety. He asked of *All the King's Men,* "Whose story is it?" and of *The Sound and the Fury,* "Who is the chief character?" The student who understands the implications of these searching questions knows a great deal about both novels.

It was typical of Mr. Stewart to suggest that some of his students should write to Edmund Wilson about Wilson's impatience with George Washington Harris and Sut Lovingood. As his fellow editors said in the Preface to the third edition of *The Literature of the United States,* "Randall Stewart was the sort of man who could love both Sut Lovingood and Henry James." I don't think that Stewart ever wrote to Wilson, but he did carry on a spirited correspondence with Malcolm Cowley and, later, with Allan Pryce-Jones about the American contributors to the special number of the *Times Literary Supplement—American Writing Today.* And he arranged the Fugitive reunion with consummate diplomacy (and very little money) largely through an astonishing correspondence which ran to several hundred letters.

Randall Stewart was also the sort of man who could celebrate the virtues of *The American Tradition in Literature* (a textbook edited by his friend Richmond Beatty, among others) and use it during his last ten years at Vanderbilt as a token of his affection for Beatty, never once alluding to one of its chief rivals, his own *The Literature of the United States*. In similar manner one doubts that his undergraduates ever realized who was the general editor of *The Literature of the South*: Stewart mentioned only his friends who were the editors, not himself. So there was kindness and modesty as well as grace and style, and all were perfectly joined.

Kindness was instinctive for Randall Stewart. Included in his correspondence is a letter from a twelve-year-old boy who was running for president of his seventh-grade class. He wrote in a childish hand, with great seriousness, addressing Mr. Stewart as The Honorable Randall Stewart, and asking what he should say in his campaign speech. Stewart promptly wrote back, giving the boy sensible and kind advice. Years later, when he was asked to write a recommendation for a Vanderbilt English major who wanted to enter the law school, he described the student—who was a very casual and intellectually undistinguished fellow—as a "nice, friendly lad" and only that, rather than say anything ill of him. At about the same time he wrote dozens of letters in an attempt to get Richmond Beatty's book review column syndicated.

It is perhaps most characteristic of Stewart's modesty and his devotion to his profession that he carefully saved every roll book that he ever used over the years, including the many summer sessions he taught; yet he did not often retain carbon copies of his manuscripts, nor did he save a large proportion of his reviews and essays. In fact, it is a cause for some amazement that Stewart did not even bother to keep an accurate record of his publications. One sees that Randall Stewart did not take himself too seriously. His humor and wit and common sense always prevailed. What finally did matter to him was good literature and its serious students.

In his memorial essay for Randall Stewart, Roy Blount characterized his departed teacher as a clearly discernible constellation, and although Stewart himself would be the first to say that he does not belong in quite the same galaxy as Melville and Hawthorne, I like to think of him occasionally dropping by the little shady corner that Melville fancifully picked out for himself and Hawthorne, and that he described to his friend in the humorous and charming idyll contained in the letter of early June 1851. It is easy to imagine Stewart having a glass of champagne and a cigar in the celestial grass with Melville and Hawthorne, and joining them in the comic songs Melville speculated about writing in paradise. One can hear them talking far into the night—as Melville and Hawthorne once did in the sacred precincts of Mrs. Hawthorne's sitting room—about all possible and impossible matters; and if he listens long and well, one might hear Hawthorne and Stewart applauding Melville as he repeats, "I stand for the heart! To the dogs with the head!"

Randall Stewart carried his knowledge to the heart: this was his ultimate grace and the source of his great humanity.

—George Core

Davidson, North Carolina
October 1967

Editorial Note

At the request of Vanderbilt University Press, I have provided notes for every essay in this collection, save for Chapters II-V, which originally had full documentation. (The notes for Chapters II and III have been slightly revised, however: see note 1 to Chapter II.) Mr. Stewart's notes for the remaining essays are shown by the notation [R. S.]. Notes by the editor are generally not identified individually, but the usual notation [Ed.] is used on occasion. I have located all but a few of Mr. Stewart's quotations: less than half a dozen remain unassigned. Most of the documentation is simply a matter of page references, but in several cases explanatory notes of one kind and another have been added.

Every effort has been made to make the spelling, capitalization, and punctuation consistent. Obvious errors have been silently corrected. I have used sound, readily available texts whenever possible for the quoted material, hoping to satisfy the scholar and the general reader alike.

PART I *Hawthorne*

EDITING *THE AMERICAN NOTEBOOKS*

B ACK in the spring of 1928 I entered the Morgan Library with a copy of Mrs. Hawthorne's *Passages from the American Note-Books* under my arm. The Library had recently acquired the manuscripts of Hawthorne's journals, and I was curious to see if Mrs. Hawthorne had made a faithful transcription. I found, of course, that she had not: she had not transcribed, but rewritten. I proceeded with the collation as fast as my duties as instructor at Yale would permit. It was an exciting time for me. I sometimes forgot to go out for lunch.

After consultation with Stanley Williams and other professors in the Department, it was decided that I might prepare under Professor Williams's direction an edition of the American Notebooks and submit it as my doctoral dissertation. This meant that there must be an elaborate editorial apparatus. It was fun visiting libraries, copying letters, getting photostats from the Huntington (microfilm came in, a little later). Fun, too, writing the introductory chapters (and here Mr. Williams's counsel was especially helpful) on "Mrs. Hawthorne's Revisions," "The Adaptation of Material from the American Notebooks in Hawthorne's Tales and Novels," "The Development of Character Types," and "Recurrent Themes" in Hawthorne's fiction. All told, the text, introduction, and notes filled more than 1,000 typewritten pages when the completed job was submitted to the Yale Graduate Faculty in 1930.

In 1932 the Yale Press published the work substantially as it was, despite the fact that some of the introductory material went well beyond the bounds of the text of the Notebooks. The first impression of 500 copies was sold within a few months, but the second impression of 700 copies required nearly ten years to dispose of. Although the Depression was on, the Yale Press treated me with great generosity: they not only required no subsidy, but paid me the usual ten percent royalty, which (it was a five-dollar book) came to a total of $600. Obviously this wasn't much of a money-making business for either editor or publisher. The book has been out of print since 1942.

The day of publication the New York *Times* ran a story on Mrs. Hawthorne's revisions.[1] They afforded a good deal of amusement all around. I, of course, had played them up, and I think rightly so. They not only justified the new edition, but they were important in themselves. They showed the clever mind of a genteel Victorian female at work; in fact, on the strength of them, Mrs. Hawthorne has become the classic example, at least in America, of the genteel Victorian female. But the tone of my chapter dealing with these matters was wrong. It was too sharp, too castigatory.

Some years later when I read Mrs. Hawthorne's letters to James T. Fields in the Boston Public Library and excerpted and summarized them for *More Books*, it became apparent that Fields had been a fairly active collaborator in the work of editing Hawthorne's Notebooks. Whether he was aware of the extent of the rewriting is not entirely clear, but he acquiesced in the omission of certain substantial portions—for example, the "Twenty Days with Julian and Little Bunny"—which he agreed with Mrs. Hawthorne in thinking too personal for publication.[2]

The editing had been a happy employment for Mrs. Hawthorne. Her hours "sang," [3] she told Fields, as she labored over the manuscripts: "all the heavenly springtime" of her married

1. Herbert Gorman, "Hawthorne's Notebooks Are Rescued From Distortion," New York *Times Book Review*, December 25, 1932, p. 3.

2. "Editing Hawthorne's Notebooks: Selections from Mrs. Hawthorne's Letters to Mr. and Mrs. Fields, 1864–1868," *More Books*, XX (September 1945), 312.

3. Cf. *ibid.*, p. 303.

life came back to her, she said, in Hawthorne's "cadences, so rich and delicate." [4] Moreover, she needed money. Hawthorne's consulate savings were dwindling away. Fields published *Passages from the American Note-Books* in the *Atlantic Monthly* (of which he was editor) in twelve instalments in 1866 at $100 an instalment and brought out the combined instalments in book form the following year.

A good deal can be said for the view that Mrs. Hawthorne was trying not so much to misrepresent her husband, or remake his writing closer to her heart's desire, as to do the kind of revising which Hawthorne himself would have done. Of course, with her sometimes mistaken notions of language and delicacy, she made many revisions which would have been abhorrent to the author. But much of her rewriting was similar—and this point I did not sufficiently stress in the Introduction—to the kind of rewriting which Hawthorne himself had done when he adapted notebook material in his tales and novels.

This raises the question of genteelism, which was a blight in nineteenth-century American literature and which not even Hawthorne entirely escaped. From the standpoint of modern taste, at least, the prose of the Notebooks is better than that of the tales and novels, being simpler, more indigenous, nearer the colloquial, less "literary." It is seen at its best, perhaps, in the North Adams journal of 1838, where the writing is earthy and plain. *The Scarlet Letter*, I think, would be an even greater book if it had been written in this early notebook style. Not that *The Scarlet Letter* is genteel, but the prose illustrates a kind of literary genteelism. Hemingway's oft-quoted statement that modern American literature began with *Huckleberry Finn* contains much truth,[5] and I do not mean to suggest that Hawthorne's Notebooks often approach the colloquialism of Mark Twain. But I think the early notebook prose is plain enough, unliterary

4. *Ibid.*, p. 308.
5. See *The Green Hills of Africa* (New York: Charles Scribner's Sons, 1935), p. 22.

enough, to suggest a revision backward of Hemingway's famous dictum.

Another error of the Introduction was a focusing on the tributary role of the Notebooks. They were regarded as of interest and value primarily as a source of the tales and novels. Had there been no tales and novels, I seemed to imply, the Notebooks would hardly be worth attending to. But this view I believe to be quite wrong. Not that the tales and novels are to be denigrated in the least, or that any scrap of material wherever found which contributed in the slightest way to their making is not of great interest and importance, but the American Notebooks are a classic, a unique classic, in their own right. Henry James's Notebooks are interesting largely in their relation to his fiction; Hawthorne's have a certain independent value.

Hawthorne said that New England was about as large a lump of this earth as his heart could readily take in, and the American Notebooks show how truly he has taken in New England. It is the rich New Englandism, so closely observed, so precisely recorded, which makes the book a New England classic. First, New England scenes—the mountains of Western Massachusetts, the meadows of Concord, the urban sights in and around Boston—are described with pictorial art. Hawthorne thought of himself as a painter, the pen-strokes were brush-strokes, the page a canvas. Second, New England people—stagecoach drivers, hog drovers, and not only rustics but men of intellect and position, a member of Congress from Maine, a historical scholar at work in the Boston Athenaeum—these were the subjects of his portraiture. Lowell spoke of Hawthorne's "fine accipitral look," [6] and a North Adams villager told him he had something of the "hawk-eye" [7] in his mien. This art of portraiture he cultivated long and painstakingly, and with so much

6. Quoted in William Dean Howells, *My Literary Friends and Acquaintance* (New York: Harper and Brothers, 1901), p. 52.

7. *The American Notebooks by Nathaniel Hawthorne* (New Haven: Yale University Press, 1932), p. 37.

objectivity that his portraits seemed "cold" to some readers; and cold they are with (as Eliot has suggested) the coldness of art.[8]

If it is objected that the American Notebooks are not entirely satisfactory as a New England classic because there is no transcendentalism in them, it must be admitted that Hawthorne was not a transcendentalist, at least in the Emersonian sense, which is the accepted sense. Hawthorne and Emerson did not see eye to eye. They started from exactly opposite premises concerning the nature of man: Emerson from the premise of innate goodness, Hawthorne from the premise of innate sinfulness. But whatever modern New England may or may not have become, it is safe to assume, I think, that Hawthorne spoke for a vast majority of the New Englanders of his time, and Emerson for a small minority.

And now that this New England classic has been out of print for some sixteen years and more, the managers of the Columbia University Press (very commendably) have felt that a new edition is desirable. They have asked me if I would prepare one, and if so, what specific plans I would propose. I have gladly consented and have made the following proposals. First, a re-collation of the text, and the restoration of the inked-out passages, most of which can now be recovered by the aid of infra-red photography. Second, the inclusion of those passages in Mrs. Hawthorne's edition whose manuscript originals have not survived. These passages are very useful, they are (though bowdlerized) a part of the American Notebooks, and their omission from the 1932 edition was a mistake which can be explained perhaps by the youthful editor's too strict view of textual authority. Third, a large reduction of the notes, and their location at the foot of the page. The information contained in the notes is now so easily available in recent books about Hawthorne

8. See Eliot's review of *The Cambridge History of American Literature*, Vol. II, *The Athenaeum*, April 25, 1919, p. 237.

that I do not think it necessary to reprint them *in extenso*. And fourth, the omission of the old long Introduction and the substitution of a new short Introduction. The Columbia Press has approved these arrangements, and it is now expected that the new edition will appear within a reasonable length of time.

The omission of those old introductory chapters on "The Development of Character Types" and "Recurrent Themes" costs me a small pang. I am a little sentimental about them, though I haven't had the courage to reread them in many years. They were once admired by some, and used by many. They were "pioneer" work. But they, like the notes, long since became part of the public domain. To reprint them now seems quite unnecessary. There have been in recent years so many analyses of Hawthorne's characters and themes, and of such subtlety and sophistication, that those early sketches must strike the modern student as fairly rough work.

The last twenty years or so have been the golden age of Hawthorne criticism. Hawthorne's art and his "visible truth" [9] (as Melville called it) have never before been so profoundly appreciated and so skillfully explicated. I like to think that the 1932 Notebooks contributed to this modern interest in Hawthorne. They showed Hawthorne in a new light, a truer and more attractive light than he had been seen in before, and many who saw him in the new light were interested in what they saw. The 1932 Notebooks, I like to think, made new friends for Hawthorne, and these new friends helped to make the modern renaissance of Hawthorne studies.

9. Letter to Hawthorne dated Pittsfield, April 16(?), 1851, *The Portable Melville*, ed. by Jay Leyda (New York: The Viking Press, 1952), p. 427. Melville continues, "By visible truth, we mean the apprehension of the absolute condition of things as they strike the eye of the man who fears them not, though they do their worst to him. . . ."

THE DEVELOPMENT OF CHARACTER
TYPES IN HAWTHORNE'S FICTION [1]

IN reading Hawthorne's works one is impressed by the frequent recurrence of certain favorite types of character. It is the purpose of this chapter to trace the evolution of several of these types through their more noteworthy individual representatives and to indicate, wherever possible, the bearing of the notebooks on this development.

I

Perhaps the most important single type of character in Hawthorne's works is the one which may be designated as the scholar-idealist. The first example is Fanshawe, the hero of his earliest work (1828). In the characterization of Fanshawe, the author had in mind as a prototype Nathaniel Mather, whom Fanshawe resembled "in his almost insane eagerness for knowledge, and in his early death." [2] Mather's epitaph, "The ashes

1. My procedure in this and the next chapter has been to retain all of Mr. Stewart's original notes; however, I have reduced the number of notes by frequently bringing together several separate consecutive page references to the same work into the form of a single footnote. In a few instances I have silently provided pertinent cross-references from the 1932 edition of *The American Notebooks* which should be incorporated into the present text and which otherwise would be unavailable. In general, Stewart's editorial methods have been followed as closely as possible, and thus it will be seen that the notes concerning the location of certain Hawthorne letters have been retained. Obvious departures are indicated by the customary notation [Ed.].

2. *Fanshawe*, p. 217. This and all subsequent references to Hawthorne's works (unless otherwise stated) are to the Riverside Edition of *The Complete Works of Nathaniel Hawthorne*, edited by George Parsons Lathrop, 13 vols. (Boston and New York: Houghton Mifflin Company, 1883). Short title references are used throughout and are explained only when the abbreviation may not be immediately clear.

of an hard student, a good scholar, and a great Christian," with
the omission of the last qualification, was inscribed on Fanshawe's tomb.[3] In 1838 Hawthorne visited the grave of Nathaniel Mather in the burial ground adjoining Dr. Peabody's
house and recorded in the journal his thoughts on this occasion:
"It affected me deeply, when I had cleared away the grass from
the half-buried stone, and read the name. An apple-tree or two
hang over these old graves, and throw down the blighted fruit
on Nathaniel Mather's grave,—he blighted too." [4] The entry
may be taken as indicating Hawthorne's continued interest in
the historical figure whom he had used as a model for the character of Fanshawe.

The following description of Fanshawe gives us Hawthorne's
fundamental conception of the scholar-idealist:

> There was a nobleness on his high forehead, which time would have
> deepened into majesty; and all his features were formed with a strength
> and boldness, of which the paleness, produced by study and confine-
> ment, could not deprive them. The expression of his countenance was
> not a melancholy one: on the contrary, it was proud and high, perhaps
> triumphant, like one who was a ruler in a world of his own, and in-
> dependent of the beings that surrounded him. But a blight, of which his
> thin pale cheek, and the brightness of his eye, were alike proofs, seemed
> to have come over him ere his maturity.[5]

Fanshawe, then, is the indefatigable scholar whose health has
been undermined by a too close application to his studies. He
leads a solitary life, confining himself sedulously to his chamber
except for an hour at sunset, when, as was Hawthorne's practice
not only when he wrote the novel but during the entire period
of his residence in Salem, he goes for a walk.[6] But Fanshawe is

3. See *Fanshawe*, p. 217, and Cotton Mather, *Magnalia Christi Americana*.
2 vols. (New York: Russell & Russell, 1967), II, 484.
4. *Passages from the American Note-Books*, p. 118. Hereafter cited as
Passages.
5. *Fanshawe*, pp. 88–89.
6. During the twelve years following his graduation from Bowdoin College

not the ineffectual person whom one expects to find in this role. His strong, bold features and the expression of triumphant pride on his countenance indicate the presence of a power which is likely to prove formidable in his relations with less ideal characters. And the events of the story amply demonstrate this force of personality. Fanshawe wins, only to refuse, Ellen Langton's love. Moreover, he triumphs over Butler, the villain, by sheer intellectual power:

Fanshawe turned calmly, and fixed his eyes on the stranger. "Retire, sir," was all he said.

Ellen almost shuddered, as if there were a mysterious and unearthly power in Fanshawe's voice; for she saw that the stranger endeavored in vain, borne down by the influence of a superior mind, to maintain the boldness of look and bearing that seemed natural to him. He at first made a step forward, then muttered a few half-audible words; but, quailing at length beneath the young man's bright and steady eye, he turned and slowly withdrew.[7]

The next representative of the scholar-idealist type to appear in Hawthorne's writings is the anonymous wayfarer in "The Ambitious Guest" (1835). Hawthorne had doubtless heard the legend upon which he based his tale in September, 1832, when he stopped at Ethan Crawford's inn[8] during the course of his travels in the White Mountains. Although the character is very slightly sketched, the few descriptive phrases place him indubitably in the category which we are considering. He is "high-browed" and "high-souled," a "refined and educated youth," of

---

(1825–1837), Hawthorne lived in great seclusion in Salem, "seldom going out except at twilight," as he wrote in the autobiographical sketch which he prepared for Stoddard (Julian Hawthorne, *Hawthorne and His Wife,* 2 vols. [Boston: James R. Osgood and Company, 1885], I, 97). It is interesting to observe this instinctive return to his old habit of walking in the evening during his later residence in Salem.

7. *Fanshawe,* p. 108.

8. See Randall Stewart, *Nathaniel Hawthorne: A Biography* (New Haven: Yale University Press, 1948), p. 42. [Ed.]

"a proud yet gentle spirit." He leads a solitary life devoted to "a high and abstracted ambition." [9]

A third character of the same type is Aylmer, who appears in "The Birthmark" (1843). He is a "pale philosopher" who has devoted his life to scientific research in the laboratory. In order to emphasize the purely ideal qualities in this character, Hawthorne, in a contrast reminiscent of *The Tempest,* has introduced the very mundane figure, Aminadab. The antithesis is put with great explicitness in the following passage:

> With his vast strength, his shaggy hair, his smoky aspect, and the indescribable earthiness that incrusted him, he seemed to represent man's physical nature; while Aylmer's slender figure, and pale, intellectual face, were no less apt a type of the spiritual element.[10]

Aylmer's crowning scientific experiment—the attempt to remove the only flaw in his wife's beauty, a birthmark on her cheek— appeared for the moment to succeed: the mark disappeared. But simultaneously with its disappearance, Georgiana died. Aylmer, like Marlowe's Dr. Faustus, had attempted "to practice more than heavenly power permits."

Owen Warland in "The Artist of the Beautiful" (1844) is another example of Hawthorne's conception of the idealist. Like his prototypes, he is physically frail; he is often seized with "a fluttering of the nerves." Here, too, we meet with the recurrent "pale face." As in "The Birthmark" the ideality of the central character is accentuated by a contrasting figure—in this instance Robert Danforth, the blacksmith. To Danforth, Owen Warland says: "Strength is an earthly monster. I make no pretensions to it. My force, whatever there may be of it, is altogether spiritual." But whereas the antithetical characters in "The Birthmark" work together toward the end in view, Aminadab executing the commands of Aylmer, Warland is seriously disturbed by the presence of Danforth. Warland says of his op-

---

9. For these descriptive phrases, see *Twice-Told Tales,* pp. 367–374 *passim.*
10. *Mosses from an Old Manse,* pp. 53, 55.

posite: "He would drive me mad were I to meet him often. His hard, brute force darkens and confuses the spiritual element within me. . . ." The explanation, however, is perhaps obvious: Aylmer, though an idealist, must use material means to accomplish the result desired; Warland, on the other hand, is attempting completely to transcend the material realm. In this attempt, moreover, he meets his chief obstacle, not in the earthiness of the blacksmith, as unfavorable as this may be, but in the "cold, unimaginative sagacity" of Peter Hovenden who represents the "hard, coarse world." And when the infant crushes the mechanical butterfly, the curious symbol of the artist's realization of ideal beauty, the "sharp and shrewd expression" [11] of Peter Hovenden, his grandsire, is strongly marked on his face.

Because he is an idealist, Clifford in *The House of the Seven Gables* (1851), although not devoted to scholarship or scientific experimentation, belongs nevertheless in this group of characters. His nature, like Owen Warland's, is guided by a "love and necessity for the Beautiful." He has the "thin delicate fingers" of the artist. His aversion to the ugly is expressed in the instinctive turning of his eyes from the ungainly Hepzibah or in the shedding of tears upon viewing the horrible ugliness, "spiritual as well as physical," of a monkey which accompanies a hand organ. Clifford's antipathy to Judge Pyncheon recalls Warland's hostility to both Hovenden and Danforth. "Even had there been no bitter recollections . . . ," says Hawthorne, "the mere natural repugnance of the more sensitive system to the massive, weighty, and unimpressible one, must, in itself, have been disastrous to the former." Clifford is a porcelain vase; the Judge, a granite column.[12] If Clifford is the most beautiful, he is also the least effectual of Hawthorne's idealists.

The character of Dimmesdale in *The Scarlet Letter* (1850) represents in some respects the culmination of the type which I

11. *Ibid.*, pp. 509, 504, 510, 511, 514, 515, 535.
12. *The House of the Seven Gables*, pp. 135, 174, 135, 198, 287.

have designated as the scholar-idealist; but this figure is also derived in part from another sequence of characters—those who are tortured by a secret guilt. It will be necessary, therefore, before studying Dimmesdale, to trace this supplementary line of descent, which includes three figures: Reuben Bourne in "Roger Malvin's Burial" (1832), the Reverend Mr. Hooper in "The Minister's Black Veil" (1836), and Roderick Elliston in "Egotism; or, The Bosom Serpent" (1843).

Leaving Roger Malvin, who was mortally wounded, to die alone in the forest, Reuben Bourne, himself seriously wounded, had barely succeeded in reaching the settlement alive. When Reuben afterward married Roger's daughter, he forbore telling her that he had left her father before he died and that his body lay unburied in the wilderness. Hawthorne analyzes Reuben's mental state in the following characteristic manner:

> There was now in the breast of Reuben Bourne an incommunicable thought—something which he was to conceal most heedfully from her whom he most loved and trusted . . . concealment had imparted to a justifiable act much of the secret effect of guilt; and Reuben . . . experienced . . . the mental horrors which punish the perpetrator of undiscovered crime. . . . His one secret thought became . . . like a serpent gnawing into his heart. . . .[13]

Reuben's sin, therefore, consisted not in the original deed itself, but in the concealment of the deed through a disingenuousness tantamount to dishonesty.

A second character who symbolizes the sin of concealment is the Reverend Mr. Hooper. On the Sunday when the minister first wore the black veil over his face, he preached, significantly, on "secret sin, and those sad mysteries which we hide from our nearest and dearest." The black veil, Hawthorne tells us, became "the symbol of a fearful secret" between the minister and his parishioners. The mysterious emblem had the effect of rendering more powerful the minister's influence, which reached its apogee

13. *Mosses*, pp. 393–395.

on the occasion of the election sermon. But Mr. Hooper had committed no peculiar sin; the black veil symbolizes a degree of concealment, or a lack of complete openness of heart, common to all mankind.[14]

A third character who is emblematical of secret sin is Roderick Elliston in "Egotism; or, The Bosom Serpent." He is afflicted with a snake in his bosom which becomes "the type of each man's fatal error, or hoarded sin, or unquiet conscience." [15] The idea of such a character may have been suggested by Spenser's description of Envy in The Faerie Queene and particularly by the following lines:

> And in his bosome secretly there lay
> An hatefull snake, the which his taile uptyes
> In many folds, and mortall sting implyes.[16]

In 1836 Hawthorne had recorded in his notebook the following suggestion:

A snake taken into a man's stomach and nourished there from fifteen years to thirty-five, tormenting him most horribly. A type of envy or some other evil passion.

Again in 1842 the idea recurs in the journal:

A man to swallow a small snake—and it to be a symbol of a cherished sin.[17]

The story "Egotism; or, The Bosom Serpent" must have been written a short time after this entry was made.

The kinship of Dimmesdale with the three characters who have just been considered is sufficiently obvious. Although the minister's deed, unlike Reuben Bourne's, may not be justifiable, Hawthorne, so far from dwelling upon its wickedness, suggests

14. Twice-Told Tales, pp. 55, 60, 66, 69.
15. Mosses, p. 314.
16. The Faerie Queene, ed. by R. E. Neil Dodge, Cambridge Edition (Boston and New York: Houghton Mifflin Company, 1908), I, iv, 31, ll. 3–5.
17. Passages, pp. 34, 93.

extenuation in the words of Hester: "What we did had a conse-
cration of its own." Dimmesdale's sin, like Bourne's, consists in
concealment and hypocrisy. The actual conduct of Dimmesdale
before his parishioners has a striking resemblance to that of the
Reverend Mr. Hooper. The assumption of sinfulness in a general
way, without reference to specific acts, in both instances adds
power to the spiritual appeals which are made from the pulpit.
Finally, Dimmesdale's habit of holding his hand over his heart [18]
recalls Elliston's gesture by which he "clutched both hands upon
his breast as if an intolerable sting or torture impelled him to
rend it open and let out the living mischief." [19]

But Dimmesdale must be considered as belonging fundamentally with the scholar-idealists whose genealogy we have
traced from Fanshawe as a progenitor. His "white, lofty, and
impending brow," his "careworn and emaciated" countenance,
his voice "sweet, tremulous, but powerful," [20] his formidable
scholarship, his solitude—all are qualities which recall Fanshawe.
Whereas Fanshawe fails because of a physical collapse, Dimmesdale fails because of moral weakness, which in turn reacts on his
physical nature. His aspiration is as exalted as that of the ambitious guest. His intellectual application in theology is as strenu-
ous as Aylmer's in natural science. His nature is as free from
worldliness and as sensitive to beauty as Owen Warland's. It is
clear, therefore, that two separate lines of character development
culminate and unite in the character of Dimmesdale.

The type of idealistic character which we have been considering was, as we have seen, a favorite one with Hawthorne. It is
likely that he put a good deal of himself into the various representatives of this type.[21] An inference concerning his opinion

18. *The Scarlet Letter*, pp. 234, 226.
19. *Mosses*, p. 305.
20. *Scarlet Letter*, pp. 88, 140.
21. It is interesting to note that Hawthorne portrays Dimmesdale in
language very similar to that used to describe himself. He wrote to Sophia
Peabody from Salem on October 4, 1840: "But living in solitude till the
fulness of time was come, I still kept the dew of my youth and the freshness

as to the effectiveness of the idealist in practical life may be warranted. In his youthful production he represented his hero as an individual of surprising strength in dealing with more worldly natures. Fanshawe's spectacular triumph over Butler may be taken as the expression of a young man's faith in the potency of ideal qualities. But Owen Warland, Dimmesdale, and Clifford are no matches for their antagonists, Peter Hovenden, Chillingworth, and Judge Pyncheon. The frail, sensitive nature is destroyed by the superior force of unfeeling intelligence or worldly power. In the following statement, which was written to apply to Owen Warland's plight, one detects the disillusionment of Hawthorne's maturity with reference to his own relation to the world: "It is requisite for the ideal artist to possess a force of character that seems hardly compatible with its delicacy. . . ." [22]

II

Hawthorne's villains may be considered in three groups in which the culminating figures are, respectively, Westervelt in *The Blithedale Romance,* Chillingworth in *The Scarlet Letter,* and Judge Pyncheon in *The House of the Seven Gables.* Although there is, of course, some overlapping of characteristics, each group has certain traits which distinguish it from the others.

In *Fanshawe,* the villain, Butler, is vaguely described as a mysterious stranger with a dark countenance and foreign manners. "The glow of many a hotter sun than ours has darkened his brow; and his step and air have something foreign in them. . . ." His face reveals traces of "hardship, peril, and dissipation." His eye is "bold" and his smile "derisive" or "ironical." On occasion his look becomes "wilder and fiercer" or "dark and fiend-

---

of my heart . . ." (*Love Letters of Nathaniel Hawthorne, 1839–41* and *1841– 63,* ed. by W. K. Bixby. 2 vols. [Chicago: Privately printed for the Society of Dofobs, 1907], I, 225). Of Dimmesdale, Hawthorne says: "He trod in the shadowy bypaths, and thus kept himself simple and child-like; coming forth, when occasion was, with a freshness, a fragrance, and dewy purity of thought . . ." (*Scarlet Letter,* p. 88).

22. *Mosses,* p. 512.

like," or is marked by a "wild earnestness." [23] In his attempt to
seduce the heroine, Ellen Langton, Butler cites Scripture for his
purpose. Hawthorne very probably had before him no more
definite prototype than the Satan of the Bible and of *Paradise
Lost*. In contriving the situation in which Butler stands at the
foot of a precipice while Fanshawe watches from the top of the
cliff, Hawthorne may have had in mind Uriel's observation of
Satan.[24] The following sentence seems distinctly reminiscent of
Milton's passage: "There was something awful, to his [Butler's]
apprehension, in the slight form that stood so far above him, like
a being from another sphere, looking down upon his wickedness." [25]

Walter Brome, the seducer of Alice in "Alice Doane's Appeal" (1835), is described with a vagueness characteristic of
Hawthorne's portrayals of his villains. We are told only that he
had been educated in the cities of the old world, that his life
abroad had been reckless and ungoverned, and that he had been
guilty of "many varieties of wickedness." [26] Edgar Vaughan,
who has evil designs upon Sylph Etherege in the story of that
title (1838), was likewise educated in Europe. His more noteworthy characteristics are: his "dark features," "the polish of
his manners," and a smile which was an "expression of mockery
and malice." When Sylph dies, Vaughan's look of "anguish" [27]
betrays his keen disappointment at the escape of his victim.

In the notebook in 1837 Hawthorne recorded the observation
that "men of cold passions have quick eyes." [28] This entry may
have been reread when he was creating the character of Matthew
Maule whose evil eye possessed powers of witchcraft. Like Butler

23. *Fanshawe*, pp. 99, 123, 100, 145, 196, 105, 197, 186.
24. *The Complete Poetical Works of John Milton*, ed. by William Vaughn
Moody. Student's Cambridge Edition (Boston: Houghton Mifflin Company,
1924), IV, 125–130.
25. *Fanshawe*, p. 207.
26. *Tales, Sketches, and Other Papers*, p. 285. Hereafter cited as *Sketches*.
27. *The Snow Image and Other Twice-Told Tales*, pp. 511, 517.
28. *Passages*, p. 110.

and Vaughan, Maule has, as a distinctive facial expression, a "dark smile" which makes "a riddle of his countenance." By means of his mesmeric faculty he completely subjects Alice Pyncheon to his will. Upon her death, Maule walks in the funeral procession, "gnashing his teeth" [29] in bitter regret because his victim has escaped the further operation of his diabolical powers.

Westervelt in *The Blithedale Romance* (1852) conforms to the pattern the general outlines of which have been indicated in the characters already considered. The notable points of characterization are: eyes which "sparkled . . . as if the Devil were peeping out of them"; "the wicked expression of his grin"; his polished manners and foppish dress;[30] his "stick with a wooden head, carved in vivid imitation of that of a serpent";[31] and his subjection of Priscilla by mesmeric influence. Upon the death of Zenobia, who also was in some unexplained manner within his power, Westervelt, like Vaughan and Maule under similar conditions, betrays, in the remark "She is now beyond my reach," [32] chagrin at the escape of a victim. Westervelt may have been suggested to Hawthorne by an entry made in the notebook in 1838: "Character of a man who, in himself and his external circumstances, shall be equally and totally false. . . ." [33] This quality of falseness in Westervelt is symbolized by "a gold band around the upper part of his teeth, thereby making it apparent that every one of his brilliant grinders and incisors was a sham." It was indeed rumored in the neighborhood that he was a wizard whose physical appearance was merely assumed and that in reality he was "a wizened little elf, gray and decrepit." [34]

The kinship of the villains thus far considered, Butler, Brome, Vaughan, Maule, and Westervelt, is evidenced by similarities of personal appearance and by the common practice of evil designs

29. *Seven Gables*, pp. 235, 250.
30. *The Blithedale Romance*, pp. 426, 427, 428, 516.
31. *Ibid.*, p. 424. Compare *Mosses*, p. 91.
32. *Mosses*, pp. 547–550, 592.
33. *Passages*, p. 205.
34. *Blithedale*, pp. 427, 428.

against innocent girls. The second group consists of old men, stooped and gray. The two conspicuous examples of this type, Rappaccini and Chillingworth, are clearly derived from the devils and wizards of the early tales. In "The Gentle Boy" (1832), there is an allusion to the devil as "a lame man of low stature and gravely apparelled, with a dark and twisted countenance, and a bright, downcast eye." [35] In "Alice Doane's Appeal" (1835), a wizard, who is described as "a small, gray, withered man, with fiendish ingenuity in devising evil, and superhuman power to execute it," [36] contrives through his machinations to bring about incest and murder. The devil in "Young Goodman Brown" (1835) appears as a man about fifty years old, dressed in "grave and decent attire" and carrying a "staff, which bore the likeness of a great black snake." [37] It seems probable that in these descriptions Hawthorne was indebted in part to Spenser's account of Archimago, and particularly to the following lines:

> At length they chaunst to meet upon the way
> An aged sire, in long blacke weedes yclad,
> His feete all bare, his beard all hoarie gray . . .
> Sober he seemde, and very sagely sad,
> And to the ground his eyes were lowly bent,
> Simple in shew, and voide of malice bad. . . .[38]

Moreover, just as the Red Cross Knight's faith in Una is destroyed by the wiles of Archimago, so Leonard Doane's belief in his sister's purity is shattered as a result of the machinations of the wizard.

Dr. Rappaccini's physical appearance recalls that of Hawthorne's devils and wizards: he is past middle age, with gray hair and a thin, gray beard; he wears the scholar's garb of black; he moves feebly in a stooping position; and his face, though sickly and sallow, is "pervaded with an expression of piercing and

35. *Twice-Told Tales*, p. 100.
36. *Sketches*, p. 284.
37. *Mosses*, pp. 90, 91.
38. *The Faerie Queene*, I, i, 20, ll. 1–7.

active intellect." Chillingworth likewise resembles in a general way the foregoing characters in this group: he "went stooping away along the earth." "His gray beard almost touched the ground, as he crept onward." His eyes had a "strange, penetrating power." [39]

Two entries in the notebooks doubtless contributed to the development of the character of Chillingworth. In 1842 Hawthorne had recorded in the journal the following suggestion: "To symbolize moral or spiritual disease by disease of the body. . . ." [40] This idea finds its application not in disease, to be sure, but in the physical deformity of Chillingworth—a deformity which, with appropriate symbolism, increases as his moral nature becomes more degraded. At the beginning of the novel, he is only "slightly deformed, with the left shoulder a trifle higher than the right"; but as the story progresses he becomes "misshapen" and "hump-shouldered." [41] Another entry in the journal which has a significant bearing on the character of Chillingworth was made in 1847: "A story of the effects of revenge, in diabolizing him who indulges in it." [42] Chillingworth is the only villain in Hawthorne's works whose character undergoes a change during the course of the narrative: all the other villains are in substantially the same moral state at the end of the story as at the beginning. But Chillingworth, Hawthorne tells us, "was a striking evidence of man's faculty of transforming himself into a devil, if he will only, for a reasonable space of time, undertake a devil's office." This diabolical transformation of the leech's character was evidenced not only by an increasing physical deformity but by "an eager, searching, almost fierce, yet carefully guarded look," and by "a glare of red light" which was emitted, on occasion, from his eyes.[43]

39. *Mosses*, pp. 112, 124, and *Scarlet Letter*, pp. 211, 80.

40. *The American Notebooks by Nathaniel Hawthorne*, ed. by Randall Stewart (New Haven: Yale University Press, 1932), p. 89.

41. *Scarlet Letter*, pp. 80, 139, 291.

42. *American Notebooks*, p. 121.

43. *Scarlet Letter*, pp. 205, 204, 205.

It is probable that Hawthorne, in creating the character of Chillingworth, drew not only upon the notebooks but also upon his intimate knowledge of Milton and Spenser. When Uriel observed Satan on the Assyrian mount—a situation which, as I have already indicated, seems to have suggested a scene in *Fanshawe*—he saw the unrestrained actions of the Evil One who supposed himself unobserved:

> Saw him disfigured, more than could befall
> Spirit of happy sort: his gestures fierce
> He marked and mad demeanour, then alone,
> As he supposed, all unobserved, unseen.[44]

Similarly, Chillingworth, when he is alone with Dimmesdale, who is sleeping, behaves in a singularly wild and diabolical manner after he has looked at the minister's bosom:

With what a ghastly rapture, as it were, too mighty to be expressed only by the eye and features, and therefore bursting forth through the whole ugliness of his figure, and making itself even riotously manifest by the extravagant gestures with which he threw up his arms towards the ceiling, and stamped his foot upon the floor! [45]

A parallel, less close but equally striking, may be drawn between the fate of Chillingworth and that of Spenser's jealous husband, Malbecco. When the latter attempted to commit suicide by jumping from a high cliff, he received no injury from his fall because his body had wasted away to the point of insubstantiality:

> But through long anguish and selfe-murdring thought,
> He was so wasted and forpined quight,
> That all his substance was consum'd to nought,
> And nothing left, but like an aery spright,
> That on the rockes he fell so flit and light,
> That he thereby receiv'd no hurt at all. . . .[46]

44. *Paradise Lost*, IV, 127–130.
45. *Scarlet Letter*, p. 169.
46. *The Faerie Queene*, III, x, 57, ll. 1–6.

Although Hawthorne's treatment of the injured husband is very different from Spenser's, the physical change in Chillingworth after the death of Dimmesdale seems reminiscent of the somewhat similar metamorphosis of Malbecco:

> All his strength and energy—all his vital and intellectual force—seemed at once to desert him; insomuch that he positively withered up, shrivelled away, and almost vanished from mortal sight, like an uprooted weed that lies wilting in the sun.[47]

Derived from the devil and wizard of the early tales, from abstract ideas recorded in the notebooks, and from hints in *Paradise Lost* and *The Faerie Queene,* the character of Chillingworth possesses at best only a galvanic vitality. Critics agree in insisting upon the artificiality of the character.[48] Obviously, Chillingworth has no points of contact with real life or with Hawthorne's actual observations or experiences.

Still another villain to be considered in this same line of development is Miriam's persecutor, the model in *The Marble Faun.* He is described very vaguely: "a wild visage was indistinctly seen, floating away, as it were, into a dusky wilderness of mustache and beard." [49] In several respects—his bearded face, his inconspicuousness, and his inexorable pursuit of his victim— the model recalls Chillingworth. As a persecutor of women he resembles Westervelt and others. Moreover, in the treatment of the character and his relation to his victim, Hawthorne, curiously enough, has drawn upon his first work, *Fanshawe.* The model, like Butler, shrouds his face in his cloak.[50] His victim, Miriam,

---

47. *Scarlet Letter,* p. 307.

48. For example, L. Dhaleine: "Celui de ses héros qui semble le plus artificiel, et qui paraît n'exister que pour permettre le développement d'une conception abstraite de l'auteur, est le vieux Chillingworth . . ." (*N. Hawthorne, Sa Vie et Son Oeuvre* [Paris: Hachette, 1905], p. 444). And W. C. Brownell: "Chillingworth . . . is . . . the one piece of machinery of the book" (*American Prose Masters* [New York: Charles Scribner's Sons, 1909], p. 102).

49. *Marble Faun,* p. 45.

50. See *Fanshawe,* p. 188, and *Marble Faun,* p. 136.

like Ellen Langton, kneels before her enemy supplicating release.[51] And again a precipice serves in both stories as a means
of disposing of the villain.[52] The crime of Miriam and the model
—probably incest [53]—had been used once before by Hawthorne,
though very slightly, in "Alice Doane's Appeal." In one respect,
however, the villain in *The Marble Faun* is different from his
predecessors in Hawthorne's stories: the author suggests that he
has lived and perhaps sinned for centuries.[54] In ascribing this
trait to the model, Hawthorne probably had in mind the
Wandering Jew, a character in whom he repeatedly evinced an
interest. The following entry may possibly be related to the
mysterious character in *The Marble Faun* as he conceived it: "A
disquisition . . . on the manner in which the Wandering Jew has
spent his life. One period, perhaps, in wild carnal debauchery;
then trying, over and over again, to grasp domestic happiness.
. . ." [55] From the foregoing analysis it is clear that the villain of
The Marble Faun, while possessing the familiar characteristics of
Hawthorne's villains, becomes through the addition of the pre-
rogative of the Wandering Jew at once more ominous and more
unreal than any of his predecessors.

I have discovered only one character in Hawthorne's fiction
who may be regarded as a precursor of Judge Pyncheon. Peter
Hovenden in "The Artist of the Beautiful" is a man of "cold,
unimaginative sagacity," an epitome of the "hard, coarse

51. See *Fanshawe,* p. 207, and *Marble Faun,* p. 121.

52. See *Fanshawe,* p. 208, and *Marble Faun,* p. 202.

53. The reasons for so interpreting the crime are given in note 26 in the
next chapter of this book. [Ed.]

54. See *Marble Faun,* p. 180. Hawthorne seems to have taken from the
Preface to Godwin's *St. Leon* a definite idea which he used in connection with
this character. Godwin tells of a Signor Gualdi whose deathless nature one
infers from the fact that he possesses a portrait of himself drawn by Titian
one hundred and thirty years before. Similarly Hawthorne implies the early
mortality of Miriam's model by pointing out his resemblance to the demon
painted by Guido more than two centuries previous to the time of the story.
(See Preface, *St. Leon,* and *Marble Faun,* pp. 165–168.)

55. *American Notebooks,* p. 117. See also *Mosses,* pp. 76, 558.

world";[56] and the artist feels a repulsion for him similar to that which overwhelms Clifford in the presence of the judge. But the character of Pyncheon is composed of elements derived from various sources. One small descriptive detail is borrowed from *The Scarlet Letter*: "a red fire" in his eyes recalls the "glare of red light" [57] in the eyes of Chillingworth. Some of Judge Pyncheon's traits were undoubtedly suggested by the Reverend Mr. Upham.[58] Elizabeth Hawthorne wrote her brother after reading *The House of the Seven Gables*:

Louisa says that Judge Pyncheon is supposed to be Mr. Upham. I do not know Mr. Upham, but I imagined him to be a much more insignificant person—less weighty in every sense. There may be some points of resemblance, such as the warm smiles, and the incident of the daguerreotype bringing out the evil traits of his character, and his boasts of the great influence he had exerted for Clifford's release.[59]

And Julian Hawthorne praises the character as a masterpiece of personal satire:

There he stands for all time,—subtle, smooth, cruel, unscrupulous; perfectly recognizable to all who knew his real character, but so modified as to outward guise that no one who had met him merely as an acquaintance would ever suspect his identity.[60]

The notebooks contributed only slightly to the development of this character. The following entry, however, made in 1847, seems to anticipate the kind of hypocrisy exemplified in Judge Pyncheon:

56. *Mosses*, pp. 514, 515.

57. *Seven Gables*, p. 158, and *Scarlet Letter*, p. 205.

58. For a biographical sketch of Charles Wentworth Upham (1802–1875) see Essex Institute *Historical Collections*, XV (1878), 290. Upham was a leader in the movement in 1849 to expel Hawthorne from his office as surveyor in the Salem Custom House. The satirical portrait of Judge Pyncheon which was based in part upon Upham was Hawthorne's retaliation.

59. *Hawthorne and His Wife*, I, 438–439.

60. *Ibid.*, I, 339–340.

Some men have no right to perform great deeds, or think high thoughts—and when they do so, it is a kind of humbug. They had better keep within their own propriety.

Another entry, recorded in 1850, may have suggested the scene of the judge's vigil:

The sunbeam that comes through a round-hole in the shutter of a darkened room, where a dead man sits in solitude.[61]

In *The House of the Seven Gables,* the moonbeams, rather than the sunlight, reveal the dead body of Judge Pyncheon—a change made in order to allow the introduction at midnight of the ghosts of the Judge's ancestors.[62] Thus, although it is doubtless true that Upham provided Hawthorne with certain major characteristics, nevertheless, in the creation of this composite character, the author drew details from other sources as well: from the earlier characters, Hovenden and Chillingworth, and from the notebooks.

In looking back over Hawthorne's villains, one observes the repetition of certain fundamental traits. They are nearly all persecutors of women (Butler, Brome, Vaughan, Maule, Westervelt, Rappaccini, the model) or of men of feminine weakness (Hovenden, Chillingworth, Pyncheon). Hawthorne often hints through various details that his villains are incarnated devils; for example, the red fire in the eyes of Chillingworth and Judge Pyncheon, and the age of the model, who has lived many hundred years, are details which have a diabolical implication. Details of personal appearance recur with regularity within the two larger divisions. Hawthorne's process of working was such that in the creation of individual characters in his fiction after about 1850, the chief source material was supplied by prototypes and precursors in his own writings. This process has been demonstrated especially with reference to the treatment of Judge

61. *American Notebooks,* pp. 118, 130.
62. *Seven Gables,* pp. 328–332.

Pyncheon and Miriam's model. The chief weakness of Hawthorne's villains is an inadequate motivation of their deeds.
Perhaps only in three instances does the author provide adequate
motivation for the acts of his evil characters: Rappaccini's zeal
in scientific experiment, Chillingworth's desire for revenge, and
Judge Pyncheon's attempt to escape the penalty of his crime by
incriminating the innocent Clifford. The other characters in this
category seem to have been actuated merely by a motiveless
malignity.

III

Hawthorne's heroines may be classified, for the convenience
of our discussion, according to three general types: first, the
wholesome New England girl, bright, sensible, and self-reliant;
second, the frail, sylphlike creature, easily swayed by a stronger
personality; and, third, the woman with an exotic richness in
her nature.

Whether Ellen Langton in *Fanshawe* is a description of an
actual girl whom Hawthorne knew and perhaps loved, or is
merely an imaginary portrait of his youthful ideal, it is impossible to say. But it is significant of Hawthorne's preferences in
these matters that Ellen is the prototype of several heroines in
later stories, including Phoebe in *The House of the Seven Gables*
and Hilda in *The Marble Faun*, and that in many qualities she
is an anticipation of Sophia Peabody. In Ellen's dark eyes one may
read "pure and pleasant thoughts." She has "the gayety and
simple happiness, because the innocence, of a child." After she
became a member of Dr. Melmoth's somber household, "the
sunny days seemed brighter and the cloudy ones less gloomy."
She possessed both "a large fund of plain sense," and an esthetic
faculty which was expressed in the daily decoration of her room
with wild flowers.[63] Differing, however, from Mrs. Hawthorne
whose linguistic knowledge was considerable,[64] Ellen prefers

63. *Fanshawe*, pp. 82, 106, 155.
64. Mrs. Hawthorne apparently was a linguist of considerable ability. Julian

reading an old romance to pursuing a course of instruction in the learned languages[65] proffered by Dr. Melmoth.

Susan in "The Village Uncle" (1835) has an interesting place in the development of this type. She is "a frank, simple, kind-hearted, sensible, and mirthful girl," scattering sunshine upon gloomy spirits. She keeps a shop where "gingerbread men and horses, picture-books and ballads, small fishhooks, pins, needles, sugar-plums, and brass thimbles" [66] are offered for sale, thus anticipating the role of Phoebe. There is reason for believing that the sketch of Susan was based upon an actual person. Hawthorne's sister, Elizabeth, wrote Julian Hawthorne:

About the year 1833, your father, after a sojourn of two or three weeks at Swampscott, came home captivated, in his fanciful way, with a "mermaid," as he called her. He would not tell us her name, but said she was of the aristocracy of the village, the keeper of a little shop. . . . You will find her, I suspect, in "The Village Uncle." . . . He said she had a great deal of what the French call *espièglerie*.[67]

The notebooks afford abundant evidence that Hawthorne continued to observe pretty girls with interest and to record his observations. In the Augusta journal one finds lively sketches of Nancy, "a pretty, black-eyed, intelligent servant-girl" with a piquant countenance, and of the "frank, free, mirthful daughter of the landlady" with whom Hawthorne carried on a flirtation. The quality of *espièglerie*, particularly admired in Susan, is the salient characteristic of "our table-waiter, Eliza Chaseboro" [68] whom Hawthorne observed at North Adams.

Hawthorne says that she read Latin, Greek, and Hebrew (*Hawthorne and His Wife*, I, 40). In her journal at the Old Manse (August 29, 30, 1843) Mrs. Hawthorne mentions reading *Les Mémoires de Luther and Tasso*. She was studying German with her mother and sisters as early as 1838 (*Hawthorne and His Wife*, I, 185).

65. *Fanshawe*, p. 82.
66. *Twice-Told Tales*, pp. 356, 355.
67. *Hawthorne and His Wife*, I, 127–128.
68. *American Notebooks*, pp. 18–19, 22, 55.

Although such characters as Faith Brown in "Young Goodman Brown" (1835), the nameless girl in "David Swan" (1837), Faith Egerton in "The Threefold Destiny" (1838), and Eve in "The New Adam and Eve" (1843) are very lightly sketched, it is obvious that these women, like Ellen and Susan, possess cheerfulness, prettiness, and a simple-minded domesticity.

The character of Phoebe is of special interest because of its derivation from several prototypes. Just as Ellen Langton promptly assumes a large share of the domestic duties in Mrs. Melmoth's household,[69] so Phoebe "by the magnetism of innate fitness" takes Hepzibah's place in the kitchen. Phoebe and Ellen are alike also in their lack of bookishness: the educational qualifications of the former do not extend beyond those of the mistress of the village school.[70] Phoebe also recalls Susan in certain definite respects: they are alike not only in their vocation of shopkeeping but in an engaging detail of personal appearance: both have a few freckles which are becoming rather than otherwise.[71] Phoebe, however, owes more to Mrs. Hawthorne than to either Ellen Langton or Susan. The name itself was one which Hawthorne had used in writing to his wife.[72] Phoebe's nose, "slightly piquant," is modeled after Sophia's, which Hawthorne refers to in a letter as "that whimsical little nose of thine." [73] More important, Phoebe and Sophia are alike in certain spiritual qualities. Hawthorne says that his wife "is birdlike in many things." [74] Simliarly, Phoebe is "as graceful as a bird" and possesses a "natural tunefulness . . . like a bird." [75] Hawthorne compares his wife to bright sunshine and himself to a dark cloud.[76] Similarly,

69. *Fanshawe*, p. 83.
70. *Seven Gables*, pp. 99, 100.
71. See *Twice-Told Tales*, p. 355, and *Seven Gables*, p. 103.
72. See *Love Letters*, II, 113, 117, 120, 124, 129, 134, 153. These letters were written between 1844 and 1845.
73. *Seven Gables*, p. 103, and *Love Letters*, II, 7.
74. *American Notebooks*, p. 182.
75. *Seven Gables*, pp. 103, 99.
76. *American Notebooks*, p. 164, and *Love Letters*, I, 236, 237.

Phoebe is a "ray of sunshine" in a "dismal place." [77] And just as Mrs. Hawthorne with happy skill transformed the Old Manse, a "musty edifice," into a "comfortable modern residence," so Phoebe by "a kind of natural magic" [78] effected an equally remarkable transformation in the interior arrangements of the house of the seven gables. Finally, both are of a religious nature: Mrs. Hawthorne goes to church, leaving her husband at home; Phoebe likewise has "a church-going conscience." [79] From these detailed comparisons it is clear that Phoebe is a composite character whose traits are drawn partly from the fictional characters, Ellen Langton and Susan, and partly from the author's wife.

The last character in this series of wholesome New England girls is Hilda in *The Marble Faun*. She is described as "pretty at all times, in our native New England style." [80] In her religious orthodoxy and in her moral purity, symbolized by the doves which circle about her tower,[81] she derives from both Phoebe and Mrs. Hawthorne herself. It appears that in this heroine, however, Hawthorne incorporated even more of his wife than in the portrait of Phoebe. The latter is a blending of the lively village girl, such as Hawthorne often met on his adventurous journeys through rural New England and occasionally described in the notebooks, and Sophia in her capacity as a homemaker. In *The Marble Faun*, Hawthorne has apparently forgotten those earlier feminine models of his youth and the character of Hilda becomes little more than an ideal portrait of the author's wife. This identity is particularly obvious in the account of Hilda's artistic career:

Even in her school-days . . . she had produced sketches that were seized upon by men of taste, and hoarded as among the choicest treasures

77. *Seven Gables*, p. 90.
78. *American Notebooks*, p. 149, and *Seven Gables*, p. 90.
79. *American Notebooks*, p. 169, and *Seven Gables*, p. 186.
80. *Marble Faun*, p. 81.
81. This symbolism is anticipated in *Blithedale* (p. 501) in which a dove perches above Priscilla's window.

of their portfolios; scenes delicately imagined, lacking, perhaps, the reality which comes only from a close acquaintance with life, but so softly touched with feeling and fancy, that you seemed to be looking at humanity with angels' eyes.[82]

Washington Allston had encouraged Sophia in her painting; and Hawthorne may have had in mind her drawing of Ilbrahim, the gentle boy,[83] in the phrase "looking at humanity with angels' eyes." Both Hilda and Sophia succeeded better as copyists than as original painters: at times their copies surpassed the originals.[84] Although the crushing blow inflicted upon Hilda by the mere knowledge of the guilt of Miriam and Donatello finds no parallel in Sophia's life, the experience, nevertheless, is conceived in harmony with the almost too moral character of Mrs. Hawthorne, of whom her sister, Elizabeth Peabody, wrote: ". . . there was one kind of thing she could not bear, and that was, moral evil." [85]

Phoebe remains perhaps the most satisfactory heroine in the group which we have just studied. With a personality more varied and more real than Hilda's, she is closer to the New England village life which Hawthorne had observed and recorded in the tales and notebooks. Hilda is the product of a later period when the author has been almost completely deracinated from the New England soil and when his wife has become too exclusively his pattern of pure womanhood.

To trace the lineage of Alice Pyncheon and Priscilla, one must go back to three fragile maidens who are but slightly sketched in the earlier tales: Sylph Etherege in the story of that name (1838), Alice Vane in "Edward Randolph's Portrait" (1838), and Lilias Fay in "The Lily's Quest" (1839). Sylph Etherege was a "shy, sensitive, and fanciful" girl with a "slender and sylph-like figure" and a nervous organization so delicate that "every vibra-

82. *Marble Faun,* p. 72.
83. *Hawthorne and His Wife,* I, 65, 181.
84. See *Marble Faun,* pp. 76–77, and *Hawthorne and His Wife,* I, 64–65.
85. *Hawthorne and His Wife,* I, 248.

tion of her spirit was visible in her frame." [86] Being too pure
and spiritual for the earth, she was translated to the spirit world
and thereby escaped her diabolical antagonist. Alice Vane is described as "a pale, ethereal creature, who, though a native of
New England, had been educated abroad, and seemed not merely
a stranger from another clime, but almost a being from another
world." Lilias Fay, like her two precursors, was a being so
delicate that "she looked as if the summer breeze should snatch
her up and waft her heavenward." [87] Her death, like that of
Sylph Etherege, results not from an external cause, but from
mere inanition; its true *raison d'être* is the enforcement of a
moral—that all joy is attended by sorrow. It may not be fantastic
to suggest that the snow image in the story of that title (1850)
properly belongs in this group of sylph-like maidens. Such is the
ethereal grace of the image that the mother of the children sup-
poses it to be an angel, and the gradual drooping of the snow
maiden when she is brought into the warm parlor is not unlike
the waning of Sylph Etherege and Lilias Fay.

Alice Pyncheon, like Alice Vane, was educated abroad. Like
Sylph Etherege, she escapes her persecutor by death, which follows a wasting away of her frail form. Two new elements, however, are added to the type in the portrait of Alice Pyncheon: her
sin of pride, which Hawthorne had treated before in "Lady
Eleanore's Mantle" (1838), and her faculty as a medium, a role
which is elaborated in *The Blithedale Romance.*

A study of the character of Priscilla affords further illustration of Hawthorne's method of mixing ingredients derived from
various sources. Arriving at Blithedale in the midst of a snow-
storm, Priscilla recalls to the author an earlier creation, the snow
image:

The fantasy occurred to me that she was some desolate kind of a
creature, doomed to wander about in snow-storms; and that, though

86. *Snow Image,* pp. 509, 508, 514.
87. *Twice-Told Tales,* pp. 294, 502.

the ruddiness of our windowpanes had tempted her into a human dwelling, she would not remain long enough to melt the icicles out of her hair.

And again she is described, fantastically, as "this shadowy snow-maiden, who, precisely at the stroke of midnight, shall melt away . . . in a pool of ice-cold water." [88] If in her ethereality Priscilla recalls the snow maiden, in her physical frailty, particularly upon her arrival at Blithedale, she resembles the other heroines in this group from Sylph Etherege to Alice Pyncheon. Her kinship with the latter is especially significant in that, like Alice, Priscilla is a medium. But Priscilla's character has elements of strength as well as of weakness, and here she parts company with her precursors in Hawthorne's fiction. In describing her improving health at Blithedale and her pranks on the farm—her clambering upon a load of hay and her riding on the oxen—the author drew upon the account in the notebook of the seamstress at Brook Farm. [89] Thus we see that Priscilla, unlike her fictional prototypes, possessed a reserve of health and normal instincts. And in the following statement of her resiliency and fortitude, the author must have had in mind Mrs. Hawthorne herself, who had succeeded after her marriage in partly overcoming a chronic invalidism:

Thus, while we see that such a being responds to every breeze with tremulous vibration, and imagine that she must be shattered by the first rude blast, we find her retaining her equilibrium amid shocks that might have overthrown many a sturdier frame. [90]

To sum up, Priscilla blends qualities taken from sources both ideal and real: her fragility, her ethereality, and her faculty as a medium were carried over from her fictional precursors; her

88. *Blithedale*, pp. 351, 357.
89. From the account of the seamstress in the journal Hawthorne drew several suggestions for the characterization of Priscilla. See *American Notebooks*, pp. 358, 404.
90. *Blithedale*, p. 593.

fund of health and good humor and her tenacious hold on life
were suggested by actual persons—the seamstress and Sophia
Hawthorne.

The third group of Hawthorne's women, those whose nature is
marked by a certain exotic richness, includes Beatrice in "Rappaccini's Daughter," Hester in *The Scarlet Letter*, Zenobia in *The
Blithedale Romance*, and Miriam in *The Marble Faun*.

Beatrice is a young girl, "redundant with life, health, and
energy"; her voice is "as rich as a tropical sunset"; and her array
is marked by "as much richness of taste as the most splendid of
the flowers" in her father's garden. She is capable on occasion of
a "queenlike haughtiness." [91] Hester Prynne "had in her nature
a rich, voluptuous, Oriental characteristic," which is symbolized
by the elaborate embroidery on the scarlet letter. She is tall with
"a figure of perfect elegance on a large scale." [92] She too is often
haughty in her demeanor. Zenobia is a woman of "bloom, health,
and vigor" with a "spacious plan" of physical development. Her
exotic beauty is symbolized by the hothouse flower which she
wears daily in her hair. Like her predecessors she has as much
pride as a queen.[93] Miriam's beauty, finally, is remarkable for "a
certain rich Oriental character in her face." [94] Although Hester
and Zenobia are older and of a more ample physical development
than Beatrice and Miriam, there is nevertheless an obvious
similarity in appearance among the four members of this group.

These women are unique in Hawthorne's fiction, not only for
their physical appearance, but also for their mental traits: they
are the only women of marked intellectual ability in Hawthorne's
stories. Beatrice's erudition was such that she was "qualified to fill
a professor's chair." [95] Hester, in the solitude of her cottage, enjoyed "a freedom of speculation," entertaining heterodox

91. *Mosses*, pp. 113, 130.
92. *Scarlet Letter*, pp. 107, 73.
93. *Blithedale*, pp. 338, 337, 335.
94. *Marble Faun*, p. 38.
95. *Mosses*, p. 118.

thoughts which, had they been known, would have been regarded by the community as more culpable than the sin symbolized by the scarlet letter. With the future improvement of the world, Hester was hopeful that "the whole relation between man and woman" would be established "on a surer ground of mutual happiness." [96] Zenobia was also given to heterodox thinking: "She made no scruple of oversetting all human institutions, and scattering them as with a breeze from her fan." Like Hester, she was particularly interested in the subject of the relation between the sexes; but unlike Hester, she was ready to take an active part "in behalf of woman's wider liberty." [97] While it is true that Zenobia's zealous advocacy of woman's rights may have been suggested by Margaret Fuller's active interest in that subject,[98] it is obvious nevertheless that this aspect of her character may be regarded as an extension and development of a similar trait in her predecessor, Hester Prynne. Miriam likewise is a woman of independent and subversive thought, which is contrasted with the simple, trusting orthodoxy of Hilda.[99]

It is interesting and perhaps significant of his moral judgments that Hawthorne should ascribe sin, either explicit or suggested, to these women of exotic physical beauty and speculative mind. Hester's sin alone is explicitly stated. Is Beatrice angel or demon? The answer is not clear. The author himself did not know.[100] But the reader suspects that Hawthorne intended that the physical poison should symbolize spiritual poison. It is vaguely hinted that in Zenobia's past life there was some culpable relationship with Westervelt which placed her in his power. Miriam's sin is concealed by the deliberate obscurity of the author's method. In one passage, however, Hawthorne assigns to Miriam conduct

96. *Scarlet Letter*, pp. 199, 311.
97. *Blithedale*, pp. 369–370, 456.
98. See [Margaret Fuller], "The Great Lawsuit," *The Dial*, IV (July 1843), 1–47.
99. See, for example, *Marble Faun*, p. 167.
100. See *Hawthorne and His Wife*, I, 360.

similar to that of Chillingworth and perhaps indicates thereby
that she was under diabolical domination: ". . . fancying herself
wholly unseen, the beautiful Miriam began to gesticulate ex-
travagantly, gnashing her teeth, flinging her arms wildly abroad,
stamping with her foot." [101] Here again we see Hawthorne's
method of developing his characters by drawing source material
from earlier characters of his own.

IV

Since it is not the purpose of this chapter to give an account
of all of Hawthorne's characters, but to analyze the chief family
groups into which they may be divided, I propose to consider
only three additional types: the detached observer, best represented by Coverdale in *The Blithedale Romance* and Kenyon in
The Marble Faun; the reformer, embodied pre-eminently in
Hollingsworth in *The Blithedale Romance;* and the decrepit old
man, as seen especially in Uncle Venner in *The House of the
Seven Gables* and Old Moodie in *The Blithedale Romance.*

The role of the detached observer of life was particularly
congenial to Hawthorne. In "Sights from a Steeple" (1831), he
wrote: "The most desirable mode of existence might be that of
a spiritualized Paul Pry, hovering invisible round man and
woman, witnessing their deeds, searching into their hearts, bor-
rowing brightness from their felicity and shade from their sorrow, and retaining no emotion peculiar to himself." [102] As an
observer of the actual life around him, Hawthorne is seen to the
best advantage in the journal kept at North Adams in 1838.[103]
Lawyer Haynes, himself an acute observer, recognized in Hawthorne "something of the hawk-eye." [104] So accurate are his

101. *Marble Faun,* p. 186. Compare *Scarlet Letter,* p. 169. These descriptive
passages were probably suggested by *Paradise Lost,* IV, 127–130; see p. 22
herein.

102. *Twice-Told Tales,* p. 220.

103. *American Notebooks,* pp. 30–71.

104. *Ibid.,* p. 37.

accounts of the various characters in North Adams that when Professor Bliss Perry visited the town in 1893, he found that a mere line from the notebook would serve with the older citizens to identify the person described.[105] Brownell characterizes Hawthorne's mode of observing as "lynx-like."[106] That this faculty did not diminish with the passing of time is shown by his remarkably shrewd description of Lincoln written in 1862.[107]

If Hawthorne were given to direct self-portraiture in his fiction, we should expect to find many characters whose sole function is to observe and comment on the progress of the action. But he is not, as he tells us in "The Old Manse," "one of those supremely hospitable people who serve up their own hearts, delicately fried, with brain sauce, as a tidbit for their beloved public."[108] Consequently, the detached observers in Hawthorne's stories are few. There are diabolical observers, like Chillingworth, whose observation is a means of persecution; but there are, I think, only three notable characters whose role may be regarded as corresponding to that of a "spiritualized Paul Pry" or of Hawthorne himself: the artist in "The Prophetic Pictures" (1837), Coverdale, and Kenyon.

The artist in "The Prophetic Pictures" looks beneath the exterior and sees the inmost soul. Through the detection of latent traits he is able to anticipate a surprising development of character. While the artist is not malevolent, neither is he benevolent toward his subjects: "he did not possess kindly feelings; his heart was cold."[109] Similarly, Coverdale has a penetrating eye. Zenobia's remark to him recalls the author's "hawk-eye": "I have been exposed to a great deal of eye-shot in the few years of my mixing in the world, but never, I think, to precisely such

105. "Hawthorne at North Adams," *Atlantic Monthly*, LXXI (May 1893), 675–682.
106. *American Prose Masters*, p. 86.
107. See "Chiefly about War Matters," *Sketches*, pp. 309–312.
108. *Mosses*, p. 44.
109. *Twice-Told Tales*, p. 206.

glances as you are in the habit of favoring me with. . . . What
are you seeking to discover in me?" And like the artist, furthermore, Coverdale feels no affection for the human beings whom he
studies—unless we except Priscilla. He recognizes this condition
when he says: "That cold tendency, between instinct and intellect, which made me pry with a speculative interest into people's passions and impulses, appeared to have gone far towards
unhumanizing my heart." It is this cool aloofness, quite as much
as any theoretical opposition to philanthropic projects, which
prevents Coverdale from making common cause with Hollingsworth.[110] Similarly the frigid detachment of another observer,
Kenyon, prevents him from hearing Miriam's secret, lest he be
drawn into a relation so intimate as to be troublesome; where-
upon Miriam says to him with truth: "You are as cold and
pitiless as your own marble." [111]

It is doubtless significant of Hawthorne's own attitude that he
stresses the cold aloofness of these penetrating observers. In the
descriptions of persons in the notebooks, one finds, except in those
passages which refer to his wife, very few traces of affection. It
is safe to say that unfavorable portraits greatly outnumber favorable ones. One recalls in the Augusta journal the characterization
of Cilley,[112] in which the author, not without a sense of satisfaction at his detective skill, reveals the sly, scheming side of the
nature of his subject. Particularly remarkable is this quality of
cold analysis, with perhaps a predisposition for the less lovely
attributes of human nature, in the descriptions of Una,[113] where
parental affection is hardly allowed to enter in. Hawthorne was
perfectly aware that his powers of observation, combined with
his gift of satire, might easily lead not only to coldness but to
malevolence. Thus the observer Coverdale frankly avows in the
course of his study of Zenobia: "I malevolently beheld the true

110. *Blithedale,* pp. 374, 495, 469–475.
111. *Marble Faun,* p. 155.
112. *American Notebooks,* pp. 19–20.
113. *American Notebooks,* pp. 193–213, *passim.* Compare p. 326, n. 511.

character of the woman, passionate, luxurious, lacking simplicity, not deeply refined, incapable of pure and perfect taste." [114] It seems not unfair to suggest the possibility of a correspondence between the attitude of Coverdale on this occasion and that of Hawthorne when he wrote his famous sketch of Margaret Fuller.[115]

But it seems hardly necessary to identify, as Miss Amy Louise Reed attempts to do, the processes of the artist or Coverdale with those of Chillingworth or Ethan Brand,[116] or to conclude "that Hawthorne's young heroes and his mature villains are compounded of the same materials and that both are varieties of self-portraiture." [117] While the faculty *per se* which makes possible the artist's portrait in "The Prophetic Pictures" may be very similar to that by which Chillingworth discovers the minister's secret, nevertheless the difference in motive and aim is decisive: the artist gratifies an instinct for the analysis of character without intentionally inflicting injury upon his subjects; Chillingworth persecutes and destroys his victim.

An observer himself, then, Hawthorne, with his aversion to self-revelation, has introduced into his works only three noteworthy characters of this type. In his portrayal of these characters he has stressed their powers of penetrating observation and their aloofness from their subjects, and the notebooks afford abundant evidence that these are the distinctive qualities which mark his observation of actual people. One may fairly conclude, therefore, that these three characters—the artist in "The Prophetic Pictures," Coverdale, and Kenyon—are the closest approaches to self-portraiture in Hawthorne's fiction.

Another type of character in which Hawthorne manifested a keen interest, though for different reasons, is the reformer. His

114. *Blithedale*, p. 507.
115. See *Hawthorne and His Wife*, I, 259–262.
116. "Self-Portraiture in the Work of Nathaniel Hawthorne," *SP*, XXIII (January 1926), 40–54.
117. *Ibid.*, p. 51.

opposition to active reform was based upon the view that whatever is has a reason for its existence and that when an institution has ceased to serve a needful purpose it will disappear by a process of natural elimination. The activity of the reformer, from this point of view, becomes impertinent and supererogatory. Apropos of Holgrave's proposed warfare on antiquated institutions, Hawthorne says:

> His error lay in supposing that this age, more than any past or future one, is destined to see the tattered garments of Antiquity exchanged for a new suit, instead of gradually renewing themselves by patchwork; in applying his own little life-span as the measure of an interminable achievement; and, more than all, in fancying that it mattered anything to the great end in view whether he himself should contend for it or against it.[118]

Aggressive, organized movements of reform seemed futile to Hawthorne. With reference to the antislavery movement, he wrote in "Chiefly about War Matters": "No human effort, on a grand scale, has ever yet resulted according to the purpose of its projectors." [119] According to Miss Elizabeth Peabody, Hawthorne "looked at all anti-slavery literature as beneath the consideration of a reasonable man." [120]

It is not surprising, therefore, that the treatment of reformers in the tales and novels is sharply satirical. In "The Hall of Fantasy" (1843), various groups of men are introduced and described: writers, businessmen, inventors, and reformers. Among the last group, "many . . . had got possession of some crystal fragment of truth, the brightness of which so dazzled them that they could see nothing else in the wide universe." Again, in "The Procession of Life" (1843), humanity is classified according to various principles: those afflicted with like physical diseases, those united by the bond of sorrow, those joined in a

118. *Seven Gables*, p. 216.
119. *Sketches*, p. 332.
120. From an unpublished letter to Horatio Bridge, June 4, 1887. This letter is in the possession of Miss Marian Bridge Maurice.

brotherhood of crime, and, finally, those associated by the principle of love. Hawthorne observes that in the last group, where one would expect to find harmony, discord prevails, and that this discord may be attributed in part to those people whose minds are "exclusively filled up with one idea." "When a good man," Hawthorne explains, "has long devoted himself to a particular kind of beneficence—to one species of reform—he is apt to become narrowed into the limits of the path wherein he treads, and to fancy that there is no other good to be done on earth but that selfsame good to which he has put his hand. . . ." And, once more, in "A Select Party" (1844), the list of guests includes the following imaginary persons: "an incorruptible Patriot; a Scholar without pedantry; a Priest without worldly ambition; a Beautiful Woman without pride or coquetry; . . . a Reformer untrammeled by his theory. . . ." [121]

The sketches of these anonymous and abstract figures give us the theoretical basis of the character of Hollingsworth. Like his shadowy precursors, Hollingsworth "knew absolutely nothing, except in a single direction." Hawthorne deprecates "such prolonged fiddling upon one string—such multiform presentation of one idea!" When Hollingsworth implores Coverdale to join with him in his philanthropic scheme for the reformation of criminals, Coverdale refuses: ". . . cannot you conceive that a man may wish well to the world, and struggle for its good, on some other plan than precisely that which you have laid down?" [122] The besetting sin of Hollingsworth, therefore, like that of the reformers described in the three tales mentioned above, is a narrowness of mind growing out of an obsession with a single idea. The character of Hollingsworth is merely an embodiment of the traits distinctly indicated, though not incarnated, in the earlier tales.

The last type of character which I propose to consider is one of minor importance and yet one which had a particular appeal

121. *Mosses*, pp. 205, 246, 247, 78.
122. *Blithedale*, pp. 382–383, 383, 474.

for Hawthorne. The notebooks afford abundant evidence of his interest in elderly men who are feeble in body and mind and impoverished in material possessions. While walking among the hills near North Adams in 1838, Hawthorne met "an underwitted old man" who talked about his children's desertion of him to join a circus. Again, Hawthorne saw and described in detail one Captain Gavett, an elderly man who was selling butternuts at the hotel in North Adams. Having an inclination to philosophy, Captain Gavett talked about "whether it would be worth while to grow young again, and the duty of being contented with old age; about predestination and freewill, and other metaphysics." Another aged man at North Adams who attracted Hawthorne's attention was the Revolutionary pensioner, "Uncle John," who drank a glass of gin in the barroom and "grew the younger for it." The old apple dealer at the railroad station in Salem was another specimen of this type who appealed to Hawthorne's love of "the moral picturesque." This character was described in great detail in the journal. Finally, the "elderly ragamuffin" in Parker's grogshop at Boston evoked the sympathetic and imaginative interest of Hawthorne, who discovered in his appearance vestiges of a former respectability.[123] Thus, between 1838 and 1850, Hawthorne studied and described in the notebooks no less than five specimens of this type of character.

These studies bore fruit in the tales and novels. The underwitted old man who has been deserted by his children reappears in "Ethan Brand" (1850) as the father of Esther, the victim of Brand's psychological experiment.[124] The sketch of the apple dealer, after a careful rewriting, was published as an independent character study.[125] Uncle Venner in *The House of the Seven Gables* recalls two of the aged men whom Hawthorne observed at North Adams. Like one, he is deficient in his wits. Like another, he makes pretensions to wisdom. Uncle Venner resembles Captain

123. *American Notebooks,* pp. 35, 46, 64, 90–92, 248.
124. *Snow Image,* pp. 488–489.
125. *Mosses,* pp. 495–503.

Gavett particularly in his contentment with old age and in his feeble excursions into the realm of religion and metaphysics. If Captain Gavett as an observer of life enjoyed the vantage point offered by the stoop of the hotel, Uncle Venner "had studied the world at street-corners, and other posts equally well adapted for just observation." [126] Dhaleine has pointed out the significant fact that Uncle Venner is the only character in Hawthorne's works who speaks a distinctive language.[127] That the author attempted to do for this character what he did for no other may perhaps be accounted for by an intimate knowledge growing out of a protracted study of actual specimens of the type.

The "elderly ragamuffin" who haunted Parker's grogshop contributed several details to the characterization of Old Moodie in *The Blithedale Romance*: the red nose, the patch over one eye, and the aspect of a decayed gentleman.[128] But Old Moodie owes something also to other precursors. Both the old man wandering in the hills near North Adams and Moodie live in loneliness while their children are in the public gaze: the children of the former perform in a circus; Priscilla appears on the stage as "the Veiled Lady." The nameless old man in "Ethan Brand" has a daughter, Esther, who has been made the subject of a psychological experiment by Brand; similarly, Moodie's daughter, Priscilla, has been used as a medium by Westervelt. Like Captain Gavett and the apple dealer, Moodie has something to sell—silk purses made by Priscilla. Again, just as Orrin Smith gives the Revolutionary pensioner, "Uncle John," a glass of gin, so Coverdale hopes to thaw the frost in Moodie's blood by means of a glass of wine.[129] And, finally, in representing the negative qualities of the character—qualities indicated by such adjectives as "lifeless," "colorless," "torpid"—Hawthorne drew largely upon his sketch of the apple dealer in which he wrote: "The portrait must be so gen-

126. *Seven Gables,* pp. 82, 188.
127. Dhaleine, *op. cit.,* p. 445.
128. *Blithedale,* pp. 327, 525.
129. *Ibid.,* pp. 523–524.

erally negative that the most delicate pencil is likely to spoil it by introducing some too positive tint." [130] Thus we see that Old Moodie, like so many of Hawthorne's characters, was the result of an evolutionary process and that several characters previously sketched in the notebooks and tales contributed to this development.

I have been able to show that Hawthorne's leading characters for the most part can be divided into a comparatively few large groups and that within each group can be traced a process of development which is both repetitive and cumulative.

In our study of the origins of Dimmesdale we saw that Hawthorne constructed the character largely out of materials drawn from his earlier works. Dimmesdale has the frail body and the pale face of all of the "scholar-idealists." His character comprehends the scholarly instincts of Fanshawe and Aylmer and the sensitivity of Owen Warland. Moreover, Hawthorne has drawn from Reuben Bourne the idea of concealment, from the Reverend Mr. Hooper certain concomitants of the role of clergyman, and from Roderick Elliston a characteristic gesture.

Again, Hawthorne's villains represent an evolutionary process by which the later characters are compounded of ingredients drawn from earlier ones. Westervelt, for example, is a composite of preceding villains: his bold eye and evil smile are reminiscent of Butler, Vaughan, and Maule; his foppish manners are taken from Vaughan, and his mesmeric powers from Maule. The character differs from these precursors, however, in that Hawthorne has added a suggestion of the supernatural: he implies that Westervelt may be the incarnation of a fiend; and in accordance with this implication, Westervelt has a stick similar to that carried by the devil in "Young Goodman Brown." In the creation of Chillingworth, Hawthorne has drawn hints from the devils and wizards of the early tales, from two entries in the notebooks, and from his reading of Spenser and Milton. An equally wide

130. *Mosses*, p. 501.

sweep of the net provided the materials for the character of Miriam's model: suggestions are drawn from his early reading of Godwin, from *Fanshawe* and "Alice Doane's Appeal," from the notebooks, and from the preceding villains, particularly Roger Chillingworth. In the creation of Judge Pyncheon, Hawthorne made use of traits suggested by an actual person, by two preceding villains—Hovenden and Chillingworth—and by two entries in the journal.

The complexities of Hawthorne's heroines likewise may be traced to a variety of origins. The character of Phoebe is a composite of elements suggested by girls described in the notebooks; by Ellen and Susan, the heroines of earlier stories; and by the author's wife. Priscilla derives fragility from heroines of the early tales (Sylph Etherege, Alice Vane, Lilias Fay), a certain fantastic grace from the snow image, the powers of a medium from Alice Pyncheon, an occupation and a tendency to playfulness from the seamstress at Brook Farm, and wifely virtues from Sophia Hawthorne. The members of the third group of Hawthorne's heroines, unlike those of the other two groups, do not represent a development based upon the early tales and the notebooks, but here again we see Hawthorne's tendency to repetition in characterization both in the general similarity of the four women in the group and in the close resemblance of Zenobia and Hester and of Miriam and Beatrice.

I have also traced the evolution of three minor types of characters: the observer, the reformer, and the feeble and indigent old man. The artist in "The Prophetic Pictures," Coverdale, and Kenyon form a sequence of development in which the chief source of materials is the author's own character. Hollingsworth is an embodiment of abstract principles set forth in three tales. Uncle Venner and Old Moodie represent in large measure a combining of characteristics drawn from sketches in the journals.

In the foregoing analysis, we have discovered three chief sources of Hawthorne's characters: his reading, the notebooks, and his own fiction. The contribution made by his reading was apparently small: I have been able to point out instances of the influence of Spenser, Shakespeare, Milton, and Godwin. The contribution of the notebooks, which was considerable, included sketches of actual people and abstract principles of characterization. But by far the greatest contribution to the development of the various types was made by the characters themselves: each character became a source of traits for characters to follow. To trace the sequence of development in the various groups which we have studied is to see how an early character of comparative simplicity becomes gradually more complex through the addition of traits contributed by successive characters. From our study it is clear that Hawthorne reperused his published tales and novels as assiduously as the notebooks in the search for materials. The minuteness of this reperusal becomes at once evident when one considers such derivations of minutiae as Dimmesdale's gesture from "Egotism; or, The Bosom Serpent," or Phoebe's freckles from "The Village Uncle," or Westervelt's stick from "Young Goodman Brown." Indeed, the discussion in the present chapter has demonstrated that the chief source of the characters of the novels is to be found in the corresponding characters of the tales. No stronger evidence could be adduced of Hawthorne's introspective habit of mind.

RECURRENT THEMES
IN HAWTHORNE'S FICTION [1]

In the journal kept at the Old Manse one reads the following statement: "This forenoon, I began to write, and caught an idea by the tail, which I intend to hold fast, though it struggles to get free." [2] Although the idea is not mentioned, it is very probable that the struggle to which Hawthorne refers was not a fresh encounter but rather the renewal, after an interval of months or years, of an old engagement, for most of the ideas which are embodied in his fiction after 1843, the year of the entry which I have just quoted, can be found in the tales and notebooks written prior to that date. One discovers in Hawthorne's works, not a wide variety of subjects, but a comparatively few themes to which he recurs again and again. I have selected four topics which seem of major importance; and I shall attempt in this chapter to explain the author's interest in these themes, to trace their development through successive stages, and to indicate, wherever possible, the relation of the notebooks to their choice and growth.

I

A subject which finds repeated and insistent treatment in Hawthorne's works is the isolation of the individual from his fellows. It is certain that this theme bears a closer relation than any other to the author's own life.

Hawthorne's isolated life during the twelve years following

1. For the editorial procedure, see note 1 to the preceding essay. See note 2 of the same essay for matters involving texts and short titles. [Ed.]
2. *American Notebooks*, p. 177.

his graduation from Bowdoin College is well known. Writing to Longfellow from Salem on June 4, 1837, he said:

By some witchcraft or other—for I really cannot assign any reasonable why and wherefore—I have been carried apart from the main current of life, and find it impossible to get back again. Since we last met . . . I have secluded myself from society; and yet I never meant any such thing, nor dreamed what sort of life I was going to lead. I have made a captive of myself and put me into a dungeon; and now I cannot find the key to let myself out—and if the door were open, I should be almost afraid to come out . . . there is no fate in this world so horrible as to have no share in either its joys or sorrows. For the last ten years, I have not lived, but only dreamed about living.[3]

This kind of isolation, which seemed to Hawthorne from his own life to be the result of a drifting process, fortuitous and involuntary, yet inevitable, is represented often and in various forms in his fiction.

Wakefield in the story of that title (1835) is a case in point: "He had contrived, or rather he had happened, to dissever himself from the world—to vanish—to give up his place and privileges with living men. . . ." The moral which the story is designed to enforce is that "by stepping aside for a moment, a man exposes himself to a fearful risk of losing his place forever."[4] Similarly the village uncle in the sketch of that title (1835) is described as "a man who had wandered out of the real world and got into its shadow, where his troubles, joys, and vicissitudes were of such slight stuff that he hardly knew whether he lived, or only dreamed of living."[5] And again, Oberon in "The Devil in Manuscript" (1835) says: "I am surrounding myself with shadows . . . they have drawn me aside from the beaten path of the world, and led me into a strange sort of solitude—a solitude in the midst of men,—where nobody wishes for

3. This letter is in the possession of Mr. H. W. L. Dana.
4. *Twice-Told Tales,* pp. 162, 164.
5. *Ibid.,* p. 350.

what I do, nor thinks nor feels as I do." [6] It is at once apparent that in these descriptions of the lives of Wakefield, the village uncle, and Oberon published in 1835, Hawthorne used language very similar to that which he employed in the letter to Longfellow two years later to describe his own life during the period from 1825 to 1837.

It is not surprising that Hawthorne, disturbed by this acute sense of isolation, should have made a definite attempt "to open an intercourse with the world"; [7] and that such an attempt was made in 1837 is evident not only in the publication of *Twice-Told Tales* but also in the record in the notebooks of his sojourn at Augusta. In the conversations and excursions with Bridge, his host, and Schaeffer, the little Frenchman—for example, in the drinking party at a country store—Hawthorne is seen as a participant, although in a mild way, in the activities of the real world. In the journal kept at North Adams in 1838 we see him even more definitely taking a part in the life around him: witness particularly his walking in a funeral procession with his friend, Orrin Smith. The advice of the old gentleman at Worcester doubtless impressed Hawthorne as exactly suited to his needs: "He told me by all means to act, in whatever way; observing that he himself would have no objection to be a servant, if no other mode of action presented itself." [8] Very probably it was as a result of the realization of his need of action that Hawthorne in the following year entered the Boston Custom House as measurer and three years later became a laborer at Brook Farm. In a letter to Sophia Peabody dated July 3, 1839, he summed up the benefits to be expected from his work at the Boston Custom House:

. . . henceforth forever I shall be entitled to call the sons of toil my brethren, and shall know how to sympathize with them, seeing that I, likewise, have risen at the dawn and borne the fervor of the midday sun,

6. *Snow Image*, p. 576.
7. Preface to *Twice-Told Tales*, p. 17.
8. *American Notebooks*, pp. 14, 56, 30.

nor turned my heavy footsteps homeward till eventide. Years hence, perhaps, the experience that my heart is acquiring now will flow out in truth and wisdom.[9]

Hawthorne's attempt to make his life more real found expression not only in the sojourns at Augusta and North Adams and in the physical labor at the Boston Custom House and at Brook Farm but in the formation of a close relationship with another human being—Sophia Peabody, to whom he became engaged in 1838 and whom he married in 1842. If the excursions in the realm of physical action were only partially successful in establishing satisfactory relations between Hawthorne and the world, it was his belief that the experience of love had efficacy to transmute shadow into substance. He wrote to Sophia from Salem on October 4, 1840: "Indeed, we are but shadows—we are not endowed with real life, and all that seems most real about us is but the thinnest substance of a dream—till the heart is touched. That touch creates us—then we begin to be—thereby we are beings of reality, and inheritors of eternity." [10] Since the journal kept at the Old Manse affords abundant evidence that love and marriage did give to his life in considerable measure the long-sought-for reality or normality, the abnormally isolated characters who appear in the stories after 1842 may be regarded as reflecting not what the author was at the time of writing but what he had been or had feared he might become.

In "The Procession of Life" (1843) one large classification of humanity includes "all mortals, who, from whatever cause, have lost, or never found, their proper places in the world." [11] Gervayse Hastings in "The Christmas Banquet" (1844), with his cold hand [12] and cold heart, explains the tragedy of his life thus: "It is a chilliness—a want of earnestness—a feeling as if

9. *Love Letters*, I, 31.
10. *Ibid.*, I, 225.
11. *Mosses*, p. 248.
12. In 1842 Hawthorne had recorded in his notebook a suggestion utilized in the sketch of Hastings: "A person with an ice-cold hand—his right hand;

what should be my heart were a thing of vapor—a haunting perception of unreality!" [13] Another character in a similar plight is the anonymous person in "The Intelligence Office" (1844) who is seeking a place. He exclaims: "I want my place! my own place! my true place in the world! my proper sphere!" [14] Similarly, "Feathertop: A Moralized Legend" (1852) repeats the theme of unreality and isolation. Feathertop is not a real man but a mere simulacrum. Love perhaps—and here Hawthorne is drawing upon his own experience—might have made him human.[15] But deprived of this source of vitality and seeing himself as "wretched, ragged, empty," Feathertop simply ceased to exist.

The theme of isolation is extended by Hawthorne to apply not only to persons like Wakefield and Gervayse Hastings who, because of their shadowy, purposeless lives, are "on the outside of everything," but also to those who because of an exceptional or abnormal nature are deprived of human comradeship. Thus the Wandering Jew in "A Virtuoso's Collection" (1842), who enjoys the gift of earthly immortality, should in reality be regarded with pity since he is "cut off from natural sympathies and blasted with a doom . . . inflicted on no other human being." [16] Similarly it was fortunate for Septimius Felton that he was prevented from drinking the elixir of life and thereby "severing . . . the link that connected him with his race, and making for himself an exceptional destiny." [17]

The most forceful example of the isolation which results from an exceptional nature is Beatrice in "Rappaccini's Daughter" (1844). The idea of this story was suggested in part by a passage

---

which people ever afterwards remember, when once they have grasped it" (*American Notebooks*, p. 97).

13. *Mosses*, p. 345.
14. *Ibid.*, p. 365.
15. See *ibid.*, p. 277.
16. *Ibid.*, p. 558.
17. *Septimius Felton*, p. 417.

from Sir Thomas Browne which Hawthorne recorded in the notebook:

> A story there passeth of an Indian King, that sent unto Alexander a fair woman fed with Aconites and other poysons, with this intent, either by converse or copulation complexionally to destroy him.[18]

There is another passage in the notebook, however, which offers a closer parallel to the story, particularly with reference to the central theme of isolation:

> Madame Calderon de la B (in Life in Mexico) speaks of persons who have been inoculated with the venom of rattlesnakes, by pricking them in various places with the tooth. These persons are thus secured forever after against the bite of any venomous reptile. They have the power of calling snakes, and feel great pleasure in playing with and handling them. Their own bite becomes poisonous to people not inoculated in the same manner. Thus a part of the serpent's nature appears to be transfused into them.[19]

In like manner Beatrice has been inoculated with the poison of the flowers in her father's garden. Possessing immunity from this poison, she experiences great pleasure in handling the rich, exotic plants. To those whose bodies have not been so impregnated, her touch is poisonous: her fingers leave a purple mark on Giovanni's hand. As additional evidence that Hawthorne was influenced by this passage from Madame Calderon, he describes the flowers as creeping "serpent-like along the ground." A person inoculated with the poison of a rattlesnake would indeed be isolated from his fellows by virtue of his exceptional nature. And this is the tragedy of Beatrice: "There was an awful doom . . . the effect of my father's fatal love of science, which estranged me from all society of my kind." Baglioni's antidote does not succeed in

18. *Passages*, p. 209, and *Pseudodoxia Epidemica*, Bk. VII, chap. xvii (*Works of Sir Thomas Browne* [Edinburgh, 1912], III, 69). In *Passages* the words "either by converse or copulation" are omitted—probably a deletion by the editor, Mrs. Hawthorne.

19. *American Notebooks*, p. 98.

"bringing back this miserable child within the limits of ordinary nature." [20]

The idea of isolation is so pervasive in Hawthorne's works that the consideration of all possible examples would include almost all of his characters, for very few are not exceptional in some sense. To name the important characters in the novels—Hester, Dimmesdale, Pearl, Chillingworth, in *The Scarlet Letter;* Hepzibah, Clifford, Phoebe, Judge Pyncheon, Holgrave, and Uncle Venner in *The House of the Seven Gables;* Hollingsworth, Zenobia, Priscilla, Coverdale, Westervelt, and Old Moodie in *The Blithedale Romance;* Hilda, Miriam, Donatello, Kenyon, and the model in *The Marble Faun*—is to become aware of the fact that all except perhaps three—Phoebe, Holgrave, and Hilda—possess traits or perform deeds sufficiently exceptional or unsocial to effect a partial isolation from their fellows. This estrangement of the individual was a major theme—almost an obsession—with Hawthorne. It had its genesis, as we have seen, in his own experience; and it found its most powerful expression in "Rappaccini's Daughter," which was written at a time when Hawthorne, having himself been brought back only recently and with difficulty within the limits of ordinary nature, felt all the more acutely the danger of the position from which he had been rescued and to which he might very easily return.

II

The problem of sin is an equally pervasive theme in the works of Hawthorne. It is a commonplace to say that his insistent consciousness of sin was an inheritance from his Puritan ancestors. Hawthorne himself avowed an inescapable connection between his "grave, bearded, sable-cloaked and steeple-crowned" progenitors and the "writer of story-books": ". . . strong traits of their nature have intertwined themselves with mine." [21] It is

20. *Mosses*, pp. 133, 111, 143, 138.
21. *Scarlet Letter*, pp. 24, 25.

in agreement with this connection that he should have preferred the older Puritan divines to the Unitarian clergy with their repudiation of the dogma of human depravity. In a passage in the journal kept at the Old Manse, he wrote with obvious predilection concerning "the difference between the cold, lifeless, vaguely liberal clergyman of our own day, and the narrow but earnest cushion-thumper of puritanical times." [22] Hawthorne and the Puritans were in complete agreement, therefore, in the belief that human nature is radically sinful. In "Fancy's Show Box" (1837) the doctrine of universal depravity is stated with sufficient explicitness to satisfy the most rigorous theologian of the puritanical school: "Man must not disclaim his brotherhood, even with the guiltiest, since, though his hand be clean, his heart has surely been polluted by the flitting phantoms of iniquity." [23]

With external, overt acts of a sinful or criminal nature, Hawthorne has very little to do. In "The Hollow of the Three Hills" (1830) there is a wife "who had betrayed the trusting fondness of her husband";[24] but specific details are lacking. Only slightly less vague is the account of Prudence Inglefield in "John Inglefield's Thanksgiving" (1840): Hawthorne goes no farther than to allude to her presence "among the painted beauties at the theatre of a neighboring city." [25] Adultery exists in *The Scarlet Letter* only *ex hypothesi;* the author eschews all outward manifestations of adulterous passion. A murder constitutes part of the machinery in *The Marble Faun,* but the act *per se* is not dwelt upon. The vagueness of Miriam's guilt [26] is characteristic of

22. *American Notebooks,* p. 158. A similar disapproval of Unitarian theology is expressed in "The Christmas Banquet," *Mosses,* pp. 341–342.

23. *Twice-Told Tales,* p. 257.

24. *Ibid.,* p. 33.

25. *Snow Image,* p. 590.

26. Her guilt is probably incest, a crime to which Hawthorne had alluded in the briefest possible manner in "Alice Doane's Appeal" (1835). The analogy repeatedly implied between the fate of Miriam and that of Beatrice Cenci would suggest that interpretation. (See particularly *Marble Faun,* p. 85.) Again, in the following passage in which the model addresses Miriam—

Hawthorne's method. His failure to treat explicitly and circumstantially the evil deeds of his characters may doubtless be attributed to two causes: first, his lack of experience with the world of evil; and, second, the focusing of his interest on the psychological effects of the deed rather than on the deed itself.

Of the many sins treated in Hawthorne's fiction, there is one sin which is more reprehensible than the others and which the author names in "Ethan Brand" the unpardonable sin. This sin, which appears in various forms in the tales and novels, consists essentially in the violation of the sanctity of a human heart. It is, for example, the sin of Chillingworth. When Dimmesdale has been informed of the machinations of the physician, he exclaims to Hester: "We are not, Hester, the worst sinners in the world. There is one worse than even the polluted priest! That old man's revenge has been blacker than my sin. He has violated, in cold blood, the sanctity of a human heart. Thou and I, Hester, never did so!" [27] The theme set forth in this speech recurs in Hawthorne's fiction with a peculiarly insistent emphasis. The violation of the sanctity of a human heart presupposes one person's possession of a special power over another and the exercise of that power with a cold, malignant intent. Thus Chillingworth inflicts upon his victim a persecution from which there is no escape except by death.

The development of Hawthorne's interest in this conception of the subjection of one person to another can be traced through several entries in the notebooks. In 1838 he recorded a suggestion which anticipates in a sense the relation between Dimmesdale and Chillingworth:

> The situation of a man in the midst of a crowd, yet as completely in the power of another, life and all, as if they two were in the deepest solitude.

"Miriam,—for I forebear to speak another name at which these leaves would shiver above our head . . ."—the name to be supplied would seem to be "daughter" or perhaps "sister" (*Marble Faun*, p. 116).

27. *Scarlet Letter*, p. 234.

Another entry in 1842 presents a variation of the idea:

Some man of powerful character to command a person, morally subjected to him, to perform some act. The commanding person to suddenly die; and, for all the rest of his life, the subjected one continues to perform that act.[28]

Although Hawthorne never made use of the special condition mentioned in the second sentence of the entry, nevertheless the relation described in the passage of imperious command on the one hand and helpless obedience on the other anticipates in a striking manner the connection between Matthew Maule and Alice Pyncheon.[29] Again in an entry made between October 13, 1844, and March 12, 1845, the same theme recurs:

Sketch of a person, who, by strength of character, or assistant circumstances, has reduced another to absolute slavery and dependence on him. Then show, that the person who appeared to be the master, must inevitably be at least as much a slave, if not more, than the other. All slavery is reciprocal, on the supposition most favorable to the rulers.[30]

Hawthorne was repeatedly to point out the penalty imposed upon the master through the exercise of his powers: Ethan Brand's heart turned to marble; Chillingworth drew sustenance from his diabolical revenge to such an extent that upon the death of his victim he withered and died.

The possession of power by one person over another might be used plausibly, Hawthorne thought, in an utterly heartless manner for purposes of an experiment. He recorded the following suggestion in the notebook in 1842:

A moral philosopher to buy a slave, or otherwise get possession of a human being, and to use him for the sake of experiment, by trying the operation of a certain vice on him.[31]

28. *Passages,* p. 113, *American Notebooks,* p. 92.
29. See *Seven Gables,* pp. 249–250.
30. *American Notebooks,* p. 107.
31. *Ibid.,* p. 98.

Hawthorne apparently was not able to embody in fiction the precise conception of this passage, but he made use of the idea of an experiment in two stories: in "Rappaccini's Daughter" (1844), the physician conducts an experiment not only upon his daughter but upon Giovanni as well; in "Ethan Brand" (1850), Brand makes a helpless girl the subject of a "psychological experiment," the exact nature of which is not explained. In both instances the experimenter is cold and insensitive; he takes an intellectual, not an emotional interest in his subject. In "Rappaccini's Daughter" Baglioni says to Giovanni:

"For some purpose or other, this man of science is making a study of you. I know that look of his! It is the same that coldly illuminates his face as he bends over a bird, a mouse, or a butterfly, which, in pursuance of some experiment, he has killed by the perfume of a flower; a look as deep as Nature itself, but without Nature's warmth of love. Signor Giovanni . . . you are the subject of one of Rappaccini's experiments!" [32]

In thus expressing his distrust of the scientist, Hawthorne was doubtless in agreement with the romantic philosophy of the early nineteenth century. His treatment of Rappaccini recalls particularly Wordsworth's lines on the scientist:

One that would peep and botanize
Upon his mother's grave.[33]

The exercise of power by one person in the control or exploitation of a weaker personality was associated in Hawthorne's mind not only with scientific experiment but with mesmeric phenomena. His interest in mesmerism as a literary theme is evidenced in a suggestion recorded in the journal in 1842: "Questions as to unsettled points of History, and Mysteries of Nature,

32. *Mosses,* pp. 124–125.
33. "A Poet's Epitaph," ll. 19–20. There is an allusion to this passage in *Septimius Felton* (p. 291): "What . . . could be her reason for coming and sitting down by this grave, and apparently botanizing upon it[?] . . ."

to be asked of a mesmerized person." [34] This principle is applied in *The House of the Seven Gables,* where Matthew Maule attempts to obtain through Alice Pyncheon, who is in a state of mesmerism, information, not relating, to be sure, to unsettled points of history or the mysteries of nature but concerning the whereabouts of a lost document, the discovery of which would place in the possession of the Pyncheons a vast estate. The attempt is unsuccessful; but Maule, having once established his ascendancy over Alice, continues to exploit her weakness and finally brings her to her death. Again, in *The Blithedale Romance,* Westervelt uses his mesmeric power over Priscilla who appears in public theatrical exhibitions as "the Veiled Lady." Moreover, it is probable, in view of the author's interest in the subject, that Ethan Brand's "psychological experiment" had to do with mesmeric phenomena, and that the discoveries made by this means, perhaps relating to the mysteries of nature, had contributed to his "vast intellectual development" and his eminence as a philosopher.[35]

Hawthorne's interest in mesmerism reflects the vogue of mesmeric phenomena in Boston in the 1830s and 1840s[36] both in theatrical exhibitions and as a means of effecting cures. When Sophia Peabody, who suffered from severe headaches, proposed to her *fiancé* the possibility of mesmerism as a curative measure, Hawthorne, in a letter written from Brook Farm on October 18, 1841, protested with unusual vehemence:

. . . my spirit is moved to talk to thee to day about these magnetic miracles, and to beseech thee to take no part in them. I am unwilling that a power should be exercised on thee, of which we know neither the origin nor the consequence, and the phenomena of which seem rather

34. *American Notebooks,* p. 93.
35. See *Snow Image,* p. 494.
36. See *Blithedale,* p. 326; Georgiana Bruce Kirby, *Years of Experience* (New York and London, 1887), p. 161; and *Journals of Ralph Waldo Emerson,* ed. by E. W. Emerson and W. E. Forbes. Riverside Edition (Boston: Houghton Mifflin Company, 1909–1914), IV, 311, 312, 488.

calculated to bewilder us, than to teach us any truths about the present or future state of being. If I possessed such a power over thee, I should not dare to exercise it; nor can I consent to its being exercised by another. Supposing that this power arises from the transfusion of one spirit into another, it seems to me that the sacredness of an individual is violated by it; there would be an intrusion into thy holy of holies. . . .[37]

In similar language Hawthorne applauds Holgrave's abstention from the exercise upon Phoebe of mesmeric power which he obviously possessed and which would have become operative by a mere motion of the hand:

To a disposition like Holgrave's, at once speculative and active, there is no temptation so great as the opportunity of acquiring empire over the human spirit. . . . Let us, therefore . . . concede to the daguerreotypist the rare and high quality of reverence for another's individuality.[38]

If Chillingworth "violated, in cold blood, the sanctity of a human heart," this likewise was the sin of Maule, Westervelt, and Brand —practitioners of the mesmeric art by which "the sacredness of an individual is violated." And it is at once evident that Chillingworth, Rappaccini, Maule, and Westervelt, as well as Brand, committed the unpardonable sin, the doctrine of which Hawthorne had formulated in the journal as early as 1844:

The Unpardonable Sin might consist in a want of love and reverence for the Human Soul; in consequence of which, the investigator pried into its dark depths, not with a hope or purpose of making it better, but from a cold philosophical curiosity—content that it should be wicked in whatever kind or degree, and only desiring to study it out. Would not this, in other words, be the separation of the intellect from the heart? [39]

We may now attempt to summarize the foregoing account of the various ramifications of the development in Hawthorne's

37. *Love Letters*, II, 62.
38. *Seven Gables*, p. 253.
39. *American Notebooks*, p. 106.

mind of the conception of the unpardonable sin.[40] In various entries in the notebook recorded between 1838 and 1844, we have seen his interest in the situation in which one person possesses a dominating power over another. This power might be used as a means of conducting a scientific experiment as in "Rappaccini's Daughter," or of securing revenge as in *The Scarlet Letter*, or of inducing a state of mesmerism whether for theatrical exhibition as in *The Blithedale Romance* or for the revelation of the occult as in *The House of the Seven Gables* and very probably in "Ethan Brand." The exercise of such a power is fundamentally wrong because it violates the sacredness of personality. Only a person utterly lacking in love and reverence for the human soul, one in whom the intellect has been overdeveloped and the emotional nature has undergone atrophy, would be capable of thus preying upon a susceptible nature. In this "separation of the intellect from the heart" and the consequent drying up of human sympathies, Hawthorne finds the unpardonable sin. His petrified "man of adamant" and the marble heart of Ethan Brand [41] are quite literal evidence of his interest in Shakespeare's question: "Is there any cause in nature that makes these hard hearts?"

III

The theme of *The House of the Seven Gables* is likewise projected from a long background in Hawthorne's thinking, as revealed in the notebooks and tales. This theme may be stated as

40. Attempts to identify Ethan Brand with Herman Melville are unconvincing not only because the story was published seven months before Hawthorne met Melville but also because the idea of "Ethan Brand" is the result of a long process of development and finds expression in other works. For attempts at identification see Edward J. O'Brien, "The Fifteen Finest Short Stories," *Forum*, LXXIX (June 1928), 908–914; Lewis Mumford, *Herman Melville* (New York: Harcourt, Brace and Company, 1929), p. 145; Newton Arvin, *Hawthorne* (Boston: Little, Brown and Company, 1929), p. 169. For reasons opposed to such an identification see my "Melville and Hawthorne's 'Ethan Brand,' " *Saturday Review of Literature*, V (April 27, 1929), 967.

41. *Snow Image*, pp. 572, 498.

the baneful influence of the past as represented by family traditions and by old houses which have been inhabited by one family during successive generations.

Hawthorne points out repeatedly in the notebooks the decline of family fortunes, the frustration of the attempt of a progenitor to secure an estate to his posterity, and the decadence of descendants whose sustenance is pride of ancestry. In 1836 he recorded the following instance of a sudden decline in the prosperity of a family:

In 1621, a Mr. Copinger left a certain charity, an almshouse, of which four poor persons were to partake, after the death of his eldest son and his wife. . . . At the time specified, however, all but one of his sons were dead; and he was in such poor circumstances that he obtained the benefit of the charity for himself, as one of the four.[42]

Mr. Gardiner's fine residence, which Hawthorne saw in 1837, would never be enjoyed by that gentleman's descendants, he predicted, and the "edifice is likely to be known by the name of Gardiner's Folly, for centuries to come." "This subject," he suggested, "offers hints of copious reflection, in reference to the indulgence of aristocratic pomp among democratic institutions." Again, after visiting General Knox's estate in the same year, Hawthorne wrote:

The house and its vicinity, and the whole tract covered by Knox's patent, may be taken as an illustration of what must be the result of American schemes of aristocracy. It is not forty years, since this house was built, and Knox was in his glory; but now the house is all in decay, while, within a stone's throw of it, is a street of neat, smart, white edifices of one and two stories, occupied chiefly by thriving mechanics. . . . The descendants are all poor; and the inheritance was merely sufficient to make a dissipated and drunken fellow of the one of the old General's sons, who survived to middle age.[43]

42. *Passages,* p. 41.
43. *American Notebooks,* pp. 8–9, 23.

Again, after studying in 1837 some old portraits in the cabinet of the Essex Historical Society, Hawthorne observed:

> Nothing gives a stronger idea of old worm-eaten aristocracy—of a family being crazy with age, and of its being time that it was extinct—than these black, dusty, faded, antique-dressed portraits. . . .[44]

Hawthorne could point to members of his own family who exemplified a worm-eaten aristocracy—for example, old Susy Ingersoll, who was "proud of being proud." [45]

"Peter Goldthwaite's Treasure" (1838) illustrates the decline of the fortunes of a family and the foolish family pride of a degenerate descendant. The following passage is in the same line of thought with that of the excerpts from the journals given above which preceded by only a short time the composition of the story:

> As he drew back, ashamed of his outward poverty, yet proud of the secret wealth within his grasp, a haughty smile shone out on Peter's visage. . . . He endeavored to assume such a mien as his ancestor had probably worn, when he glorified in the building of a strong house for a home to many generations of his posterity.[46]

This house is almost completely torn down during the process of Peter's hunt for a treasure; and just as rows of mechanics' houses were erected where General Knox meant to have a park, so Mr. Brown, we are to suppose, will construct a "brick block" of business houses on the site of the ancestral edifice of Goldthwaite.

Another story which reflects the trend of the entries from the notebooks quoted above is "Old Esther Dudley" (1839). Esther Dudley's family, once eminent, has fallen into decay. Like Peter Goldthwaite and the people whose portraits Hawthorne saw at the Essex Historical Society, Esther is partially crazed.

44. *Passages,* pp. 88–89.
45. *American Notebooks,* p. 27.
46. *Twice-Told Tales,* pp. 446–447.

And thus she becomes a perfect representative of the decayed past—"of an age gone by, with its manners, opinions, faith and feelings, all fallen into oblivion or scorn." [47]

Passages in the notebooks dealing with the decay of families that were once flourishing recur with the repetition of an obsession. Concerning the Pepperell family, Hawthorne recorded in the journal in 1842:

Sir William had built an elegant house for his son and his intended wife; but after the death of the former, he never entered it. . . . Very anxious to secure his property to his descendants, by the provisions of his will, which was drawn up by Judge Sewell, then a young lawyer. Yet the Judge lived to see two of Sir William's grandchildren so reduced, that they were to have been numbered among the town's poor, and were only rescued from this fate by private charity.

That Hawthorne contemplated writing a story that should represent a situation suggested by the passage just quoted is shown in the following note recorded in the journal in 1843:

A young girl inherits a family grave-yard—that being all that remains of rich hereditary possessions.

Another note, made in 1844, offers a different approach to the same central idea:

The history of an Alms-House. . . . The rich of one generation might, in the next, seek for a home there. . . . Perhaps the son and heir of the founder might have no better refuge.

A visit to the old residence of Sir William Pepperell in 1845 was the occasion of further observations in the notebook on the decline of the Pepperell family:

Precisely a hundred years since, he [Sir William Pepperell] was in his glory. None of the name now exist here—or elsewhere, that I know of. A descendant of the Sparhawks, one of whom married Pepperell's daughter, is now keeper of a fort in the vicinity—a poor man.[48]

47. *Ibid.*, p. 433.
48. *American Notebooks*, pp. 94, 99, 100, 116.

The interest with which Hawthorne contemplated physical evidences of the decline of aristocratic families is revealed again in his lengthy account, written in 1847, of the remains of a mansion on Browne's Hill. He contrasts the surviving traces of the old house, consisting of two cellars, with the former splendor of the edifice, particularly when its owner celebrated the King's birthday, and remarks that the structure "has perpetuated an imputation of folly upon the poor man who erected it, which still keeps his memory disagreeably alive, after a hundred years." [49]

These citations from the notebooks and tales foreshadow the situation presented in *The House of the Seven Gables* (1851). Colonel Pyncheon, like General Knox, Sir William Pepperell, and the others, erected a family mansion which was "calculated to endure for many generations of his posterity." Like the many families, both historical and imaginary, mentioned in the notebooks, the Pyncheon "breed had not thriven"; in fact, at the time of Hawthorne's story "it appeared rather to be dying out." The only surviving members of the family when the narrative opens are Judge Pyncheon, a man of wealth and prominence; his son, who is traveling in Europe; Clifford, whose life has been wrecked by a thirty years' imprisonment; Hepzibah, the elderly owner of the house of the seven gables, who is so wretchedly poor that she is forced to open a cent shop; and, finally, Phoebe, whose father "died early and in poor circumstances" and who because of extreme poverty seeks a home with Hepzibah. Since in the course of the narrative both the Judge and his son die, the family line, properly speaking, is shortly to disappear. Although the Pyncheons have contrived to continue their residence in the ancestral mansion for a longer period of time than had the families mentioned by Hawthorne in the notebooks, nevertheless gradual decay and ultimate extinction are the common lot. At the end of the novel the old house is abandoned, and the final scene

49. *Ibid.*, pp. 119–120.

shows us with characteristic symbolism Uncle Venner, an embodiment of decrepitude, "passing slowly from the ruinous porch." [50]

So, far from deploring such changes in the fortunes of families as those described in the passages cited from the notebooks and works of fiction, Hawthorne regards them as a necessary part of the progress of society. The following passage from *Dr. Grimshawe's Secret,* appertaining to the visit of Redclyffe, an American, to his ancestral home in England, may be taken as expressing the author's firmly established conviction on the subject:

Redclyffe could not compare this abode, and the feelings that it aroused, to the houses of his own country; poor tents of a day, inns of a night, where nothing was certain, save that the family of him who built it would not dwell here, even if he himself should have the bliss to die under the roof, which, with absurdest anticipations, he had built for his posterity. Posterity! An American can have none.

"All this sort of thing is beautiful; the family institution was beautiful in its day," ejaculated he . . . "but it is a thing of the past. It is dying out in England; and as for ourselves, we never had it. Something better will come up; but as for this, it is past." [51]

Hawthorne's belief that the disintegration of old families is for the good of society may be explained partly as a result of his democratic sympathies. In "Earth's Holocaust" the first articles of "wornout trumpery" to be thrown into the fire are the insignia of rank. The speech of a nameless "rude figure," who represents the people, may be regarded as a statement of the attitude of the author himself:

". . . henceforth let no man dare to show a piece of musty parchment as his warrant for lording it over his fellows. . . . No mortal must hope for place and consideration by reckoning up the mouldy bones of his ancestors." [52]

50. *Seven Gables,* pp. 21, 39, 40, 378.
51. *Dr. Grimshawe's Secret,* p. 230.
52. *Mosses,* p. 433.

So strongly anti-aristocratic, indeed, were Hawthorne's social views that his reference to himself in "The Custom House" as "the Locofoco Surveyor" [53] may be taken as something more than an attempt at facetiousness. One infers from a letter written by Longfellow to George W. Greene that Hawthorne was identified with the "Locofocos" in 1839.[54] Two years earlier, he had been impressed by, though perhaps he had not fully acquiesced in, the opinions of Eben Hawthorne; he had written in the journal:

> Eben passed from the matters of birth, pedigree, and ancestral pride, to give vent to the most arrant democracy and locofocoism, that I have happened to hear; saying that nobody ought to possess wealth longer than his own life, and that then it should return to the people &c.[55]

Hawthorne ascribes to Holgrave in *The House of the Seven Gables* views somewhat similar to those of Eben: the daguerreotypist says to Phoebe:

> "But we shall live to see the day, I trust . . . when no man shall build his house for posterity. . . . If each generation were allowed and expected to build its own houses, that single change, comparatively unimportant in itself, would imply almost every reform which society is now suffering for." [56]

Not only views so democratic as to approach the socialistic but also the belief that the influence of the past on the present is intrinsically bad determined Hawthorne's attitude toward old families and ancestral mansions. In 1844 Hawthorne wrote in the journal a paragraph beginning, "To represent the influence which Dead Men have among living affairs." [57] The thought of this paragraph, which constitutes the central theme of *The House of*

53. *Scarlet Letter*, p. 23.
54. See *American Notebooks*, p. 288, n. 62.
55. *Ibid.*, p. 27.
56. *Seven Gables*, p. 220.
57. *American Notebooks*, p. 106.

the Seven Gables, is expanded in the novel in several speeches by Holgrave:

> "Shall we never, never get rid of this Past?" cried he. . . . It lies upon the Present like a giant's dead body! . . . Just think a moment, and it will startle you to see what slaves we are to bygone times. . . . The house [of the seven gables], in my view, is expressive of that odious and abominable Past, with all its bad influences. . . ." [58]

In coming into possession of their ancestral mansion, therefore, the Pyncheon descendants have inherited—as Hawthorne puts it —not a great fortune, but a great misfortune.[59]

If the present is to be freed from its slavery to the past, the living must vindicate all claims to recognition and reward through their own efforts. Hawthorne demonstrates repeatedly the folly of seeking in ancestral arcana the clue to success. When Peter Goldthwaite in "Peter Goldthwaite's Treasure" (1838) opens the treasure-chest, he finds it filled with worthless paper money.[60] Again, when in *The House of the Seven Gables* (1851) the lost document which was to make the Pyncheons owners of a vast estate in Maine is at length found, it proves to be "an ancient deed, signed with the hieroglyphics of several Indian sagamores," [61] and therefore quite without value. And, finally, when in *Dr. Grimshawe's Secret* Redclyffe at the end of a long quest obtains the mysterious coffer, he discovers that its contents consist of luxurious golden ringlets, beautiful but worthless.[62] Thus in these three instances Hawthorne expresses symbolically the idea that the expectation of benefits to be received through ancestral channels must prove delusive.

58. *Seven Gables,* pp. 219–221.
59. Compare *Seven Gables,* p. 34: "Would it not be a far truer mode of expression to say of the Pyncheon family, that they inherited a great misfortune, than the reverse?"
60. *Twice-Told Tales,* p. 453.
61. *Seven Gables,* p. 374.
62. *Dr. Grimshawe's Secret,* p. 342. (The novel was written in 1861.)

The positive side of the same moral is clearly stated in the speech of Governor Hancock in "Old Esther Dudley" (1839):

". . . I, and these around me—we represent a new race of men—living no longer in the past, scarcely in the present—but projecting our lives forward into the future. Ceasing to model ourselves on ancestral superstitions, it is our faith and principle to press onward, onward!" [63]

Again in *The Ancestral Footstep* Hawthorne states explicitly the moral to be drawn from Middleton's attempt to regain his ancestral heritage in England:

Let the past alone: do not seek to renew it; press on to higher and better things,—at all events, to other things; and be assured that the right way can never be that which leads you back to the identical shapes that you long ago left behind. Onward, onward, onward! [64]

And a similar moral is enforced in *The House of the Seven Gables:* Holgrave, like General Hancock, belongs to a new race of men who have ceased to model their lives on ancient superstitions; and at the close of the novel he and Phoebe face the future together, leaving behind them the old house, which is the symbol of the outworn past.

We have followed the development of the theme of the past in the notebooks, tales, and novels. We have seen that Hawthorne recorded in the notebooks, again and again, instances of the decline of aristocratic families and that this conception had its fruition in the central situation of *The House of the Seven Gables.* We have seen also that his democratic sympathies and his belief that the influence of the past is intrinsically bad resulted in the conviction that the disintegration of old families is necessary to the progress of society. Although Hawthorne best expressed these ideas in *The House of the Seven Gables,* he returned to the theme

63. *Twice-Told Tales*, p. 341.
64. *Ancestral Footstep*, pp. 488–489. (This fragmentary novel was written in 1858.)

of the past in *Dr. Grimshawe's Secret* and *The Ancestral Footstep,* in both of which an American attempts to get possession of an ancestral estate in England. Here again he emphasizes the folly of seeking aid or guidance from bygone times. In the light of the discussion in this chapter, the cry of "Onward!" in *The Ancestral Footstep* becomes, instead of the facile or casual exclamation that it might otherwise seem to be, the distilled essence of the thought of a lifetime.

IV

Another theme in which Hawthorne manifested a prolonged and intense interest is that of earthly immortality made possible by the elixir of life. This theme did not find expression in a masterpiece comparable to "Rappaccini's Daughter" or "Ethan Brand" or *The House of the Seven Gables*—to mention the most notable embodiments of the three themes already considered: namely, isolation from one's fellows, the unpardonable sin, and the influence of the past—but it is, nevertheless, a topic of major importance in the study of Hawthorne's work.

Hawthorne's interest in this subject was very probably awakened by William Godwin's *St. Leon: A Tale of the Sixteenth Century,* which he had read as early as 1820, for in a letter to his sister Elizabeth, dated October 31 of that year, he wrote: "I have read Hoggs Tales, Caleb Williams, St. Leon, & Mandeville. I admire Godwin's Novels, and intend to read them all." [65] Imbibing the elixir at the age of fifty-four, the hero of *St. Leon* is made younger by thirty-two years.[66] Hawthorne of course treated the subject in an independent manner, but his reading of the novel may have suggested to him the feasibility of using this theme in fiction.

Early references to the subject point out undesirable effects which an earthly immortality would have on human life. The

65. This letter is in the possession of Miss Rebecca Manning.
66. See the edition (London, 1799), III, 274 ff.

abolishment of death would result in serious complications in
human society, as the following passage from the notebook of
1836 suggests:

Curious to imagine what murmurings and discontent would be
excited, if any of the great so-called calamities of human beings were
to be abolished—as, for instance, death.

In 1840 Hawthorne points out a specific source of discontent
consequent upon an indefinite prolongation of life:

The love of posterity is a consequence of the necessity of death. If
a man were sure of living forever here, he would not care about his
offspring.[67]

Another argument against the elixir of life is that the rejuvenation which it produces does not bring about a real improvement in character. Captain Gavett, a natural philosopher
with whom Hawthorne conversed at North Adams in 1838,
raised the question, "whether it would be worth while to grow
young again." [68] The subject was of particular interest to
Hawthorne at that time because only a short while before he
had attempted to answer this very question in "Dr. Heidegger's
Experiment" (1837). His conclusion in this story is that no real
advantage would be achieved by regaining one's youth: Mr.
Medbourne, Colonel Killigrew, Mr. Gascoigne, and the Widow
Wycherly, all give unmistakable evidence, when under the influence of the elixir, of returning to the evil ways of their early
life. Dr. Heidegger concludes:

". . . if the fountain [of youth] gushed at my very doorstep, I
would not stoop to bathe my lips in it—no, though its delirium were
for years instead of moments. Such is the lesson ye have taught me!" [69]

In "A Virtuoso's Collection" (1842) Hawthorne again rejects

67. *Passages,* pp. 36, 212.
68. *American Notebooks,* p. 46.
69. *Twice-Told Tales,* p. 270.

the elixir. When the virtuoso proffers a draught of the potent cordial, the writer says in refusing it:

"No; I desire not an earthly immortality. . . . Were man to live longer on the earth, the spiritual would die out of him. The spark of ethereal fire would be choked by the material, the sensual. There is a celestial something within us that requires, after a certain time, the atmosphere of heaven to preserve it from decay and ruin. I will have none of this liquid." [70]

And, once more, in "The Birthmark" (1843) we are told why Aylmer regards as unwise the application of the principle of the elixir to human life:

He [Aylmer] more than intimated that it was at his option to concoct a liquid that should prolong life for years, perhaps interminably; but that it would produce a discord in Nature which all the world, and chiefly the quaffer of the immortal nostrum, would find cause to curse. [71]

Thus, in his thinking on the subject of the elixir in the period from 1836 to 1843, Hawthorne had formulated various objections to the indefinite extension of human life: the application of such a principle would destroy parental affection; it would not result in the betterment of character; on the contrary, it would evenually annihilate the life of the spirit; and, finally, it would produce a discord in nature. A different point of view from which the subject of the elixir of life might be regarded was suggested apparently by the death of Washington Allston, who left unfinished his painting, "Belshazzar's Feast," upon which he had been engaged for twenty-six years: namely, that a longer term of life than man now possesses is necessary for the accomplishment of a great task. The following two notes were made in the journal presumably soon after Allston's death on July 9, 1843:

70. *Mosses*, pp. 551–552.
71. *Ibid.*, p. 58. Hawthorne is thinking here of the isolation of the drinker of the elixir as a result of his exceptional nature. See pp. 50–51.

The advantages of a longer life than is allotted to mortals—the many things that might then be accomplished;—to which one life-time is inadequate, and for which the time spent is therefore lost; a successor being unable to take up the task when we drop it.

Allston's picture of Belshazzar's Feast—with reference to the advantages, or otherwise, of having life assured to us, till we could finish important tasks on which we were engaged.[72]

This view of the subject is referred to incidentally in "The Artist of the Beautiful" (1844): Owen Warland "was incited to toil the more diligently by an anxiety lest death should surprise him in the midst of his labors." And Hawthorne adds: "This anxiety, perhaps, is common to all men who set their hearts upon anything so high, in their own view of it, that life becomes of importance only as conditional to its accomplishment." That the death of Allston suggested this trend of thought to the author becomes apparent in a direct reference a little farther in the same paragraph: "The poet leaves his song half sung. . . . The painter—as Allston did—leaves half his conception on the canvas to sadden us with its imperfect beauty. . . ."[73]

The transition from the idea of the extension of life for the accomplishment of a task to the conception of the Wandering Jew is not difficult. In a passage in the notebook written in 1845, Hawthorne speculates on the various possible occupations of the Wandering Jew: "One period, perhaps, in wild carnal debauchery; then trying, over and over again, to grasp domestic happiness; then a soldier; then a statesman &c—at last, realizing some truth."[74]

Notwithstanding the fact that the idea of the elixir of life, as we have seen, had been the subject of numerous entries in the notebooks and of several incidental references in the tales, it had furnished thus far the central theme of only one story—"Dr.

72. *American Notebooks*, pp. 100, 101.
73. *Mosses*, pp. 525–526.
74. *American Notebooks*, p. 117.

Heidegger's Experiment." It was not until after his return from England that Hawthorne began to construct a novel around this subject which he had been pondering for over twenty-five years. The immediate suggestion which led to the resumption of this old theme came from his occupancy of the Wayside where, as Thoreau had told him, there had lived at one time a man who believed he would never die.[75] An unpublished memorandum written in July, 1863, obviously continues the trend of thought which we have traced through the tales and notebooks:

> He must have been a man of high purposes, which he hates to leave unaccomplished. This nostrum to bring back his youth is a thing to which he otherwise attaches no importance. He knows that it is inconsistent with the plan of the world, and, if generally adopted, would throw everything into confusion; he therefore considers it justifiable only in his own exceptional case. . . .

> It might be a metaphysical discovery that he wishes to complete. Perhaps physical. He might have imagined a way to clear disease out of the world; some great beneficence, at all events. Perhaps the object for which he wants renewed youth may appear to the reader ridiculously trifling compared with the means used, as for example, to find out the solution of an algebraic sum. No; better to confer a material benefit on the world, how to get rid of poverty, or slavery, or war. . . .[76]

In the discussion of this subject in *Septimius Felton* we find that Hawthorne has restated and elaborated most of the argu-

75. Hawthorne wrote George William Curtis from Concord on July 14, 1852: "I knew nothing of the history of the house [the Wayside], except Thoreau's telling me that it was inhabited a generation or two ago by a man who believed he should never die" (George Parsons Lathrop, *A Study of Hawthorne* [Boston: Houghton Mifflin and Company, 1876], p. 244). Hawthorne wrote Fields from Concord on October 24, 1863: "From a tradition which he [Thoreau] told me about this house of mine, I got the idea of a deathless man. . . ." (This letter is in the Huntington Library.)

76. This memorandum is written on the back of a letter from Fields dated July 22; the year is 1863, since Fields writes in praise of "Civic Banquets," which appeared in the *Atlantic Monthly* (August 1863). The manuscript is in the Huntington Library. The note refers to the hero of the proposed novel.

ments, for and against, which he had noted in the journals or used in the tales. If death were abolished, he had pointed out in the notebook, the parent would no longer cherish his offspring; in *Septimius Felton* he shows that the converse of this proposition is also true: "How could Death be spared?—then the sire would live forever, and the heir never come to his inheritance, and so he would at once hate his own father, from the perception that he would never be out of his way." [77] The indefinite prolongation of life, he had reasoned before, would produce "discontent" and "discord"; in *Septimius Felton,* the author specifies an objectionable condition that would arise in governmental affairs: ". . . the same class of powerful minds would always rule the state, and there would never be a change of policy." [78]

On the other hand, arguments in favor of a longer life are set forth at great length in the novel. The following passage, in which Septimius is talking to the minister, repeats the thought which we have traced beginning with the entry in the notebook on the death of Allston:

And how is this rich world thrown away upon us, because we live in it such a moment! What mortal work has ever been done since the world began! Because we have no time. No lesson is taught. We are snatched away from our study before we have learned the alphabet. As the world now exists . . . it seems to me all a failure, because we do not live long enough.[79]

The passages in which Septimius discusses with Sibyl Dacy his occupations during successive centuries are derived partly from the note on the Wandering Jew and partly from the memorandum. The Wandering Jew would devote a portion of his life to "wild carnal debauchery"; similarly, Septimius would pass

77. *Septimius Felton,* pp. 363–364.
78. *Ibid.,* p. 364. Following this passage, according to the editor's note, several pages of the manuscript of *Septimius Felton* are missing. It is probable that in these pages the author gave further arguments against the principle of the elixir.
79. *Ibid.,* p. 238.

one century in being "what men call wicked." He explains:
"How can I know my brethren, unless I do that once? I would
experience all. Imagination is only a dream. I can imagine myself
a murderer, and all other modes of crime; but it leaves no real
impression on the heart. I must live these things." Again, the
Wandering Jew would play the roles of soldier and statesman
during a part of his existence; similarly, Septimius "would try
the life of power, ruling men"; for one century he would be the
ruler of the earth. Once more, the Wandering Jew would at last
realize some truth; and Septimius would "contrive deep
philosophies," "build a system . . . by which mankind shall look
far into the ways of Providence," and become a religious teacher
greater than Mahomet.[80]

But this last parallel is also a contrast: the Wandering Jew is a
lost soul who may finally be redeemed; Septimius, on the other
hand, is to be a benefactor of mankind. Like the character described in the memorandum, who wishes a longer life in order to
accomplish "some great beneficence," perhaps the abolishment
of such evils as disease, poverty, slavery, and war, Septimius contemplates spending one century "in devising and putting in
execution remedies" [81] for all the ills of the human race. Thus
the character of Septimius is compounded largely of hints drawn
from the sketch of the Wandering Jew in the notebook and from
the description of the benefactor of the race in the memorandum.
In this attempt to combine in one character the selfishness and
evil nature of the former with the altruism and innocence of
the latter, Hawthorne scarcely succeeded. An inescapable
dichotomy destroys the consistency and unity of the character
of Septimius.

In spite of all that might be said in favor of the experiment,
Hawthorne decided finally that such an attempt should not be
allowed to succeed; accordingly, the elixir concocted by Sep-

---

80. *Ibid.*, pp. 409, 405, 407, 408, 409.
81. *Ibid.*, p. 406.

timius proves to be a poison which is fatal to Sibyl and which Septimius is saved from drinking only by Sibyl's breaking the goblet which contains it.

In *The Dolliver Romance,* which was begun late in 1863 and of which only three fragmentary chapters were written, Hawthorne, perhaps dissatisfied with *Septimius Felton,* was obviously undertaking another treatment of the theme of the elixir of life. Although it is impossible to infer his plan for the whole work from the existing fragments, it is clear that he was approaching the subject from a point of view altogether different from that employed in *Septimius Felton.* Hawthorne had recorded the following suggestion in the notebook in 1848:

A man, arriving at the extreme point of old age, grows young again, at the same pace at which he has grown old; returning upon his path, throughout the whole of life, and thus taking the reverse view of matters. Methinks it would give rise to some odd concatenations.[82]

A passage in the memorandum from which I have already quoted contributed to the development of *The Dolliver Romance:*

As he returns down the road of life, he meets all mankind full in the face coming towards him . . . he is reluctant to leave a baby, entrusted to him, friendless in the world, and therefore avails himself of this secret, which he had discovered in the course of his researches, but would not, on his own account, have thought of using it.[83]

Hawthorne undoubtedly had in mind for Dr. Dolliver some such scheme of gradual rejuvenation. The apothecary, who takes just one drop of the elixir at regular intervals, is growing perceptibly younger; for example, his eyebrows, which were snow

82. *American Notebooks,* p. 125.
83. This memorandum appears to have served a double use: we have already seen the incorporation of part of its contents in *Septimius Felton,* which in large measure doubtless antedates it; *Septimius Felton* having been abandoned, another portion of the memorandum furnished the starting point of *The Dolliver Romance.*

white, are getting dark again.[84] The motivation of such a procedure suggested in the memorandum—namely, the necessity of rearing a baby entrusted to his care—is not stated explicitly in the fragmentary romance; but the author implies that Dr. Dolliver feels an "uneasiness about the future of little Pansie," [85] and it is probable that Hawthorne intended to find in the dependence of the child the justification of the rejuvenation of the old man. The story breaks off before any "odd concatenations" mentioned in the notebook have arisen; it appears, however, from the following passage in the memorandum that Hawthorne intended to continue the process of rejuvenation until the doctor should be a child again[86] in order that he might discover some secret apprehensible only in childhood:

> . . . there must be some mystery, which perhaps, missing it all through maturity, he discovers when he is a little boy again; and as the story ends, you shall see it in his childish eyes.[87]

Thus, by means of two notations, one an entry made in the journal in 1848, the other a memorandum written in 1863, we are able better to understand the fragment of the romance and to predict the probable course of the narrative had Hawthorne completed it.

We have traced the growth of Hawthorne's interest in the theme of the elixir of life. The results of this interest are a story, a novel, complete though unrevised, and a fragment of a novel consisting of three chapters. Having rejected the principle of

84. *Dolliver Romance,* p. 60.
85. *Ibid.,* p. 55.
86. Since the process of rejuvenation is to proceed at the same rate at which one grows old, when the doctor becomes a child, little Pansie, of course, will have passed long before beyond the need of his protection.
87. There is a suggestion here of the influence of Wordsworth's "Ode: Intimations of Immortality." Mrs. Hawthorne quotes from this poem in her letters and journals: Julian she apostrophizes as "Thou eye among the blind!" (See "Ode," 1. 111; Rose Hawthorne Lathrop, *Memories of Hawthorne* [Boston and New York: Houghton Mifflin and Company, 1897], p. 172.) Her husband is "the light of all our seeing" (cf. "Ode," 1. 156).

rejuvenation in "Dr. Heidegger's Experiment," Hawthorne, after the death of Allston, began to ponder the subject with reference to the advantages of a longer life on earth. These advantages were urged in *Septimius Felton;* but whether because he wished to show as in "The Birthmark" the sinfulness of an attempt to circumvent the laws of nature or because a story involving the success of such a scheme would become pure extravaganza, the author thwarted the ambition of Septimius by turning his elixir into poison. In *The Dolliver Romance,* finally, Hawthorne returned to the theme of "Dr. Heidegger's Experiment," but with the difference that the rejuvenation was to be gradual and should have a happy issue. What Hawthorne would have made of *The Dolliver Romance,* one can only conjecture; the Wordsworthian suggestion in the memorandum—that the old man when transformed into a child would discover some secret which he had lost upon reaching maturity—might or might not have been carried out, if he had completed the story. Although the theme of the elixir of life was not productive of Hawthorne's best work, it is of special interest because of his persistent though unsuccessful attempts to give it a satisfactory embodiment in the final phase of his literary career.

In our consideration of four major themes in Hawthorne's fiction, we have traced the gradual growth of certain ideas over considerable periods of time. The themes discussed—the isolation of the individual, the unpardonable sin, the influence of the past, and the elixir of life—are most notably embodied, respectively, in "Rappaccini's Daughter," *The Scarlet Letter* and "Ethan Brand," *The House of the Seven Gables,* and *Septimius Felton.* We have found that a long background of thinking and writing preceded these culminating works. Main lines of development and ramifications of the central themes have been traced through the notebooks, tales, and novels. We have found that the notebooks were useful, both as a repository of hints which might be incorporated in the fiction, and as a necessary agency in the growth of his ideas, since the journals afforded a means of recording the stages of development.

Upon the comparatively few themes which one finds treated in the tales and novels, Hawthorne expended long and patient thought. He was incapable of making a quick and facile disposition of his subject: his judgments were reached only after arduous effort. When he made Holgrave say in *The House of the Seven Gables*, ". . . a man's bewilderment is the measure of his wisdom," [88] he had in mind the difficult processes by which he clarified his own thinking. We have seen that the isolation of Beatrice, the sin of Chillingworth or of Ethan Brand, the evil influence of the Pyncheon house, and Septimius Felton's quest of earthly immortality are themes which acquire added significance when studied genetically. The examples discussed in this chapter, though not exhaustive, are sufficiently representative to establish the principle that rightly to interpret the major fiction of Hawthorne, one must consider the tale or the novel, not *in vacuo*, but in relation to the process of development of which it is a culminating expression.

88. *Seven Gables*, p. 214.

HAWTHORNE AND
THE FAERIE QUEENE

H AWTHORNE'S acquaintance with *The Faerie Queene*[1] dated from early boyhood: there was a tradition in the family that it was the first book which he bought with his own money.[2] Precisely at what age he read the poem for the first time is not known, but it is certain that he reread it many times during his life. For example, he wrote to Sophia Peabody from Boston on June 11, 1840: "I came home and lay down on the bed with the Faery Queen in my hand." [3] And on June 22, 1840, he wrote: "I took a nap, with a volume of Spenser in my hand." [4] During the first winter at the Old Manse, 1842–1843, Hawthorne read Spenser aloud to his wife.[5] And during their residence in England, he read *The Faerie Queene* to his children.[6]

The naming of their first child, Una, reflects, of course, an interest in Spenser's poem on the part of the parents, although Hawthorne wrote to his friend, George S. Hillard, in explanation: "After all, I like the name, not so much from any association with Spenser's heroine, as for its simple self—it is as simple as a name can be—as simple as a breath—it is merely inhaling a breath

1. Hawthorne nowhere refers to Spenser's other works, and it seems unlikely that he was influenced by them.
2. G. P. Lathrop, *A Study of Hawthorne* (Boston: James R. Osgood and Company, 1876), p. 73.
3. *Love Letters of Nathaniel Hawthorne, 1839–41 and 1841–63*, ed. by W. K. Bixby (Chicago: Privately printed for the Society of Dofobs, 1907), I, 206.
4. *Ibid.*, 212.
5. See Rose Hawthorne Lathrop, *Memories of Hawthorne* (Boston and New York: Houghton Mifflin Company, 1897), p. 54.
6. See Julian Hawthorne, *Nathaniel Hawthorne and His Wife* (Boston: James R. Osgood and Company, 1885), II, 9.

into one's heart, and emitting it again, and the name is spoken." [7]
Other names from *The Faerie Queene* became household terms:
for example, a dog at the Old Manse was known in the family as
"Una's lion";[8] and a certain publisher, whose name I have not
discovered, was referred to by Hawthorne and his wife as "the
Blatant Beast." [9]

There are a few direct allusions to Spenser in the tales and
novels. Spenser's name occurs twice in Hawthorne's fiction: in
"The Hall of Fantasy" he is described as "meet guest for an
allegoric structure," [10] and in "A Virtuoso's Collection" the
virtuoso rebukes his visitor for not being able to identify a certain
lovely lamb in his museum. "Methinks you have but carelessly
read Spenser . . . or you would at once recognize the 'milk-white
lamb' which Una led." [11] Other direct allusions to Spenser occur
in *The Blithedale Romance*, where "allegoric figures from the
Faery Queen" appear among the masqueraders,[12] and in "A
Select Party," where the author refers to "the unwritten cantos
of the Fairy Queen." [13]

There is a sufficient amount of external evidence, therefore,
to show that Hawthorne knew *The Faerie Queene* and that the
poem made an uncommonly deep impression upon his mind. But
when we search in the tales and novels for evidence of the
influence of the poem, we find comparatively little that is
tangible. Hawthorne's reading was completely assimilated. He is
one of the least allusive of modern writers, and in both the con-

---

7. The manuscript of this letter, dated Concord, March 24, 1844, is in the
collection of the Maine Historical Society.

8. See *Love Letters, II*, 130.

9. See *Memories*, p. 77, and *The Faerie Queene*, Books V and VI. All references to *The Faerie Queene* are to the Cambridge Edition, ed. by R. E. Neil
Dodge (Boston and New York: Houghton Mifflin Company, 1908).

10. *Mosses from an Old Manse*, p. 198. All references to Hawthorne's
works are to the Riverside Edition, ed. by George Parsons Lathrop (Boston
and New York: Houghton Mifflin Company, 1883).

11. *Mosses*, p. 539.

12. *Blithedale Romance*, p. 557.

13. *Mosses*, p. 83.

ception and the execution of his fiction he maintained a sturdy independence. Since he was no learned plagiary of other writers, the student of Hawthorne must not expect, in any obvious way, to track him in their snow. Shadowy traces of Hawthorne's reading, however, may be found in his works; and although in this case parallel passages are even more inconclusive than they usually are, since Hawthorne's language is rarely derivative, the attempt to discover vestiges of Spenserian influence may serve to emphasize and illuminate some of his characteristic interests and methods.

It is a truism to observe that Hawthorne's conceptions of his characters are fundamentally allegorical, and *The Faerie Queene* was for him certainly, among other things, a great pageant of allegorical figures. One might reasonably expect to find, and one does find, I think, suggestions of Spenserian influence in several of Hawthorne's characters.

In 1836 Hawthorne recorded in his notebook the following suggestion: "A snake taken into a man's stomach and nourished there from fifteen years to thirty-five, tormenting him most horribly. A type of envy or some other evil passion." [14] Again, in 1842, the idea recurs in the journal: "A man to swallow a small snake—and it to be the symbol of a cherished sin." [15] The story, "Egotism; or, the Bosom Serpent," which was published in March 1843, must have been written a short time after this entry was made. Roderick Elliston in the tale is afflicted with a snake in his stomach which becomes the symbol of "a tremendous Egotism, manifesting itself . . . in the form of jealousy." [16] Two

14. *Passages from the American Note-Books*, p. 34.
15. *The American Notebooks by Nathaniel Hawthorne*, ed. by Randall Stewart (New Haven: Yale University Press, 1932), p. 93. For other passages in the journals which seem reminiscent of Spenser, see *ibid.*, pp. 294 and 295. Discussions of the genesis of Elliston and of Chillingworth similar to those presented in this article occur, though in different contexts, in the Introduction to my edition of the American notebooks. [See pp. 15, 20, 22–23, Ed.]
16. *Mosses*, p. 320.

passages in *The Faerie Queene* may have suggested this conception
to Hawthorne. One passage is the following description of Envy:

> And in his bosome secretly there lay
> An hatefull snake, the which his taile uptyes
> In many folds, and mortall sting implyes.[17]

Another passage presents the idea of jealousy with similar
imagery:

> O hatefull hellish snake! what Furie furst
> Brought thee from balefull house of Proserpine,
> Where in her bosome she thee long had nurst,
> And fostred up with bitter milke of tine,
> Fowle Gealosy! [18]

Spenser recommends that jealousy be supplanted by love:

> O let him far be banished away,
> And in his stead let Love for ever dwell. . . .[19]

Similarly in Hawthorne's story the serpent of jealousy is
exorcised by the touch of Rosina, the victim's loving wife.[20]
The unusualness of the conception, combined with the fact that
the story was written at a time when we know Hawthorne to
have been rereading *The Faerie Queene*, seems to make more
plausible the conjecture of Spenserian influence.

Again, Lady Eleanore, the personification of pride in "Lady
Eleanore's Mantle," recalls in several descriptive details Spenser's
Lucifera. In Hawthorne's story, the proud lady makes her
entrance in a coach, "surrounded by the prancing steeds of half
a dozen cavaliers." [21] Lucifera appears in a coach drawn by "six
unequall beasts" on which ride "six sage counsellours." [22] Lady
Eleanore's embroidered mantle matches Lucifera's "royall robes

17. *Faerie Queene*, I, iv, 31.
18. *Ibid.*, III, xi, 1.
19. *Ibid.*, III, xi, 2.
20. *Mosses*, p. 320.
21. *Twice-Told Tales*, p. 310.
22. *Faerie Queene*, I, iv, 18.

and gorgeous array." [23] Both characters display an exquisite hauteur. Lady Eleanore "gazed carelessly [at the spectacle of the ball given by the Governor in her honor], and with now and then an expression of weariness or scorn, tempered with such feminine grace that her auditors scarcely perceived the moral deformity of which it was the utterance." [24] Of Lucifera Spenser writes:

> With loftie eyes, halfe loth to looke so lowe,
> She thancked them in her disdainefull wise. . . .[25]

Hawthorne and Spenser employ somewhat similar acts of symbolism: Lucifera sits on a throne with her feet resting upon a dragon;[26] Lady Eleanore, as she leaves her coach, places her foot upon the body of Jervase Helwyse.[27] Finally, it is not a far cry from the epidemic of smallpox in Hawthorne's story to "the dreadfull spectacle of that sad House of Pryde" in Spenser's poem—"a donghill of dead carcases" of "murdred men"

> Which al through that great princesse pride did fall
> And came to shamefull end.[28]

Hawthorne, to be sure, may have been familiar with the conventional attributes of the Seven Deadly Sins from sources other than *The Faerie Queene*. But when one considers his long familiarity with Spenser, it seems unlikely that he could have created Lady Eleanore the embodiment of Pride, without remembering Spenser's famous pageant. Moreover, there is, as we have seen, a broad parallelism in details which suggests an adaptation by Hawthorne of Spenser's general plan of description.

The vagueness and unreality of Hawthorne's villains imply a literary origin. It is unlikely that Hawthorne found prototypes

23. *Twice-Told Tales*, p. 314; *Faerie Queene*, I, iv, 8.
24. *Twice-Told Tales*, p. 315.
25. *Faerie Queene*, I, iv, 14.
26. *Ibid.*, I, iv, 10.
27. *Twice-Told Tales*, p. 312.
28. *Faerie Queene*, I, v, 53.

in his comparatively innocent New England environment. More-over, his limited contact with the world of men would almost preclude such a possibility. In what was for him, therefore, a peculiarly difficult task, the creation of a villain, what was more natural than that he should remember Spenser's arch-villain, Archimago? And there is reason to believe that he was influenced by Archimago in the portrayal of a group of wicked characters, all of whom are marked by a venerable age and an apparently innocent demeanor.

The type includes the devils and wizards of the early tales and reaches its culmination in Rappaccini and Chillingworth. In "The Gentle Boy," there is an allusion to the devil as "a lame man of low stature and gravely apparelled, with a dark and twisted countenance, and a bright, downcast eye." [29] In "Alice Doane's Appeal," a wizard, who is described as "a small, gray, withered man, with fiendish ingenuity in devising evil, and superhuman power to execute it," [30] contrives to bring about incest and murder. The devil in "Young Goodman Brown" appears as a man about fifty years old dressed in "grave and decent attire" [31] and carrying a "staff, which bore the likeness of a great black snake." [32] Dr. Rappaccini's physical appearance recalls that of Hawthorne's devils and wizards: he is past middle age, with gray hair and a thin, gray beard; [33] he wears the scholar's garb of black; he moves feebly in a stooping posi-tion; and his face, though sickly and sallow, is "pervaded with an expression of piercing and active intellect." [34] Chil-lingworth, likewise, resembles in a general way the foregoing characters in this group: he "went stooping away along the earth." "His gray beard almost touched the ground as he crept

29. *Twice-Told Tales*, p. 100.
30. *Tales, Sketches, and Other Papers*, p. 284.
31. *Mosses*, p. 90.
32. *Ibid.*, p. 91.
33. *Ibid.*, p. 112.
34. *Ibid.*, p. 124.

onward." [35] His eyes had a "strange penetrating power." [36] It seems probable that in these descriptions Hawthorne was indebted in part to Spenser's account of Archimago, and particularly to the following lines:

> At length they chaunst to meet upon the way
> An aged sire, in long blacke weedes yclad,
> His feete all bare, his beard all hoarie gray . . .
> Sober he seemde, and very sagely sad,
> And to the ground his eyes were lowly bent,
> Simple in shew, and voide of malice bad. . . .[37]

Hawthorne's treatment of Chillingworth may have been influenced by another character in *The Faerie Queene*, Malbecco, who is also a jealous husband. Of the transformation of Malbecco, Spenser writes that he

> Is woxen so deform'd, that he has quight
> Forgot he was a man. . . .[38]

In a similar manner the deformity of Chillingworth, with appropriate symbolism, increases as his moral nature becomes more degraded. At the beginning of the novel, he is only "slightly deformed, with the left shoulder a trifle higher than the right"; [39] but as the story progresses, he becomes "misshapen" [40] and "hump-shouldered." [41] Furthermore, when Malbecco attempts to commit suicide by jumping from a high cliff, he receives no injury from his fall because his body has wasted away to the point of insubstantiality:

> But through long anguish, and selfe-murdring thought,
> He was so wasted and forpined quight,

35. *Scarlet Letter*, p. 211.
36. *Ibid.*, p. 80.
37. *Faerie Queene*, I, i, 29.
38. *Ibid.*, III, x, 60.
39. *Scarlet Letter*, p. 80.
40. *Ibid.*, p. 139.
41. *Ibid.*, p. 291.

> That all his substance was consum'd to nought,
> And nothing left, but like an aery spright,
> That on the rockes he fell so flit and light,
> That he thereby receivd'd no hurt at all. . . .[42]

The physical change in Chillingworth after the death of Dimmesdale seems reminiscent of the somewhat similar metamorphosis of Malbecco:

All his strength and energy—all his vital and intellectual force—seemed at once to desert him; insomuch that he positively withered up, shrivelled away, and almost vanished from mortal sight, like an uprooted weed that lies wilting in the sun.[43]

There are, of course, many points of difference between Chillingworth and Malbecco. But in both characters physical deformity is a symbol of moral depravity, and they are alike in their fantastic fates.

Another character from whom emanates a Spenserian aura is Donatello, whose lineage recalls the parentage of Satyrane. The parents of Satyrane were a satyr and a mortal woman, Thyamis by name. When "fayre Thyamis" was searching for her husband in the forest,

> A Satyre chaunst her wandring for to finde,
> And kindling coles of lust in brutish eye,
> The loyall linkes of wedlocke did unbinde,
> And made her person thrall unto his beastly kind.
>
> So long in secret cabin there he held
> Her captive to his sensuall desyre,
> Till that with timely fruit her belly sweld,
> And bore a boy unto that salvage syre. . . .[44]

Hawthorne's account of the beginning of the Monte Beni family appears to be a euphemistic rendering of Spenser's story:

---

42. *Faerie Queene*, III, x, 57.
43. *Scarlet Letter*, p. 307.
44. *Faerie Queene*, I, vi, 22–23.

A sylvan creature, native among the woods, had loved a mortal maiden, and—perhaps by kindness, and the subtile courtesies which love might teach to his simplicity, or possibly by a ruder wooing—had won her to his haunts. In due time, he gained her womanly affection; and, making their bridal bower, for aught we know, in the hollow of a great tree, the pair spent a happy wedded life in that ancient neighborhood where now stood Donatello's tower.[45]

The descendants of this pair were "a pleasant and kindly race of men, but capable of savage fierceness." [46] Similarly Satyrane, after a savage youth spent in the taming of wild animals, acquired with maturity all the knightly virtues; he was

> Plaine, faithfull, true, and enimy of shame. . . .[47]

If the reader has recognized Spenser's influence in the conception and description of the four characters considered (Elliston, Lady Eleanore, Chillingworth, and Donatello), he may find plausible also the conjecture that *The Faerie Queene* suggested a favorite device of characterization which Hawthorne employed repeatedly in the tales and novels. This device consists in the use of a material adjunct which in association with the character acquires a symbolical significance. One recalls many examples: Reverend Mr. Hooper's black veil, Lady Eleanore's mantle, Owen Warland's mechanical butterfly, Hester's embroidered letter *A*, Zenobia's exotic flower, Westervelt's dental gold band, and Hilda's doves. Spenser frequently employs a similar method of characterization. Conspicuous examples occur in the pageant of the deadly sins to which reference has already been made. Each character carries a significant object: Idlenesse, a "portesse"; Gluttony, "a bouzing can"; Lechery, "a burning heart"; Avarice, "an heap of coine"; Envy, "an hatefull snake"; and Wrath, "a burning brond." [48]

45. *Marble Faun*, p. 269.
46. *Ibid.*, p. 270.
47. *Faerie Queene*, I, vi, 20.
48. *Ibid.*, I, iv, 18–33.

But many other instances of this allegorical device may be found in the poem: the Red Cross Knight's bloody cross, the palmer's virtuous staff, Talus's iron flail, to mention only a few obvious examples. It may be urged, doubtless, that the use of this method is widespread in allegorical literature, and that Hawthorne could have caught the trick from another source. He was not, however, a multifarious reader: he tended rather to reperuse his favorite authors, among whom Spenser held a high place. Moreover, Hawthorne's symbolic concomitants bear a striking resemblance to Spenser's in their general nature and function.

The influence of *The Faerie Queene* in the contrivance of situation is less demonstrable than in characterization: Spenser's situations would doubtless be less adaptable to the purpose of modern fiction, however allegorical, than his characters. Without pretending to exhaust the possibilities of the subject, I profess, quite undogmatically, to find Spenserian hints in two scenes in Hawthorne.

One scene is in *The Scarlet Letter* and embodies a favorite theme of the author's—namely, moral error. Hester and Pearl go into the forest to meet the minister:

[The footpath] straggled onward into the mystery of the primeval forest. This hemmed it in so narrowly, and stood so black and dense on either side, and disclosed such imperfect glimpses of the sky above, that, to Hester's mind, it imaged not amiss the moral wilderness in which she had so long been wandering.[49]

Later, when Hester and Dimmesdale are talking together, a storm comes on:

The forest was obscure round them, and creaked with a blast that was passing through it. The boughs were tossing heavily above their heads. . . .[50]

Referring to Hester's "latitude of speculation," Hawthorne observes:

49. *Scarlet Letter,* p. 220.
50. *Ibid.,* p. 234.

She had wandered, without rule or guidance, in a moral wilderness; as vast, as intricate and shadowy, as the untamed forest, amid the gloom of which they were now holding a colloquy that was to decide their fate.[51]

Could Hawthorne have written this scene without remembering the similar plight of Una and the Red Cross Knight? At the very beginning of the poem, Una and her knight lose their way in Errour's Wood whither they have gone to seek shelter from a storm:

> The day with cloudes was suddeine overcast,
> And angry Jove an hideous storme of raine
> Did poure into his lemans lap so fast,
> That everie wight to shrowd it did constrain,
> And this faire couple eke to shroud themselves were fain.
>
> Enforst to seeke some covert nigh at hand,
> A shadie grove not farr away they spide,
> That promist ayde the tempest to withstand:
> Whose loftie trees, yclad with sommers pride,
> Did spred so broad, that heavens light did hide. . . .[52]

When the storm has ceased, Una and the Knight are unable to find the path by which they entered the forest; continuing on their way, they at length reach a hollow cave. Here Una warns the Knight:

> This is the wandring wood, this Errours den. . . .[53]

Thus in both *The Faerie Queene* and *The Scarlet Letter* a man and woman wander in a dense forest where they are sheltered from a raging storm; and in both works, such a wandering symbolizes bewilderment leading to, or resulting from, moral error.

A second scene in Hawthorne which recalls Spenser is in *Dr. Grimshawe's Secret*. Here we have external evidence (the passage

---

51. *Ibid.*, p. 239.
52. *Faerie Queene*, I, i, 6–7.
53. *Ibid.*, I, i, 13.

in this respect is unique in Hawthorne's writings) that he was thinking of *The Faerie Queene,* for he wrote the following memorandum in connection with Chapter XI of the novel: "Compare it with Spenser's Cave of Despair.[54] Put instruments of suicide there." [55] If we make the suggested comparison, we find a correspondence similar to those parallelisms already noted. Spenser depicts the cave of Despayre as

> Darke, dolefull, dreary, like a greedy grave. . . .[56]

Hawthorne describes a mysterious chamber:

It was dim, dim as a melancholy mood. . . . You detected that it was within very narrow boundaries, though you could not precisely see them; only you felt yourself shut in, compressed, impeded, in the deep centre of something; and you longed for a breath of fresh air.[57]

The only inhabitant of Spenser's cave is Despayre:

> That cursed man, low sitting on the ground,
> Musing full sadly in his sullein mind:
> His griesie lockes, long growen and unbound,
> Disordred hong about his shoulders round,
> And hid his face; through which his hollow eyne
> Lookt deadly dull. . . .[58]

---

54. The fascination which Spenser's story of Despayre had for Hawthorne may doubtless be explained by the fact that he himself was subject to periods of despondency. For example, a letter from Horatio Bridge, dated Augusta, October 22, 1836, indicates that Hawthorne at that time may have been contemplating suicide: "I have just received your last, and do not like its tone at all. There is a kind of desperate coolness in it that seems dangerous. I fear that you are too good a subject for suicide, and that some day you will end your mortal woes on your own responsibility" (*Nathaniel Hawthorne and His Wife,* I, 142). In *The American Magazine of Useful and Entertaining Knowledge,* II (August 1836), 507, Hawthorne wrote in an article on "Caverns": "In the spacious gloom of this cave [Mammoth Cave in Kentucky], the innumerable wretches who are weary of the light of day might build a city of Despair. . . ."
55. *Dr. Grimshawe's Secret,* p. 354.
56. *Faerie Queene,* I, ix, 33.
57. *Dr. Grimshawe's Secret,* pp. 130–131.
58. *Faerie Queene,* I, ix, 35.

The sole occupant of Hawthorne's chamber is a nameless young man:

> He sits dull and motionless . . . his hair long and dishevelled. His beard has grown, and curls round his face. . . . A dull, dreamy reverie seems to have possessed him.[59]

In Spenser's poem the "instruments of suicide" which Despayre offers to the Red Cross Knight are swords, ropes, poison, fire, and a dagger.[60] In Hawthorne's novel, the "implements of self-destruction" are pistols, an Italian dagger, a vial containing poison, a drug, and a noose.[61]

The parallels cited are intended to be illustrative rather than exhaustive: another reader of Hawthorne and Spenser might very well choose other passages to exemplify the influence of the poet on the novelist. The examples given above, however, make plausible, I think, the conjecture that Hawthorne's creative conceptions were colored by his recollections of *The Faerie Queene*. His typical villain, the bearded, venerable man of apparent guilelessness, seems to have been suggested by Spenser's arch-villain, Archimago. His best personification of Pride, Lady Eleanore, inevitably recalls Lucifera. Rich in the lore of fauns and satyrs, *The Faerie Queene* seems the most likely source of the lineage of Donatello. More convincing because of the grotesque-ness of the subject matter are the similarities between passages in *The Faerie Queene* and the accounts of Chillingworth's transformation and Elliston's affliction. Again, Hawthorne's favorite trick of the symbolical concomitant is very like Spenser's stock device. Moreover, it is not difficult to believe that in portraying symbolically the moral aberration of Hester and Dimmesdale, Hawthorne remembered Spenser's Wood of Errour. And finally, in the dark, dismal scene in *Dr. Grimshawe's Secret*, we have

---

59. *Dr. Grimshawe's Secret*, p. 135.
60. *Faerie Queene*, I, ix, 50–51.
61. *Dr. Grimshawe's Secret*, pp. 135–138.

external evidence that Hawthorne was thinking of the Cave of Despayre.

These passages illustrate the common ground of moral allegory where the two writers meet. There are, of course, important traits peculiar to each author: to Spenser, for example, the rich, sensuous imagery of the Renaissance; and to Hawthorne, a Puritan somberness and an element of hard realism. But as moral allegorists—and no one heretofore has adduced evidence bearing on this relationship—they are closely allied. Envy, pride, moral error, despair—in the contemplation of these and similar abstractions, Hawthorne was drawn, whether consciously or unconsciously, to Spenser; and Hawthorne's allegorical representations not infrequently took form and color, there is reason to believe, from the imagery of *The Faerie Queene*.

HAWTHORNE AND THE CIVIL WAR [1]

A F T E R an absence from America of nearly seven years, Hawthorne arrived at the Wayside in Concord in June 1860. During his residence abroad, he had kept informed concerning events at home by a careful reading of the American newspapers,[2] which his friend and publisher, W. D. Ticknor, sent to him at frequent intervals. He was not, therefore, altogether unprepared for the outbreak of war, though the shock of events would probably have been less disturbing if his contact with the American scene during the preceding years had been closer.

An account of Hawthorne's life in relation to the Civil War, I believe, has never been given in adequate detail. It is the purpose of this article to set forth his views of the war, and the effect of certain environmental conditions brought about by the war upon the writer and the man.

I

The opening of hostilities had the immediate effect upon Hawthorne, quite naturally, of producing an excited and even belligerent frame of mind. Repeatedly in letters to friends he

1. I am indebted for helpful suggestions to Professor Frank L. Owsley of Vanderbilt University and Professor Gregory Paine of the University of North Carolina.

2. A popular misconception is reflected in the opinion expressed by E. W. Emerson that Hawthorne "probably had—as a man living in his dreams, remote from politics—little knowledge" of Franklin Pierce's "political misdeeds with regard to Kansas and Nebraska." See *The Early Years of the Saturday Club, 1855–70* (Boston and New York: Houghton Mifflin Company, 1918), p. 345.

expressed regret that he himself was too old to enlist. To Ticknor he wrote on May 16, 1861, "If I were younger, I would volunteer." [3] To Horatio Bridge he declared on May 26, "I regret . . . I am too old to shoulder a musket myself." [4] And, once more, to Francis Bennoch in August he said, "Were it not for certain silvery monitors hanging by my temples, suggesting prudence, I feel as if I could catch the infection, shoulder a musket, and be off to the war myself!" [5] Upon hearing the news of the Battle of Bull Run, he gave way to a feeling of extraordinary belligerency in a letter to Lowell, dated July 23, 1861: "If last evening's news puts all of us into the same grim and bloody humor that it does me, the South had better have suffered ten defeats than won this victory." [6] In his letters he spoke repeatedly also of the stimulating and engrossing effect of the war: "the war . . . has had a beneficial effect upon my spirits," [7] "the excitement had an invigorating effect on me for a time," [8] "the war at first drew my thoughts wholly to itself" [9] —are some of the comments which reflect his state of mind during the spring and summer of 1861. Apparently then during the early months of the war Hawthorne was not unresponsive to the popular feeling.

It was impossible at first to think of creative work; but in the autumn, partly because the winter months had always been for him the most favorable period of the year for writing and partly

3. *Letters of Hawthorne to William D. Ticknor, 1851–1864* (Newark: Privately printed for the Carteret Book Club, 1910).

4. Horatio Bridge, *Personal Recollections of Nathaniel Hawthorne* (New York: Harper and Brothers, 1893), p. 169.

5. Moncure D. Conway, *Emerson at Home and Abroad* (Boston: James R. Osgood and Company, 1882), p. 274.

6. The original manuscript is in the Harvard Library.

7. *Personal Recollections*, p. 168.

8. *Letters to Ticknor* (May 26, 1861).

9. From a letter to Henry Bright, dated November 14, 1861. The original manuscript is in the possession of the Earl of Crewe. [The entirety of the letter appears in Edward Mather, *Nathaniel Hawthorne, A Modest Man* (New York: Thomas Y. Crowell Co., 1940), pp. 315–318. Ed.]

because the initial excitement had subsided somewhat, he began to contemplate a new novel. "As the autumn advances," he wrote to Bridge on October 12, "I find myself sitting down to my desk and blotting successive sheets of paper, as of yore";[10] and to Henry Bright, he confided, on November 14, "Latterly, I am meditating a Romance." [11] The work in hand was very probably *Septimius Felton*. But even in the writing of a romance, Hawthorne was unable to dissociate himself or his story from the events which surrounded him; for, although the theme of the novel—the elixir of life—was one which he had used twenty-five years before in "Dr. Heidegger's Experiment," the background was the Revolutionary War, which was in a sense a civil war. And Septimius's reflections on the Revolutionary War and his relation thereto were, *mutatis mutandis,* Hawthorne's own thoughts on the present crisis.

"The war" he wrote in the novel "put everybody into an exaggerated and unnatural state";[12] it "filled the whole brain of the people and enveloped the whole thought of man in a mist of gunpowder." [13] As the mist in his own mind cleared away and his partisan feeling yielded by degrees to sober second thought Hawthorne could see all too clearly the evils of war. He was depressed first of all of course by the homicidal aspect:

"O heavens, Mr. Felton!" whispered Rose, "why should we shoot these men, or they us? . . . Each of them has a mother and sisters, I suppose, just like our men."

"It is the strangest thing in the world that we can think of killing them," said Septimius. "Human life is so precious." [14]

Moreover he was acutely aware of the social ills which attend and follow war:

10. *Personal Recollections*, p. 171.
11. From the letter cited in note 9.
12. *Septimius Felton*, p. 299. All references to Hawthorne's works are to the Riverside Edition, ed. by George Parsons Lathrop (Boston and New York: Houghton Mifflin Company, 1883).
13. *Ibid.*, p. 285.
14. *Ibid.*, p. 248.

In times of revolution and public disturbance . . . the measure of calm sense, the habits, the orderly decency, are partially lost. . . . Offences against public morality, female license, are more numerous; suicides, murders, all ungovernable outbreaks of men's thoughts, embodying themselves in wild acts, take place more frequently, and with less horror to the lookers-on.[15]

Hawthorne was particularly apprehensive of a degrading influence upon women and young girls (his own daughter, Una, was just seventeen):

Any breaking up of the ordinary state of things is apt to shake women out of their proprieties, break down barriers, and bring them into perilous proximity with the world.[16]

The gravity of his conviction on this point was reaffirmed by Mrs. Hawthorne, who after her husband's death told Henry Bright "how he felt that, when the soldiers returned, the quiet rural life of the New England villages would be spoiled and coarsened." [17] Nor did he overlook the most tragic consequence of the fact that many soldiers would never return:

The girls that would have loved them, and made happy firesides for them, will pine and wither, and tread along many sour and discontented years, and at last go out of life without knowing what life is. . . . Every shot that takes effect . . . kills one and worse than kills the other.[18]

Thoughts like these, we may be sure, were uppermost in Hawthorne's mind as he wrote *Septimius Felton*.

II

In March 1862 Hawthorne went on a journey of several weeks' duration to Washington. One finds a vivid record of this

15. *Ibid.*, p. 299.
16. *Ibid.*, p. 246.
17. *The Life, Letters, and Friendships of Richard Monckton Milnes*, ed. by T. Wemyss Reid (London: Cassell & Company, Ltd., 1890), II, 242.
18. *Septimius Felton*, p. 278.

excursion to the theatre of war in the essay, "Chiefly About War Matters." [19] He had been compelled, he tells the reader in the opening paragraph, "to suspend the contemplation of certain fantasies," because he felt that there was "a kind of treason in insulating one's self from the universal fear and sorrow, and thinking one's idle thoughts in the dread time of civil war." [20] In Washington he would be able to look a little more closely at matters with his own eyes. He arrived on March 11, just a few hours after the movement of a large body of troops across the Potomac, and only two days after the epochal battle between the *Monitor* and the *Merrimac*.

Two spectacles evoked his enthusiasm. One was McClellan reviewing his troops, and in the essay he deprecated the popular detraction and expressed complete confidence in his soldiership and courage—a confidence which seemed to him to be confirmed by the cheers with which the soldiers greeted McClellan's appearance on parade: "They believed in him, and so did I; and had I stood in the ranks, I should have shouted with the lustiest of them." [21] A second spectacle, more stirring than the first, which came into view from a steamer's deck in the course of a voyage to Fortress Monroe, was "the masts of the Cumberland rising midway out of the water, with a tattered rag of a pennant fluttering from one of them." [22] Moved by this reminder of the *Cumberland's* gallant action against the *Merrimac,* he wrote to his son: "A braver thing was never done; and I only wish I could write a song about it—or you either." [23]

But despite these moments of enthusiasm, the prevailing mood of the essay is one of perplexity with respect to war issues—a perplexity which was increased by a disposition to see both sides

19. Published with the subtitle, "By a Peaceable Man," in *The Atlantic Monthly,* X (July 1862), 43–61.

20. *Ibid.,* p. 43.

21. *Ibid.,* p. 52.

22. *Ibid.,* p. 59.

23. Letter to Julian Hawthorne, dated Washington, March 27, 1862. The original manuscript is in the Huntington Library.

of the conflict. Accordingly, numerous passages in "Chiefly About War Matters" reflect a sympathetic attitude toward some phases of the Southern position. Hawthorne clearly recognized, for example, the primacy, from the emotional point of view, of the claim of one's state or section upon one's allegiance:

We inevitably limit to our own State, or, at farthest, to our own section, that sentiment of physical love for the soil which renders an Englishman . . . so intensely sensitive to the dignity and well-being of his little island.[24]

This was so, because

the State comes nearest home to a man's feelings, and includes the altar and the hearth, while the General Government claims his devotion only to an airy mode of law, and has no symbol but a flag.[25]

He freely confessed, therefore, his admiration of the Southerner's loyalty to his state:

If a man loves his own State . . . and is content to be ruined with her, let us shoot him, if we can, but allow him an honorable burial in the soil he fights for.[26]

Again, Hawthorne saw that the problem of emancipation was much more complex than the abolitionists represented it as being. John Brown's mistake, which quite justified his being hanged, was "his preposterous miscalculation of possibilities." [27] And when Hawthorne actually encountered in Virginia a group of Negroes plodding northward, he was more than ever perplexed by the difficulties presented by their newly acquired freedom:

I felt most kindly towards these poor fugitives, but knew not precisely what to wish in their behalf, nor in the least how to help them. For the sake of the manhood which is latent in them, I would not have

24. *Atlantic Monthly*, X, 48.
25. *Ibid.*
26. *Ibid.*
27. *Ibid.*, p. 54.

turned them back; but I should have felt almost as reluctant, on their own account, to hasten them forward to the stranger's land.[28]

Still other passages in the essay betray more than a modicum of sympathy with the Southern point of view. He "tried to imagine how very disagreeable the presence of a Southern army would be in a sober town of Massachusetts." [29] Apropos of the striking contrast between the neatness of a New England village and the somewhat untidy appearance of a Virginia town, he reflected that after all the difference was perhaps largely superficial: white paint, which was used in larger quantities in New England than in the South, was "prodigiously efficacious in putting a bright face upon a bad matter." [30] And he was apparently impressed by his observation that "very excellent people" in Washington spoke with feeling of "the genial courtesy, the warm and graceful freedom" of the Southern character as contrasted with "the frigidity of . . . Northern manners." [31]

"Chiefly About War Matters," [32] then, reveals a divided mind

28. *Ibid.*, p. 50.
29. *Ibid.*, p. 48.
30. *Ibid.*, p. 53.
31. *Ibid.*, p. 61. He parenthetically professed disagreement with this view of the Northern character.
32. James T. Fields, then editor of the *Atlantic,* deleted from the article sketches of Lincoln and of certain cabinet members and congressmen. Nine years later, he printed the sketch of Lincoln ("Our Whispering Gallery," *Atlantic Monthly*, XXVII, April 1871, 510–512). It is a good-humored and remarkably acute portrait written in Hawthorne's best descriptive vein. The following sentence sums up his attitude toward Lincoln at this time: "On the whole, I liked this sallow, queer, sagacious visage, with the homely human sympathies that warmed it; and, for my small share in the matter, would as lief have Uncle Abe for a ruler as any man whom it would have been practicable to put in his place" (p. 511). The article was accompanied by footnotes mildly castigating the author for certain expressions of opinion. These comments were naturally believed by many readers to have been written by the editor, but in reality they were supplied by Hawthorne himself (see *ibid.*, p. 510) in a spirit of sardonic humor, either to protect the political reputation of the magazine or (supposing their authorship to be detected) to add a deceptive ambiguity to his position.

I have been unable to locate the original manuscript of "Chiefly About War

which was disposed, at least for the nonce, to allow no little weight to Southern claims.

III

But inasmuch as Hawthorne was a realist rather than a sentimentalist, he was not content merely to deprecate an unwelcome state of affairs. "If compelled to choose," he said, "I go for the North." [33] And as a Northern man, he formulated early in the war and held consistently a definite opinion as to the most feasible course open to the federal government. "Amputation seems to me much the better plan," he wrote to Bridge on October 12, 1861; "and all we ought to fight for is the liberty of selecting the point where our diseased members shall be lop't off." [34] In a letter to Bright, dated November 14, he set forth this view more explicitly: "Maryland, Virginia, Kentucky, Missouri . . . are fully capable of being made free soil," he declared; the war, he thought, ought to be prosecuted until "we have established our boundary lines to our satisfaction"; and after this has been accomplished, he went on to say, "I trust we shall cast off the extreme Southern States. . . . I want no more of their territory than we can digest into free soil." [35] One finds the same view again in a letter to Bridge dated February 14, 1862: "I (if we can only put the boundary far enough south) should not much regret an ultimate separation." [36] Once more, in the concluding sentence of "Chiefly About War Matters," published in July, Hawthorne implied his reluctant acquiescence in the (as it seemed to him) inevitable dissolution of the Union: ". . .

Matters." Fields apparently destroyed it; and in that event, the passages on the cabinet members and congressmen would seem to be irrecoverable. The article, with the sketch of Lincoln restored to its proper place, is included in *Tales, Sketches, and Other Papers*, pp. 299–345.

33. Julian Hawthorne, *Nathaniel Hawthorne and His Wife* (Boston: James R. Osgood and Company, 1885), II, 271.

34. *Personal Recollections*, p. 170.

35. From the letter cited in note 9.

36. *Personal Recollections*, p. 172.

heaven was heaven still, as Milton sings, after Lucifer and a third part of the angels had seceded from its golden palaces. . . ." [37] And again in a conversation with F. B. Sanborn and others in December 1862, Hawthorne expressed the view that "the North and the South were two distinct nations in opinion and habits, and had better not try to live under the same institutions." [38]

In the following year, he seems to have been even more convinced of the impossibility of the restoration of the Union; and as this conviction grew, he became more reconciled to a permanent division. In the original form of the dedicatory letter to Pierce dated July 2, 1863, and intended as a Preface to *Our Old Home,* Hawthorne said, "I might even deem it allowable for myself, in the last resort, to be content with half the soil that was once our broad inheritance." [39] And in a remarkable letter to Elizabeth Peabody, dated July 20—his longest and frankest epistolary pronouncement on war matters—he declared:

The best thing possible, as far as I can see, would be to effect a separation of the Union, giving us the west bank of the Mississippi and a boundary line affording as much Southern soil as we can hope to digest into freedom in another century. . . . I am very often sensible of an affectionate regard for the dead old Union . . . though I had as lief see my grandfather's ghost as have it revive.[40]

From the above quotations it is clear that during the years 1861, 1862, and 1863, Hawthorne held consistently and with growing conviction the opinion that the dissolution of the Union into two nations was a regrettable necessity and that Northern military success was desirable in order that the federal government might dictate the location of the boundary line.

37. *Tales, Sketches, and Other Papers,* pp. 344–345.
38. F. B. Sanborn, *Hawthorne and His Friends* (Cedar Rapids: The Torch Press, 1908), p. 61.
39. See note 51.
40. The letter was printed in the Boston *Post,* April 18, 1887.

IV

When Hawthorne wrote his *Life of Pierce* in 1852, he was in substantial agreement with Pierce's view of the legal rights of slavery under the Constitution; and nowhere in his writings, so far as I am aware, is there a hint of disapproval of the policies of Pierce's administration. But it is important to observe that after the outbreak of war Hawthorne's political views were clearly different from those of his friend. Pierce opposed the continuation of the war. Hawthorne, in the letter to Miss Peabody already referred to, said, "I always thought that it should have been avoided, although since it has broken out I have longed for military success as much as any man or woman of the North." [41] Pierce advocated a restoration of the Union on the basis of the *status quo ante bellum*. Hawthorne, as we have seen, believed that the political separation of the North and South was the only feasible plan; Pierce, he thought, was "bigoted to the Union." [42]

These facts notwithstanding, certain events in the summer and autumn of 1863 brought the two men together in such a way as to lead the public to suppose that their positions were identical.

On July 4, when Hawthorne was visiting his friend in Concord, New Hampshire,[43] Pierce delivered a speech in which he maintained that "aggression by arms" was not "a suitable or possible remedy for existing evils" and that "the great objects for which . . . the Constitution was formed" could be achieved "through peaceful agencies . . . alone." His view of the future of his country was dark to the point of defeatism. In his peroration, perhaps the supreme oratorical effort of his career, he declared that if all agencies of war and peace should fail, then

41. *Ibid.*
42. See the letter to Bridge, dated February 14, 1862, in *Personal Recollections*, p. 172.
43. See R. F. Nichols, *Franklin Pierce* (Philadelphia: University of Pennsylvania Press, 1931), p. 523.

. . . we will, at least, in the effort to defend our rights, as a free people, build up a great mausoleum of hearts to which men who yearn for liberty will in after years, with bowed heads and reverently, resort, as Christian Pilgrims to the sacred shrines of the Holy Land.[44]

It so happened that Hawthorne sat on the speakers' platform during the delivery of this "treasonable" speech.[45]

On the first day of July, Hawthorne had written to Fields: "I intend to dedicate the book [*Our Old Home*] to Frank Pierce, come what may." [46] And on the following day, he had composed and dispatched to Fields the dedicatory letter. He intended that the dedication should be a secret between himself and the publisher. "Even Sophia did not know it," he wrote to Miss Peabody after the secret was out, "and I have never whispered it to Gen. Pierce, nor meant that it should be known till the publication of the book." [47] Fields remonstrated with Hawthorne, pointing out the fact that Pierce's unpopularity would react unfavorably upon the sale of the book; and lest his own unaided efforts should prove insufficient, he asked the assistance of Ellery Channing. Apparently lacking the courage to approach Hawthorne on the subject, Channing transferred the mission to the more than willing Miss Peabody, who also addressed to Hawthorne a communication of remonstrance.

We have, therefore, two letters by Hawthorne (one to Fields, dated July 18; the other to Miss Peabody, dated July 20) in which he defended his position with respect to the dedication. A notably courageous passage in the letter to Fields has been often quoted:

I find that it would be a piece of poltroonery in me to withdraw either

44. From the account of the speech given in *The New Hampshire Patriot and Gazette*, July 8, 1863. While Pierce was speaking, the audience received reports of events at Gettysburg. See Nichols, *op. cit.*, p. 523.

45. See F. B. Sanborn, *op. cit.*, p. 61.

46. James T. Fields, *Yesterdays With Authors* (Boston: James R. Osgood and Company, 1882), p. 106.

47. From the letter cited in note 40.

the dedication or the dedicatory letter. My long and intimate personal relations with Pierce render the dedication altogether proper, especially as regards this book, which would have had no existence without his kindness; and if he is so exceedingly unpopular that his name is enough to sink the volume, there is so much the more need that an old friend should stand by him. I cannot, merely on account of pecuniary profit or literary reputation, go back from what I have deliberately felt and thought it right to do; and if I were to tear out the dedication, I should never look at the volume again without remorse and shame. As for the literary public, it must accept my book precisely as I think fit to give it, or let it alone.[48]

To Miss Peabody, he said:

I determined upon [the dedication] long since, as a proper memorial of our lifelong intimacy, and as especially suitable in the case of this book, which could not have been in existence without him. I expressly say that I dedicate the book to the friend, and decline any present colloquy with the statesman, to whom I address merely a few lines expressing my confidence in his loyalty and unalterable devotion to the Union—which I am glad to have the opportunity of saying, at this moment, when all the administration and abolition papers are calling him a traitor.[49]

Quite obviously, the question of Pierce's loyalty depended upon the point of reference—loyalty to what? Hawthorne continued:

A traitor! Why, he is the only loyal man in the country, North or South. Everybody else has outgrown the old faith in the Union . . . but Pierce retains it in all the simplicity with which he inherited it from his father. . . . It would ruin a noble character (though one of limited scope) for him to admit any ideas that were not entertained by the fathers of the Constitution and the Republic. Knowing that he is eternally true to them, I say so, and that is all I say of his political character.[50]

Hawthorne, however, had yielded to his remonstrators to the

48. *Yesterdays With Authors*, pp. 107–108.
49. From the letter cited in note 40.
50. *Ibid.*

extent of rewriting the concluding paragraph of the dedicatory letter.[51] The revision did not bear upon his attitude toward his friend, for in both versions he expressed his confidence in Pierce's loyalty to the Union, historically considered. The essential alteration was the omission of certain sentences in which he definitely contemplated the likelihood of the permanent disruption of the Union and suggested his own more or less reluctant acceptance of such an outcome. With the exception of this change (which was, in fact, the excision of a somewhat intrusive expression of his personal views, though the first form of the paragraph would have had the desirable effect of indicating to readers wherein he and Pierce differed), the book with dedication and dedicatory letter exactly as Hawthorne had originally written them appeared on September 19.[52]

A cruel coincidence in connection with the publication of *Our Old Home* has not, I believe, been previously noticed. On

51. The paragraph in its original form was as follows:

"And now farewell, my dear friend, and excuse, if you think it needs any excuse, the freedom with which I thus publicly assert a personal friendship between a private individual, and a Statesman, who has filled what was then the most august position in the world. Can it be, that no man shall hereafter reach that elevated seat!—that its platform, which we deemed to be so firmly laid, has crumbled beneath it!—that a chasm has gaped wide asunder, into which the unbalanced Chair of State is about to fall! In my seclusion, accustomed only to private thoughts, I can judge little of these matters, and know not well what to hope, although I can see much to fear. I might even deem it allowable for myself, in the last resort, to be content with half the soil that was once our broad inheritance. But you, as all men may know by the whole record of your life, will hope steadfastly while there shall be any shadow or possibility of a country left, continuing faithful forever to that grand idea, which, as you once told me, was the earliest that your brave father taught you; and whether the Union is to be henceforth a living giant, or a mangled and dismembered corpse, it will be said of you that this mighty Polity, or this miserable ruin, had no more loyal, constant, or single-minded upholder than Franklin Pierce.

The Wayside, July 2d, 1863."

From the manuscript in the Huntington Library.

52. See "Advertisements" in the Boston *Daily Advertiser,* September 19, 1863: "Messrs. Ticknor & Fields publish this day OUR OLD HOME. . . ."

the same day, the New York *Evening Post* and other leading newspapers in the North carried the story of the discovery, following the seizure of the house of Jefferson Davis near Jackson, Mississippi, of a rather remarkable letter from Pierce to Davis dated January 6, 1860, in which the writer had said:

Let me suggest that in the morning debates of Congress, full justice seems to me not to have been done to the Democracy of the North. I do not believe that our friends at the South have any just idea of the state of feeling hurrying at this moment to the pitch of intense exasperation between those who respect their political obligations, and those who have apparently no impelling power but that which fanatical passion on the subject of domestic slavery imparts. Without discussing the question of right,—of abstract power to secede, I have never believed that actual disruption of the Union can occur without blood; and if through the madness of Northern abolitionists that dire calamity must come, the fighting will not be along Mason and Dixon's line merely. It will be within our own borders, in our own streets, between the two classes of citizens to whom I have referred. Those who defy law and scout constitutional obligations, will, if we ever reach the arbitrament of arms, find occupation enough at home.[53]

Lengthy editorials in the *Evening Post,* the *Tribune,* and other papers uniformly denounced Pierce as a traitor and maintained that the secession of the Southern states had been brought about through the collusion or with the encouragement of Pierce and other Northern Democrats. It was indeed an unlucky hour for the appearance of Hawthorne's book. And it was to be expected that Hawthorne would share in large measure the political odium visited upon his friend, for the newspaper editors and the reading public either ignored or failed to grasp the distinction be-

53. First printed in *The Independent Democrat* (Concord, New Hampshire), September 17, 1863, under the caption, "Letter from Ex-President Pierce to Jeff. Davis. A Deposit for the Corner-Stone of the 'Mausoleum of Hearts.' " Copied by the New York *Evening Post* (September 19), the New York *Daily Tribune* (September 19), the Salem *Gazette* (September 22), the Boston *Daily Advertiser* (September 23), and other papers. See also Nichols, *op. cit.*, pp. 510–511, 525.

tween two kinds of loyalty—loyalty to the Northern side of
the war, and loyalty (attributed to Pierce by Hawthorne) to
the "grand idea of an irrevocable Union" [54] as conceived by the
founding fathers.

The sensational news of the discovery of this fresh and overwhelming evidence of Pierce's "treason" was not long in reaching
Concord. "We took Bryant's paper," wrote Miss Peabody in a
reminiscent letter to Horatio Bridge dated June 4, 1887,

and when this copy arrived, it happened that Sophia was calling at our
house, & Mary pointed out this letter to her & offered to let her take
it home to Mr. Hawthorne. But Sophia exclaimed that it was a "forgery
of course" & she wondered Mr. Bryant could give it a place in his
paper. About an hour after she returned home, however, she sent down
for it, saying, "Mr. Hawthorne wanted to see the paper" & we sent
it up & from that day to the end of his life—Mr. Hawthorne never
named Franklin Pierce to either *Mary or me*.[55]

                                   V

"If the public of the North," Hawthorne with clear foresight
had written to Fields on July 18, "see fit to ostracize me for
this, I can only say that I would gladly sacrifice a thousand or
two of dollars rather than retain the good-will of such a herd of
dolts and mean-spirited scoundrels." [56] Well, the ostracism, it
would seem, was pretty complete.

A few Democratic papers spoke out in defense of the dedication. The Boston *Post* (September 26) referred to the prefatory
letter as "exceedingly to the point . . . mellow, kindly, easy,
original." The same paper on October 10 quoted with approval
the view of the Newburyport *Herald* that Hawthorne's de-
tractors were "political scavengers whose bosoms never knew

54. *Our Old Home*, p. 18.
55. The original manuscript is in the possession of Miss Marian Bridge
Maurice.
56. *Yesterdays With Authors*, p. 108.

such a sensation as gratitude." But the adverse critics were in the majority. On September 30 the Boston *Daily Courier* reported that "already the abolition partizan presses" had "opened upon [the dedication] in terms either of reprobation or of mockery."

Newspaper reviewers, while generally admiring the sketches of English life in *Our Old Home,* were quick to pounce upon the offending dedication. The Boston *Daily Advertiser* (September 30) regarded "the intrusion of Mr. Hawthorne's hardly pardonable illusions respecting President Pierce" as a "blemish upon the volume." The New York *Daily Tribune* (October 3) observed: "The gratuitous affirmation of the loyalty and patriotism of the ex-President is a gush of Quixotic enthusiasm which will expose Mr. Hawthorne to ridicule as mistaking a windmill for a giant." The Salem *Register* (quoted in the Boston *Liberator,* October 2) commented sarcastically: "Mr. Hawthorne is good at fiction." And the New York *Evening Post* (October 7), devoting a greater amount of space to the dedication than to the book itself, asserted that the concluding paragraph "was either written before the exposure of Pierce's letter to Jeff. Davis, or is to be regarded as a fine bit of ironical writing."

A fine bit of ironical writing! Here indeed was an interpretative twist perhaps not anticipated by Hawthorne. The enemies of Pierce would say that Hawthorne's tribute was ironical. Not that any reader could seriously suppose that to have been Hawthorne's intention. But the passage, by means of such a deliberate misinterpretation, might actually be turned to account against his friend. In a letter to G. W. Curtis written on September 21, Charles Eliot Norton commented, almost clairvoyantly, on this aspect of the case:

To-night I am half annoyed, half amused at Hawthorne. . . . His dedication to F. Pierce . . . reads like the bitterest of satires; and in that I have my satisfaction. The public will laugh. "Praise undeserved" (say the copy books) "is satire in disguise,"—and what a blow his friend has dealt to the weakest of ex-Presidents.[57]

Instead therefore of shielding his friend from unjust attack, Hawthorne's dedication had apparently placed in the hands of Pierce's opponents a new weapon, which was none the less damaging for its being a weapon of rhetoric.

A personal friendship, dramatized by an appearance on a speakers' platform and the dedication of a book, became the object of open derision or silent contempt: such was the war hysteria of 1863. An anonymous correspondent sent a collection of newspaper clippings denouncing Pierce, which Hawthorne tossed aside unread, thinking *that* "the best method of disappointing his malice." [58] Moncure Conway bore testimony to the "sharp words concerning Hawthorne" which he heard daily among the abolitionists.[59] But if it was perhaps not too difficult to ignore the harsh criticism of newspapers or of oral report, it must have been less easy to endure the unspoken condemnation of neighbors and friends. Julian Hawthorne, who remembered the "local odium" [60] incurred by his father at this time, attributed his reluctance to attend the meeting of the Saturday Club, of which he had been elected a member in 1859, partly to his desire "to avoid the political discussions which would be apt to arise." [61] And Elizabeth Hawthorne, an acute commentator on matters pertaining to her brother, noted the distressing absence of social contacts between Hawthorne and the Concord community.[62] The atmosphere of popular disapproval which hemmed Hawthorne in during the final period of his life is

57. *Letters of Charles Eliot Norton,* ed. by Sara Norton and M. A. De Wolfe Howe (Boston: Houghton Mifflin Company, 1913), I, 264–265.

58. Hawthorne's letter to Pierce, dated July 26, 1863. The original manuscript is in the collection of the New Hampshire Historical Society.

59. Moncure D. Conway, *Life of Nathaniel Hawthorne* (London: W. Scott, 1890), p. 205.

60. *Nathaniel Hawthorne and His Wife,* II, 272.

61. *Ibid.,* 276.

62. See *ibid.,* 327, 335.

perhaps most vividly suggested by a comment and an act of Emerson's. The comment was recorded in his journal shortly after Hawthorne's death:

Lately he had removed himself the more by the indignation his perverse politics and unfortunate friendship for that paltry Franklin Pierce awakened, though it rather moved pity for Hawthorne, and the assured belief that he would outlive it, and come right at last.[63]

The act was the excision of the dedicatory pages from his copy of *Our Old Home* before admitting the volume to his library shelves.[64]

Hawthorne's isolation in this last phase was perhaps even more painful than that of the early Salem years since it resulted, not from choice, but from political ostracism. After having enjoyed in England and Italy a comparatively active and varied social experience, Hawthorne must have returned to America with the expectation of a richer and more spontaneous relationship with people than he had before known. The war, however, set up barriers which prevented this fulfilment. But it is pleasant to recall that Annie Fields, refusing to join in the hue and cry of the moment, recorded in her diary her admiration of Hawthorne's motives,[65] and that during the last months of his life he enjoyed on several occasions the sympathetic hospitality of her house.

In the foregoing paragraphs, we have seen something of Hawthorne's reactions to the impact of the Civil War. Sensitively aware of the inevitable evils of the war and sympathetically disposed to allow considerable weight to the claims of the

63. *Journals of Ralph Waldo Emerson*, ed. by E. W. Emerson and W. E. Forbes (Boston: Houghton Mifflin Company, 1909–1914), X, 40–41.
64. See M. A. De Wolfe Howe, *Memories of a Hostess* (Boston: Atlantic Monthly Press, 1922), p. 15n.
65. See *ibid.*, pp. 14–15. "Friendship of the purest stimulates him"; "such adherence is indeed noble"; "it is a beautiful incident in Hawthorne's life"— these are some of the comments in Mrs. Fields's diary of July 26, 1863.

South, he nevertheless took his stand with the North and adopted and consistently maintained a view of Northern objectives which seemed to him a realistic and practical one: the division of the Union in accordance with a boundary line dictated by a victorious North. This view, of course, differed from that of the abolitionists. It differed quite as radically from Pierce's view, though certain events in 1863 conspired to identify in the popular mind Hawthorne's attitude toward public affairs with that of his friend and consequently to heap upon Hawthorne and Pierce alike a general opprobrium.[66]

It is not the intention of the writer to imply that the war killed Hawthorne,[67] but the inference seems inescapable that it crippled his creative faculties and hastened his death.[68] In the light of the present study, Hawthorne stands revealed against the background of the Civil War as, it may not be too much to say, a tragic figure, possessed of dignity and strength and a clear, and in some respects a prophetic, perception of events.

66. Unlike Pierce (see, for example, Nichols, *op. cit.*, p. 526), Hawthorne made no attempt to strike back at his critics.

67. An inquiry into the nature of the mysterious malady of which he died on May 19, 1864, does not come within the province of this article.

68. Compare the statement attributed to Lowell by G. P. Lathrop in his *A Study of Hawthorne* (Boston: James R. Osgood and Company, 1876), p. 319: "Hawthorne's life was shortened by the war."

MELVILLE AND HAWTHORNE [1]

Iᴛ is fitting that Nathaniel Hawthorne should be mentioned on the occasion of the centenary of *Moby-Dick* for at least two reasons: one is the personal friendship between Melville and Hawthorne, which reached its full development during the writing of *Moby-Dick* and was witnessed by the book's dedication; a second reason is the probable (though not exactly demonstrable) influence of Hawthorne and his works upon the shaping of Melville's masterpiece.

Earlier writers on Melville—notably Raymond Weaver and Lewis Mumford—accused Hawthorne of coldness and regarded the relationship of the two men as a tragic disappointment to Melville. To Mumford, especially, Hawthorne was the villain in Melville's tragedy; Hawthorne committed, Mumford said, the unpardonable sin of friendship when he portrayed Melville as Ethan Brand, and Melville recoiled from his false friend with a sense of injury and frustration from which he never fully recovered. Fortunately for both Hawthorne and Melville, such was not the case. Melville did not sit, wittingly or unwittingly, for the portrait of Ethan Brand, for the story of that title was published before the meeting of Hawthorne and Melville and was fully adumbrated in the author's notebooks before the publication of *Typee*. Melville praised the story in a letter to Hawthorne, and it seems strange indeed that a supposition that he felt injury should ever have been entertained.[2]

1. Read at Pittsfield, September 4, 1951, at the centenary celebration held under the auspices of the Melville Society and Williams College.
2. See Randall Stewart, "Melville and Hawthorne's 'Ethan Brand,'" *Saturday Review of Literature*, V (April 27, 1929), 967.

As a matter of fact, the two men were on very friendly terms between August 1850, when they first met, and November 1851, when Hawthorne left the Berkshires. After the latter date they apparently saw each other only twice: once at the Wayside in 1852, where they discussed the Agatha story, and again in England in 1856, during Hawthorne's consulship. It is futile to ask why a stimulating friendship should have lapsed into comparative desuetude after fifteen months. One can only point out a few things by way of extenuation: that geographical proximity counted for more then than it does now, that Hawthorne was in Europe for seven years, and that when he returned to America he was a sick man. It is less than honest not to admit the importance of external accidents in the formation and maintenance of most human connections. If Hawthorne had remained in the Berkshires, the issue might have been different. If he had been able or willing to use the Agatha story, or if he had succeeded in his attempts to get a consular appointment for Melville or the job of putting into publishable form the memoirs of Commodore Perry, the issue might have been different, for little external ties like these may lead to the resumption of friendly exchanges. The best explanation of the lapse is simply the absence of opportunities to meet and smoke and drink and talk together. Friendships of an Emersonian kind may flourish indefinitely by epistolary means alone, but friendships of the Hawthorne-Melville sort seem to require a vis-à-vis basis and the accoutrements of conviviality.

The record of the friendship is not as complete as one could wish, consisting chiefly, as it does, of a few letters by Melville to Hawthorne and a few passages in Hawthorne's notebooks. One can still hope—though with little prospect of realization, I fear—that letters by Hawthorne to Melville may yet be found; the discovery in particular of Hawthorne's letter to Melville about *Moby-Dick* (which Melville called "joy-giving and exultation-breeding")[3] would have added a unique éclat to this

3. Letter to Hawthorne dated Pittsfield, November 17(?), 1851, *The*

occasion, if it could have been arranged. The records that survive, though, tell a good deal. Hawthorne's accounts in the American Notebooks of the Berkshire meetings are not copious, but they suggest a happy and fruitful association. The two men talked of time and eternity, Hawthorne said, and books and publishers, and all possible and impossible matters until far into the night. They drank Mr. Mansfield's gin. They smoked cigars even within the sacred precincts of the sitting room, a privilege allowable only during Mrs. Hawthorne's absence and suggestive surely of a very easy, friendly, and confidential relationship.[4]

Melville's letters are eloquent and overwhelming. In one famous passage (these letters are full of famous passages) he describes a jolly meeting in the next world, with which, one must suppose, the Berkshire meetings were not entirely out of keeping:

If ever, my dear Hawthorne, in the eternal times that are to come, you and I shall sit down in Paradise, in some little shady corner by ourselves; and if we shall by any means be able to smuggle a basket of champagne there (I won't believe in a Temperance Heaven), and if we shall then cross our celestial legs in the celestial grass that is forever tropical, and strike our glasses and our heads together, till both musically ring in concert,—then, O my dear fellow-mortal, how shall we pleasantly discourse of all the things manifold which now so distress us,—when all the earth shall be but a reminiscence, yea, its final dissolution an antiquity.[5]

Another famous passage describes Melville's sympathetic reaction to Hawthorne's letter about *Moby-Dick*:

Whence come you, Hawthorne? By what right do you drink from my

Portable Melville, ed. by Jay Leyda (New York: The Viking Press, 1952), p. 452.

4. See *The American Notebooks by Nathaniel Hawthorne,* ed. by Randall Stewart (New Haven: Yale University Press, 1932), p. 220.

5. Letter to Nathaniel Hawthorne dated June 1(?), 1851, *The Portable Melville,* p. 431.

flagon of life? And when I put it to my lips—lo, they are yours and
not mine. I feel that the Godhead is broken up like the bread at the
Supper, and that we are the pieces. Hence this infinite fraternity of
feeling.[6]

Hawthorne's sympathetic understanding obviously meant a great
deal to Melville. Possibly it was the first sympathetic understanding that he had experienced, and his expression of appreciation,
for this reason, took a hyperbolical and somewhat extravagant
form.

Melville's letters to Hawthorne are for the most part preserved
only in Julian Hawthorne's biography of his father. It is
curious to recall that, when this book was reviewed by T. W.
Higginson in the *Atlantic* in 1884, the author was rebuked for
padding the biography with worthless letters by one Herman
Melville. Well, opinions concerning Melville have changed a
good deal since 1884, and readers today are likely to think of
Julian's printing of Melville's letters as one of his more praise-
worthy deeds.

Hawthorne's record in the English Notebooks of the last meeting at Southport, England, in November 1856 is sad and memorable and contains some of the best things ever said about
Melville:

He stayed with us from Tuesday till Thursday; and, on the intervening
day, we took a pretty long walk together, and sat down in a hollow
among the sand hills (sheltering ourselves from the high, cool wind)
and smoked a cigar. Melville, as he always does, began to reason of
Providence and futurity, and of everything that lies beyond human
ken, and informed me that he had "pretty much made up his mind to
be annihilated"; but still he does not seem to rest in that anticipation;
and, I think, will never rest until he gets hold of a definite belief. It
is strange how he persists—and has persisted ever since I knew him,
and probably long before—in wandering to-and-fro over these deserts,
as dismal and monotonous as the sand hills amid which we were sitting.
He can neither believe, nor be comfortable in his unbelief; and he is

6. *The Portable Melville*, p. 453.

too honest and courageous not to try to do one or the other. If he were a religious man, he would be one of the most truly religious and reverential; he has a very high and noble nature, and better worth immortality than most of us.[7]

One might well ask, To what extent is this passage a description of Hawthorne himself? For Hawthorne himself had reasoned much concerning Providence and futurity and the things that lie beyond human ken, and although in the present passage he seems to imply the futility and unwisdom of such an occupation, he continued to be deeply concerned with these matters until the end of his days. The passage, therefore, cannot be taken as deprecatory of Melville unless it is taken as equally deprecatory of Hawthorne. It was Hawthorne's dilemma as well as Melville's —and indeed the dilemma of many other serious minds—to find it difficult either to believe or to be comfortable in unbelief.

Their friendship began in the summer of 1850 under the most favorable auspices. Before their meeting at a Berkshire party in early August, each, thanks to the good offices of Evert Duyckinck, had been reading the works of the other. The reaction of each to his reading was most favorable: witness Melville's rhapsodic "Hawthorne and His Mosses" and Hawthorne's report to Duyckinck—less rhapsodic but perhaps more just, as in the following:

No writer ever put the reality before his reader more unflinchingly than he does in "Redburn" and "White Jacket." "Mardi" is a rich book, with depths here and there that compel a man to swim for his life. It is so good that one scarcely pardons the writer for not having brooded long over it, so as to make it a great deal better.[8]

The mutuality of interest and good will may be supposed to have

7. *The English Notebooks by Nathaniel Hawthorne*, ed. by Randall Stewart (New York: The Modern Language Association of America, 1941), pp. 432–433.

8. Letter to Evert Duyckinck dated August 29, 1850, *Herman Melville: Representative Selections*, ed. by Willard Thorp. American Writers Series (New York: American Book Company, 1938), p. 423.

increased during the succeeding months and reached its full development in the summer of 1851 when Melville was finishing *Moby-Dick*. From one standpoint, it was a happy, bucolic time: the beauties of nature were everywhere displayed; the Berkshire world was one of innocence and simplicity. If there is anything in the environmental theory, it would seem that the writings of Hawthorne and Melville composed at this time ought to reflect an Emersonian benevolence. It seems a bit incongruous to hear Melville declare grimly while lying in the haymow, "It is that blackness in Hawthorne . . . that so fixes and fascinates me." [9] But it is a fallacy, of course, to suppose that natural beauties— even those of Berkshire, which are truly resplendent—are a panacea for human ills. I like, nevertheless, to think of Hawthorne and Melville, each at the height of his powers, engaged in friendly converse among these hills and enjoying them together. All told, it is one of the most fortunate and picturesque conjunctions (or possibly one might say "intersections," in the Eliot sense) in our literary history.

In his excellent edition of Melville in the American Writers Series, Willard Thorp listed what he called "five determining influences" in Melville's literary career, as follows:

. . . the religious orthodoxy of his home, which left its imprint though he revolted from it; his contact with the brutalities of a sailor's life and with savage societies which impelled him to question the premises of western civilization; his reading in philosophy and belles-lettres, which though unmethodical, was prodigious between 1846 and 1851; his friendships with artists and men of letters in New York who advanced his interests and educated him in his craft; and the sympathy of Hawthorne, which more than any other factor contributed to the fruition of his genius.[10]

I applaud the importance which Mr. Thorp gives to the sympathy of Hawthorne; it comprehends, I take it, both points which I

9. "Hawthorne and His Mosses," *The Portable Melville*, p. 407.
10. Pages xxxix–xl.

mentioned at the beginning, the friendship and the influence of
Hawthorne's writings. The friendship, as we have seen, is plain
and palpable enough; the literary influence is impalpable and
conjectural. (Since Hawthorne, being fifteen years older, had
reached full maturity as a writer before he met Melville, and his
subsequent career showed no radical change, it is reasonable to
suppose that Melville did not greatly influence his work. Whether
significant in this connection or not, it is interesting that Hawthorne wrote not his darkest but his brightest book, *The House
of the Seven Gables,* in the period of his association with
Melville.)

Shakespeare's influence was very great and might have been
included in Mr. Thorp's list. It was not, of course, a personal
influence, as Hawthorne's was in part, and the influence of
Shakespeare's plays upon what Melville wrote is, I imagine,
more demonstrable than the influence of Hawthorne's tales and
novels. At any rate, more has been done with it. A good deal
in fact has been done with the influence of Shakespeare's works,
and almost nothing, so far as I know, with Hawthorne's. I have
no intention of attempting to make good this deficiency in the
present paper. The subject would require long and patient
study. The results would doubtless be interesting, but more
effort would be required than anyone is likely to be willing
to give today to an "influence" subject. If the late Professor
Lowes had heard of this subject thirty years ago, and if the
authors concerned had been as respectable then as they are now,
we should have had long since a Harvard monograph—solid,
weighty, and buttressed with parallel passages.

After reading *Mosses from an Old Manse,* Melville wrote,
"Already I feel that this Hawthorne has dropped germinous
seeds into my soul." [11] He singles out many pieces and passages
for admiration (he apparently liked just about everything in
the book) and praises especially "Young Goodman Brown,"

11. *The Portable Melville,* p. 417.

which he says is "deep as Dante." [12] Additional evidence of the germinous seeds referred to could be had by consulting the numerous marked passages in Melville's copy of *Mosses from an Old Manse*, now preserved in the Houghton Library at Harvard. But this, as I have said, is a subject for a monograph or dissertation.

Two general lines of influence occur to me, though I am wondering if the Hawthorne influence may have been stimulating and encouraging rather than "germinous," as Melville himself called it, for the germs were already there. One is allegory: the allegorical development in Melville may very well have been stimulated by his reading of Hawthorne. It is interesting to note that in his comment on "Young Goodman Brown" he speaks of Young Goodman's "allegorical pursuit of his Puritan wife";[13] in speaking of "A Select Party," he says, "there is nothing in Spenser that surpasses it," [14] thereby recognizing and praising the allegorical excellence of the work. It would seem too that the subject of allegory may have been discussed in their conversations: at any rate, Hawthorne analyzed the allegorical aspects of *Moby-Dick* in his acknowledgment to the author, and Melville replied in the famous letter to Mrs. Hawthorne:

I had some vague idea while writing it, that the whole book was susceptible of an allegorical construction, & also that *parts* of it were— but the specialty of many of the particular subordinate allegories, were first revealed to me after reading Mr. Hawthorne's letter . . . which intimated the part-and-parcel allegoricalness of the whole.[15]

Hawthorne was perhaps to Melville, among other things, a teacher of allegory. It is true that the author of *Mardi* was well versed in allegory before he met with Hawthorne's *Mosses from*

12. *Ibid.*, p. 418.
13. *Ibid.*
14. *Ibid.*, p. 419.
15. *Ibid.*, pp. 455–456.

an Old Manse, but he may have learned from the old master
some refinements of the art, and he may have been encouraged
to venture further in that direction.

A second line of possible influence is suggested by what
Melville called the "blackness" in Hawthorne. He quotes from
"Young Goodman Brown" and applies to the author himself
the following words: "It is yours to penetrate, in every bosom,
the deep mystery of sin." [16] When Melville wrote "Ego non
baptizo te in nomine patris, sed in nomine diaboli" in the scene
where Ahab tempered the barbs in the blood of the harpooners,
and "the malignant iron scorchingly devoured the baptismal
blood" (Chapter CXIII, "The Forge"), he must have remembered the baptismal rite clearly alluded to in the account of the
witches' Sabbath in "Young Goodman Brown." Melville, like
Hawthorne, studied the deep mystery of sin. Captain Ahab
recalls in various ways certain characters in Hawthorne, the
closest parallel being Ethan Brand. As Matthiessen has remarked:
"Ahab suffers, but unlike Hawthorne's Hester or Miriam, he is
not purified by his suffering. He remains, like Ethan Brand,
damned." [17] Melville read "Ethan Brand" in the summer of
1851. The story evoked the fervent comment in a letter to
Hawthorne: "I stand for the heart. To the dogs with the head! I
had rather be a fool with a heart, than Jupiter Olympus with
his head." [18] There would seem to have been agreement between
the two men as to the nature of the unpardonable sin.

But despite such examples as I have mentioned, it may be a
question if Hawthorne's influence was "germinous" (to come
back to Melville's word) or only fostering and stimulating. The
author of *Redburn* and *White Jacket* had discovered evil before
he discovered Hawthorne. His reading of Hawthorne no doubt
enriched his thinking on the subject. It must also have fortified

16. *Ibid.,* p. 418.
17. F. O. Matthiessen, *American Renaissance* (New York: Oxford University Press, 1941), p. 457.
18. *The Portable Melville,* p. 432.

him in an honesty and even boldness of treatment not too common in mid-nineteenth-century American literature. I should like to express the hope that some student will work out in such detail of example and proof as the subject will bear the whole question of the influence on Melville of his reading of Hawthorne.

It is interesting and perhaps a little surprising to find in Melville's article on Hawthorne such a frank emphasis of the patriotic note: surprising, that is, after the mild castigations of Vivenza in *Mardi*. But here are patriotic pronouncements which, curiously enough, place Melville—in this particular—in the tradition of Emerson's "American Scholar" and Whitman's 1855 Preface. "Call him [Hawthorne] an American," he says, "and have done, for you cannot say a nobler thing of him." He urges Americans to do away with "the leaven of literary flunkeyism towards England." [19] (Melville's first draft, Mr. Thorp tells us in his notes, read "Bostonian leaven of literary flunkeyism," [20] where the author must have recalled that Lowell's *Fable for Critics,* published just two years earlier, had almost invariably assessed American writers in terms of their resemblances to English writers.) Melville goes on to speak of Hawthorne very much as Whitman might have spoken, not of Hawthorne assuredly, but of himself, in the following passage: "The smell of your beeches and hemlocks is upon him; your own broad prairies are in his soul; and if you travel away inland into his deep and noble nature, you will hear the far roar of his Niagara." He pleads for the generous recognition of this great American author by his fellow Americans. "And by confessing him," Melville adds, "you thereby confess others; you brace the whole brotherhood." [21] Melville doubtless felt the need of such a bracing even more than did Hawthorne. When the article on the

---

19. *Ibid.,* p. 413.
20. *Melville: Representative Selections,* p. 424, n. 10.
21. *The Portable Melville,* p. 414.

Mosses was published in August 1850, *The Scarlet Letter* had received greater acclaim than any of Melville's books (greater, alas, than any of Melville's books would receive during his lifetime).

But questions of patriotism and patriotic duty aside, it would be appropriate and rewarding to think of Hawthorne and Melville as *American* writers. More has been done with Melville, I believe, than with Hawthorne with respect to the author's Americanism and the distinctively American elements which inform his work. Professor Ralph Gabriel devoted a chapter to Melville in his excellent book, *The Course of American Democratic Thought.* The late F. O. Matthiessen regarded Ahab, among other ways of regarding him, as symbolical of the empire builders of post-Civil War America. I quote Matthiessen at some length because this interpretation seems to have gained in popularity since it was first advanced in *American Renaissance,* just ten years ago:

The captain's career is prophetic of many others in the history of later nineteenth-century America. Man's confidence in his own unaided resources has seldom been carried farther than during that era in this country. The strong-willed individuals who seized the land and gutted the forests and built the railroads were no longer troubled with Ahab's obsessive sense of evil, since theology had receded even farther into their backgrounds. But their drives were as relentless as his. . . . They tended to be as dead to enjoyment as he, as blind to everything but their one pursuit, as unmoved by fear or sympathy, as confident in assuming an identification of their wills with immutable plan or manifest destiny, as liable to regard other men as merely arms and legs for the fulfillment of their purposes, and, finally, as arid and exhausted in their burnt-out souls.[22]

This view is developed and extended in Richard Chase's book, which contains, among many other valuable insights, the fullest

22. Page 459.

treatment I happen to know of the native American elements, especially the folk elements, present in *Moby-Dick*.[23]

My impression, as I have said, is that the native Americanism of Hawthorne has been studied somewhat less and has been less recognized. He has been thought of as a parochial New Englander—the product of certain New England and Puritan influences and also of certain English literary influences. But his work could be profitably studied with broad national references in mind. Granted that he never created a character whom we can call (as Matthiessen calls Ahab) a "symbolical American hero." [24] Granted that Hawthorne's men seem too small and specialized to be included in a gallery of American heroes: Dimmesdale being too neurotic, Judge Pyncheon too wooden, Kenyon too much a dilettante, and so on. But if one turns to his women, one finds not a few characters who are broadly and significantly symbolical of female development in this country (a development which some observers have regarded as peculiar to our civilization): one need only mention Hester, who stands in the popular mind, I suppose, for the woman more sinned against than sinning; or Zenobia, "the high-spirited Woman," as Hawthorne described her, "bruising herself against the narrow limitations of her sex";[25] or Hilda, the fictional prototype of countless American girls, fresh and independent, who have boldly and innocently ventured out into the world alone, or nearly so, in search of culture and a career. Hawthorne could not compete with Melville in the creation of a character like Ahab; his Ethan Brand never comes to life. But his female characters (and in this department Melville has comparatively little to show) take on a significance which has impressed later

23. See *The American Novel and Its Tradition* (Garden City: Doubleday & Company, 1957), pp. 89–113.

24. *American Renaissance*, p. 458.

25. Preface, *The Blithedale Romance*, *The Novels and Tales of Nathaniel Hawthorne*, ed. by Norman Holmes Pearson (New York: The Modern Library, 1937), p. 440.

writers, notably Henry James, and which might well recommend him to students of American civilization.

The connection of Hawthorne and Melville was a fruitful one for both of them, and can be equally so for the student of American letters. I have touched upon their friendship during Hawthorne's residence in the Berkshires. I have suggested the likelihood of the influence of Hawthorne's writings on Melville and a few of the directions which an inquiry into the subject might take. And I have mentioned the Americanism of these writers: a point about Hawthorne which Melville emphasized in his historic essay and in so doing implied that he was proud to think of himself, and wished himself to be thought of, in the same light.

The mid-nineteenth century now appears to us as the greatest period in our literary history and Hawthorne and Melville as the period's greatest writers. It is pleasant to think of them as friends, stimulating and encouraging each other and sharing a high ambition for the literary reputation of their country. And it is rewarding to study comparatively their works, which (as Melville said of Shakespeare's) probe "at the very axis of reality." [26]

26. *The Portable Melville*, p. 407.

HAWTHORNE AND FAULKNER

THE subject of this paper was first broached by George Marion O'Donnell in a pioneering essay, "Faulkner's Mythology," where he dropped the comment that "Mr. Faulkner resembles [Nathaniel Hawthorne] in a great many ways." [1] The suggestion, merely thrown out by O'Donnell, has since been picked up by Malcolm Cowley, Richard Chase, and others, and has received a rather general endorsement, but without any attempt (so far as I know) to extend the endorsement beyond a sentence or two. The present paper attempts to extend it to a few pages.

The assertion of similarity between two authors apparently so dissimilar was a little surprising to many of us, I imagine, when we first read it back in 1939. The contrasts indeed are flagrant enough when these two writers are juxtaposed: reticence is contrasted with a shocking frankness, obscenity even; readability with abstruseness; normal narrative procedure with complicated time arrangements; authorial omniscience with the stream of consciousness; a style calm and restrained with passionate, dithyrambic utterance. It is hardly worth while to pursue these obvious differences beyond saying that they stem from fairly obvious causes: if Hawthorne had the Puritan coldness, Faulkner belongs to the passionate South; if Hawthorne inherited a neo-classic neatness and objectivity, Faulkner reflects the experimentation and subjectivity of the age of Joyce; if Hawthorne was cabined, cribbed, and confined in Victorian genteelness, Faulkner has enjoyed the new freedom of subject and

1. *Kenyon Review*, I (Summer 1939), 292.

treatment which was won chiefly by exponents of naturalism (like Dreiser) earlier in the century. Paradoxically, although Faulkner's works could hardly be what they are had they not been preceded by the great works of Dreiser and the other naturalists, Faulkner, in a deeper sense, represents a break with naturalism and a return to the older tradition of Hawthorne.

The similarities, indeed, are more interesting and significant than the differences, and it will be more rewarding to do our exploring in that direction.

Perhaps I should say that I am not concerned with "influences." I have made no attempt to ascertain whether Faulkner likes Hawthorne, or has read him much, or little, or not at all. It is true that Faulkner's first volume (which consists of quite undistinguished verse) was entitled *The Marble Faun,* but I do not attach much importance to this fact. For the purposes of this paper, the extent of his acquaintance with Hawthorne is of no great consequence, for we are concerned not so much with actual influence as with a common view of the human condition. It cannot be too much insisted upon, I think, that the common view of the human condition held by these two writers is the point to be emphasized most in a comparative study such as I am trying to suggest or adumbrate. And it is particularly noteworthy that Faulkner, in recapturing the older view of Hawthorne, overleaped not only a century, but also the whole naturalistic movement which appeared so triumphant at the time when he began to write.

Germane to our subject are the two regions, and the relation of each author to his respective region. The South in the second quarter of the present century (and after) resembled in many ways New England a century earlier. In both cases, a rampant industrialism was transforming the traditional social structure. A marked progressivism was in the air. Making money had become very important. Abbot Lawrence said to Daniel Webster in 1828, "If we can get this tariff through Congress, we will put the West and the South in debt to New England for a hundred years." [2] It was a true prediction, but by the expiration of that period, a good deal of New England's wealth had moved to the South, and the South was trying to figure out ways by which she might put New England in *her* debt. The whirligig of Time was bringing in his revenges. Descendants of proud old families in the South, as formerly in New England, were caught up in the money craze. It would be interesting to compare Jaffrey Pyncheon and Jason Compson as representatives of the money mania in their respective regions and epochs. Both are rats in a rat-race, and both are treated by their authors about as contemptuously as any characters one is likely to meet with anywhere in fiction.

(Incidentally, it would be interesting to compare also two brilliant, incisive works of social criticism dealing with these progressive eras: one with the advancing South, and the other, a century earlier, with advancing New England. I refer to *Walden* and *I'll Take My Stand*. Thoreau's lament—"Where is this division of labour to end?" [3]—is a lament in which the Nashville Agrarians joined heartily.)

If the regions are comparable, the relations of the two authors to their respective regions are comparable, too. Both are loyal sons, inheritors, patriots. Faulkner is the more ardent celebrator. The passage in *Intruder in the Dust* about the Southern boy who imagines Gettysburg still unfought is justly famous:

For every Southern boy fourteen years old, not once but whenever he wants it, there is the instant when it's still not yet two o'clock on that July afternoon in 1863, the brigades are in position behind the rail fence, the guns are laid and ready in the woods and the furled flags are already loosened to break out and Pickett himself with his long oiled ringlets and his hat in one hand probably and his sword in the other

2. The relevant passage is quoted in Jay B. Hubbell, *The South in American Literature, 1607–1900* (Durham: Duke University Press, 1954), p. 171.

3. *Walden and Civil Disobedience*, ed. by Sherman Paul. Riverside Edition (Boston: Houghton Mifflin Company, 1957), p. 31.

looking up the hill waiting for Longstreet to give the word and it's all in the balance, it hasn't happened yet. . . .[4]

Justly famous also is the passage in *The Bear* which celebrates the Southern seasons and the Southern fertility:

. . . this land this South for which He [God] had done so much with woods for game and streams for fish and deep rich soil for seed and lush springs to sprout it and long summers to mature it and serene falls to harvest it and short mild winters for men and animals. . . .[5]

Faulkner abounds in passages like these.

Hawthorne is less ardent but none the less doting. In his notebooks he described the New England scenery with loving care. His New Englandism was intensified by his residence abroad. At the outbreak of the Civil War, he declared, "We never were one people." [6] And a few years earlier he had said, "The States are too various and too extended to form really one country. New England is quite as large a lump of earth as my heart can really take in." [7]

If Faulkner relived the Civil War, Hawthorne relived the Witch Trials. Both had ancestors who had figured prominently in these momentous events. Both, too, are sensitively aware of the sin and the wrong—the sin of Negro slavery, the crime of Salem in 1692. Each, too (it may be added), had certain important lineal relations, as a writer, to the regional literature which preceded him. If Hawthorne's relation to his New England predecessors (to Cotton Mather, for example) is clearer than Faulkner's relation to his Southern predecessors (to G. W. Harris, for example), it is because the former subject has been a good deal more studied than the latter. The latter subject—a whole new field—has scarcely been studied at all.

4. New York: Random House, 1948, pp. 194–195.
5. *The Faulkner Reader* (New York: Random House, 1954), p. 318.
6. Letter to Horatio Bridge dated Concord, May 26, 1861, in his *Personal Recollections of Hawthorne* (London: James R. Osgood, McIlvaine & Co., 1893), p. 189.
7. Letter to Horatio Bridge dated Liverpool, January 15, 1857, *Ibid.*, p. 173.

Both Hawthorne and Faulkner see the past as inescapable, as one's inevitable inheritance. It was a romantic fallacy to suppose that the past could be brushed aside, a fresh start made, the world's great age begun anew. (It was a curiously American fallacy to suppose that the New World would produce sinless beings.) The inheritance of the Pyncheons and Maules, the Compsons and Sutpens, is an inexorable thing. In these writers, the past is not dead, it is not even past, it is a continuous living force.

Faulkner's past seems more colorful than Hawthorne's. Life in the house of the seven gables was a drab and mouldy affair. Young Holgrave (a progressive who later turned conservative) was oppressed by the weight of the Puritan centuries: "Shall we never get rid of this Past?" he exclaimed. "It lies upon the Present like a giant's dead body." [8] Faulkner's past emphasizes the heroic, the chivalric, the romantic. Hightower cherished obsessively the vision of "wild bugles and clashing sabres and the dying thunder of hooves." [9]

The New England past, however, was not without its heroisms to Hawthorne, less spectacular though they may have been. If Faulkner's heroic vision drew upon the Civil War, Hawthorne's went back to colonial times, and celebrated heroes like Endicott and the Gray Champion, whose exploits prefigured the great deeds of the American Revolution. "The Gray Champion," said the author, "is the type of New England's hereditary spirit; and his shadowy march on the eve of danger must ever be the pledge that New England's sons will vindicate their ancestry." [10] Endicott was a hero when he tore the Red Cross from New England's banner. Yes, New England had her heroisms, too.

But human experience to these writers is ambiguous; its meaning is double. It is both heroic and unheroic, noble and ignoble,

8. *The Novels and Tales of Nathaniel Hawthorne*, ed. by Norman Holmes Pearson (New York: The Modern Library, 1937), p. 352.
9. *Light in August* (New York: The Modern Library, 1937), p. 352.
10. *Novels and Tales*, p. 866.

sublime and ridiculous. It was ridiculously ironic that Hightower's grandfather—the hero of the wild bugles, clashing sabres, and dying thunder of hooves—should have been shot and killed while raiding a chicken house. The two narratives which make up *The Bear* reflect this ambiguity: the fine traditionalism of the hunting story contrasts sharply with the sordidness revealed by the old ledgers, and both the fine traditionalism and the sordidness are true. Hawthorne has no story with the dual structure of *The Bear* (a structure so admirably designed to show both sides of the picture, both halves of the truth), but he manages nevertheless to achieve a wholeness which does justice to both man's strength and his weakness. Hawthorne, like Faulkner, is very careful to check the debits against the credits. When you think he has given one of his characters a clean bill of health, look again, and you will see the tell-tale blemish, the sign of imperfection. The foot-travelers to the Celestial City (to take a small illustration from "The Celestial Railroad") would seem to have a better chance than most of escaping denigration, but Hawthorne reminds us that these candidates for sainthood prided themselves on their martyrdom —they liked it when Apollyon squirted the steam in their direction.

Much has been said of the heart-head antithesis in Hawthorne. His villains, like Ethan Brand, stand for the head. It is not, of course, that the author is opposed to the intellect *per se,* or that his fictions are arguments in behalf of that bugaboo of our time, anti-intellectualism. The stories are concerned, rather, with an imbalance between head and heart: Ethan Brand "became a fiend" because "his moral nature had failed to keep the pace of improvement with his intellect." [11] But perhaps a character like Peter Hovenden in "The Artist of the Beautiful" is even more villainous than a great villain like Ethan Brand: he is shrewd, scheming, utterly cold, the foe of all generous acts, the arch-

11. *Ibid.,* p. 1194.

enemy of the beautiful. It is interesting to note that Faulkner's purest villain, Flem Snopes, is a somewhat similar sort of person. Flem is unheroic, acquisitive, cruel; nothing human or lovely can flourish within the scope of his blighting influence. It seems to me not a little remarkable that the actual descriptions of these two characters have certain points of similarity in that both are presented as dehumanized: Flem had "a broad still face . . . and eyes the color of stagnant water, and projecting from among the other features in startling and sudden paradox, a tiny predatory nose like the beak of a small hawk." [12] Hovenden's facial expression, reproduced in the grandchild when he destroyed the butterfly, had a "certain odd sagacity," and of the child at the moment when he most perfectly reincarnated his grandfather, Robert Danforth whispered to his wife, "How wise the little monkey looks!" [13]

Contrasted with villains like Flem Snopes and Jason Compson are the idiot Benjy and the Negress Dilsey, who are beatified at the Easter Service, where Benjy sat "rapt in his sweet blue gaze," and Dilsey cried "rigidly and quietly in the annealment and the blood of the remembered lamb." [14] These redemptive characters, these symbols of innocence and goodness, stand at the opposite pole from the Jasons and the Snopeses, and point the way to Christ and salvation.

Hawthorne has no characters quite like Benjy and Dilsey. His chief examplar of pure innocence is the early Donatello. But the problem of evil dominates the works of both writers. Both writers are concerned with the fall of man, with man's struggle toward redemption, with the regeneration occasioned by sin itself, with the *felix culpa*. "Is sin, then, like sorrow," Kenyon asks in *The Marble Faun*, "an element of human education, through which we struggle to a higher and purer state than we

12. *The Hamlet* (New York: Random House and the Modern Library, 1954), p. 52.
13. *Novels and Tales*, p. 1155.
14. *The Sound and the Fury, The Faulkner Reader*, p. 220.

could otherwise have attained?" [15] It is a question which might be inscribed as an epigraph to the writings of both Hawthorne and Faulkner.

For man's struggle toward redemption is the grand subject of both. Faulkner said in the Stockholm speech, "I believe that man . . . will prevail." [16] A reviewer in the *New Yorker* magazine professed to be puzzled by the word *prevail*, and decided that it is vague and meaningless. I would suggest, however, that it might be helpful to look up the word in Cruden's *Concordance* to the Bible, and then read the passages (there are 65 altogether) in which it occurs. In general, *prevail* occurs in contexts where a victory is won with God's help. *Prevail*, as Faulkner uses it, has nothing to do with modern technology; it is a Biblical word, and has a religious, or Biblical, connotation.

Prevailing in Faulkner is never an easy matter. His protagonists are nearly always surrounded by hell and high water. But they tower, they enhance our conception of the human potential. This is perhaps what John Crowe Ransom meant when he said that Faulkner shows us man "under the aspect of magnificence." [17]

Does Hawthorne ever quite show us man under the aspect of magnificence? Do his important actors ever quite tower? There is indeed a more marked heroic strain in Faulkner: moving accidents by flood and field; battle, murder, and sudden death. Faulkner's characters have a Shakespearean super-stature which Hawthorne's characters seem to lack. It would be untrue, however, to say that Hawthorne's characters totally lack this kind of appeal. I shall not call the roll, looking for candidates, but content myself with nominating one person to stand with the battle-scarred, distraught, bedeviled heroes of Faulkner—Arthur Dimmesdale. Arthur's stature, it seems to me, has been greatly

15. *Novels and Tales*, p. 854.
16. *The Faulkner Reader*, p. 4.
17. "William Faulkner: An Impression," *The Harvard Advocate*, CXXX (November 1951), 17.

underestimated. While his paramour has been admired for her strength, Arthur has been despised for his weakness, yet Hester never did anything which required a tithe of the courage which Arthur's last sermon and confession required. If he walked less firmly than Hester, his burden was much heavier. Hester's struggle with the community was infinitely less toruresome than Arthur's struggle with himself. It is a far cry—at least on the surface—from Arthur Dimmesdale to Joe Christmas, but Dimmesdale is perhaps the one Hawthorne character who can be compared with Christmas, who would have understood him and who exemplifies with something approaching Faulknerian power the destruction wrought by civil war within the soul.

We read these two writers allegorically. This approach to Hawthorne was recognized almost from the start, but it was not at first recognized as appropriate to Faulkner, because many readers insisted (and some perhaps still insist) upon reading him as sociology, as a report on "conditions" in the South. But his work now, like Hawthorne's, is seen by most readers to be not so much a sociological record of a particular region as a report on the human race. Recent criticism has done much to elaborate and enrich the symbolical interpretation of both Hawthorne and Faulkner. The last decade or so has been indeed a golden age in criticism for both of these authors. More than most authors, both Faulkner and Hawthorne compel a symbolical reading.

We see these two writers, finally, as working in the orthodox Christian tradition, a tradition which posits original sin. It doesn't much matter, perhaps, whether the tradition is called Protestant or Catholic, Calvinist or Augustinian, though it is probably true that both authors (whether consciously or not) hark back to a view of Man and God which is older than the Protestant movement. Adherence to such a tradition was natural enough in Hawthorne's case (despite the heresies of the romantic age which surrounded him) because of his strong hereditary sense. Faulkner's adherence is not surprising either (despite the naturalistic amoralism which dominated the early decades of this century) because certain fundamentalist beliefs had persisted longer in the South than elsewhere, and naturalism as a philosophy had failed to gain much of a foothold there. Religious liberals can with justice affix the label "reactionary" to Hawthorne and Faulkner alike.

Faulkner said in the Stockholm speech that "the problems of the human heart in conflict with itself alone can make good writing because only that is worth writing about, worth the agony and the sweat." [18] The remark is curiously reminiscent of Hawthorne, who said in the famous Preface to *The House of the Seven Gables* that the fiction writer "sins unpardonably" if he deviates from "the truth of the human heart." [19] The business of writers like Hawthorne and Faulkner (as indeed of Shakespeare himself) is not to change the world, but to describe the human condition, to anatomize the human heart, to contemplate our common imperfections.

18. *The Faulkner Reader*, p. 3.
19. *Novels and Tales*, p. 243.

THE GOLDEN AGE
OF HAWTHORNE CRITICISM

T H E marked interest in Hawthorne is one of the more striking phenomena of our time. It is an interest which is evident among undergraduates as well as graduate students, among
teachers as well as professing critics. The interest of which I
speak is hardly at all biographical: readers of Hawthorne today
are not interested primarily in the facts of Hawthorne's life,
nor do they read the works to discover "autobiographical" passages, or glimpses of the personality of the author, or characters
who may be taken as "spokesmen" for the author, or traces of
the author's use of this or that "source." Readers today, rather,
read a work by Hawthorne to get the total impression of the
work itself. They are interested in the tale *qua* tale, the novel
qua novel. They find the meaning, the value, in the totality of
the work, in the work's composite structure.

To say these things is merely to repeat the truisms of the
critical revolution. This revolution began (for practical purposes) about two decades ago with *Understanding Poetry*. It
has since spread to include the understanding of fiction, but
the approach has been the same, and the kind of fiction which
has especially attracted critical attention has been "poetic" fiction. In this high, non-realistic realm, it was soon pointed out,
Hawthorne occupies an exalted place. Mrs. Q. D. Leavis, for
example, wrote an important study called "Hawthorne as
Poet." [1] Hyatt H. Waggoner says pointedly that Hawthorne's
fiction "conveys the kind of knowledge poetry conveys, in
symbolic terms not essentially different from those poetry uses,"

1. *Sewanee Review*, LIX (Spring and Summer 1951), 179–205, 426–458.

and that Hawthorne, therefore, must be read, as the modern critics have taught us to read poetry, "with the closest attention to texture." [2] Richard Harter Fogle's recent *Hawthorne's Fiction: The Light and The Dark* [3] approaches Hawthorne's fiction with this same kind of awareness, as do excellent recent studies by Roy R. Male, Jr., Norman Holmes Pearson, Roy Harvey Pearce, John William Shroeder, Marius Bewley, and still others. These immediate years are the golden age of criticism in America, and Hawthorne (along with Melville, James, and Faulkner) is obviously a chief beneficiary.

To undertake to distinguish the special contribution of each of the critics of Hawthorne just named would be a task greatly in excess of the limits imposed by the present notice. Such an undertaking, too, would be premature,[4] and would entail an invidiousness which I, for one, should be happy to avoid. As between the book-length studies by Fogle and Waggoner, both contain so many valuable insights that I should be reluctant to express a preference. To a certain extent, the two books are supplementary: among the tales, Fogle selects for special analysis "Young Goodman Brown," "The Minister's Black Veil," "Ethan Brand," "The Maypole of Merry Mount," "The Artist of the Beautiful," and "Rappaccini's Daughter"; Waggoner also analyzes "Rappaccini's Daughter" while he gives major treatment to certain less familiar tales—"Alice Doane's Appeal," "The Canterbury Pilgrims" (whose merit, I think, he exaggerates), "Roger Malvin's Burial," "The Man of Adamant," and "My Kinsman Major Molineux" (which the author is not entirely alone, now, in believing to be "among the greatest stories in the language"). Both writers study the four major novels,

2. *Hawthorne: A Critical Study* (Cambridge: The Belknap Press of Harvard University Press, 1955), pp. 117, 174.

3. Norman: University of Oklahoma Press, 1952.

4. Nearly ten years later the undertaking was appropriate and necessary. See Randall Stewart and Seymour L. Gross, "The Hawthorne Revival," *Hawthorne Centenary Essays,* ed. by Roy Harvey Pearce (Columbus: Ohio State University Press, 1964), pp. 335–366. [Ed.]

while Waggoner examines, in addition, the posthumous works, taking them up, in their chronological place, at the end of his book. This last procedure makes a kind of anticlimax (though Waggoner thinks that Hawthorne's powers were already failing in *The Marble Faun*), and seems, in a sense, regrettable. It was, moreover, perhaps avoidable, since the primary purpose of the book, I take it, is not to show the literary career of the author, or the development, in time, of his genius or craft, but rather his essential achievement in its more notable manifestations.

But the object of this little notice is not to compare these two books (however much they invite comparison), but to draw especial attention to Hyatt Waggoner's excellent *Hawthorne: A Critical Study*. Waggoner's exposition is lucid and free of jargon. He is particularly good at setting forth patterns of imagery: in *The House of the Seven Gables*, for example, the straight lines and angles (in the house itself, in the angular Hepzibah), and the curves and circles (in the Pyncheon elm, in Phoebe, in Clifford's oval face); in *The Blithedale Romance*, the fire imagery, and the imagery of masks and veils. One remembers (I can testify, already) insights like these (of which there are many) and applies them rewardingly in the rereading of the works. Waggoner's demonstration of patterns is more than the work of a virtuoso: the demonstration throws new light upon Hawthorne's meanings. The meanings (as suggested in the contrasting images cited above) are inevitably ambiguous, for Hawthorne's thought cannot be reduced to a few simple propositions. The famous question which Mrs. Hawthorne put to her husband, "Is Beatrice to be demon or angel?",[5] requires a double answer.

Waggoner is a formal critic, but he goes beyond formalism (as many of the formalists are beginning to do), because he is interested in the moral meanings, too. Hawthorne's moral meanings are not only inseparable from the formal aspects of

5. Julian Hawthorne, *Nathaniel Hawthorne and His Wife* (Boston: James R. Osgood and Company, 1885), I, 360.

his art; they are to Waggoner intrinsically important, for he is quite sympathetic, I take it, with the new orthodoxy, and he might have quoted for his purpose Melville, who said in the great essay on Hawthorne, "No man can weigh this world without throwing in something, somehow like Original Sin, to strike the uneven balance." [6] Waggoner finds Hawthorne Christian in his recognition of man's sinfulness, and democratic in his insistence upon a brotherhood which stems not from the traditional natural goodness of Jefferson and romantics like Emerson and Whitman but from an older doctrine contained in the proposition that all have sinned and come short of the glory of God.

The following passage from *A Critical Study* seems especially worthy of quotation:

It might be worth while today to look into Hawthorne to see how solid a case for democratic values and democratic safeguards can be made on the basis of a belief in the reality of evil in man. Emerson admitted in his private journal that he had never been able to make evil seem real to himself. It was very real to Hawthorne, whose politics were Jacksonian democratic, not Whig like Emerson's. Attempts today to defend democracy, against the charges of Communist and Fascist alike, on the basis of Emersonian philosophy suggest to me that the self-proclaimed "philosophers of democracy" like Emerson and Whitman are less serviceable to us than traditional conservatives like Hawthorne or skeptical conservatives like Melville.[7]

As this view of the matter gains ground (as it appears to be doing very generally at the present time), we may expect to see several well-thumbed historical interpreters (Parrington, particularly, among them) relegated to the obsolescent shelf.

I have heard one respected critic object to the ideological bias of Waggoner's book. I do not object to the bias, possibly because I find myself in hearty agreement with it. The re-

6. "Hawthorne and His Mosses," *The Portable Melville,* ed. by Jay Leyda (New York: The Viking Press, 1952), p. 406.
7. Page 16.

emergence of some of the basic tenets of Christian theology I regard as one of the more hopeful signs of our time. This radical ideological shift is finding important support (in imaginative American literature) not only in the work of contemporaries like Faulkner and Warren, but in perceptive rereadings of Melville and Hawthorne. If the critic actually thinks the ideological shift is a good thing, it is making a fetish of critical disinterestedness to insist that he refrain from saying so.

But be this as it may, the critical job is here to appraise and admire. To Hawthorne, fiction is an art form. As practiced by him, the art form employs the indirection of image and symbol. Waggoner finds in Hawthorne's best work "a depth and completeness of symbolization rare in fiction." [8] Meaning is a function of image, and image a function of meaning. Waggoner shows us Hawthorne's wholeness, his artistic totality, and he shows us too (as indeed a part of this) what Melville so aptly called "Hawthorne's visible truth." [9]

---

8. Page 254.

9. Letter to Hawthorne dated Pittsfield, April 16(?), 1851, *The Portable Melville*, p. 427. Melville continues, "By visible truth, we mean the apprehension of the absolute condition of present things as they strike the eye of the man who fears them not, though they do their worst to him . . ." (p. 427).

PART II *Aspects of American Literature*

REGIONAL CHARACTERISTICS IN
THE LITERATURE OF NEW ENGLAND [1]

T H E subject is so large that I find it necessary to impose certain arbitrary limitations. My present aim is a comparatively restricted one: to venture a few generalizations which seem to hold true for a select number of New England writers —some of the better-known writers of the colonial period and of the "Flowering." I shall not be concerned specifically with the "Indian Summer," [2] unless Emily Dickinson belongs to that period; nor shall I attempt to resolve the dilemma of present-day New England writers, so cogently stated by Professor Jones in a recent *Atlantic* article. [3]

The word "regional" in the title may possibly warrant certain expectations which this paper will disappoint. If the term means "peculiar to the region," "not possessed by another region," it is misleading, for I do not mean to imply that the characteristics to be considered cannot be found, in varying degrees, elsewhere. If the term requires a consideration of popular literature, it is inapplicable to the present paper, because I shall not attempt to discuss the literature of the folk. Moreover, if the word implies the treatment of the whole region and the local variations within the region, it is inapplicable, for the writers whom I have in mind were, almost without excep-

1. Read on September 11, 1940, at a meeting of the English Institute held at Columbia University.
2. In his *Makers and Finders* series Van Wyck Brooks has written volumes entitled *The Flowering of New England* and *New England: Indian Summer* which respectively cover the years 1815–1865 and 1865–1915.
3. Howard Mumford Jones, "New England Dilemma," *The Atlantic Monthly*, CLXV (April 1940), 458–467.

tion, Massachusetts writers. The literature presented in that extremely useful anthology *The Puritans,* edited by Professors Miller and Johnson, was, with a comparatively few exceptions, produced in Massachusetts; and Mr. Brooks's book could have been named more accurately "The Flowering of Eastern Massachusetts."

The subject thus limited becomes: "Some Characteristics of the More Classic Writers of Massachusetts from the Beginning to about 1880."

In the first place, the writers whom I have in mind exemplify, to a greater or less degree, the New England tradition of learning. The individual writer may or may not "pretend" (to quote Cotton Mather) "unto reading, yet he could not have writ as he does if he had not read very much in his time." [4] New England has not, I believe, produced a great untutored genius in literature; has not produced, for example, a Mark Twain. One Southern poet once said of another Southern poet (with how much justice I shall not attempt to decide) that "he didn't *know* enough." [5] The charge could scarcely be made against a New England writer, if by "knowledge" one means the knowledge obtainable from books.

The foundations of the tradition of learning were firmly laid in early colonial times, as one may discover in Professor Morison's *History of Harvard College in the Seventeenth Century* and in Professor Miller's *New England Mind,* both amazingly learned records of colonial New England learning. To the unsympathetic and uninformed modern, much of this learning may appear to have been rubbish; but it was good solid learning, nevertheless. The most delightful and revealing pas-

4. "Of Poetry and Style," *The Puritans,* ed. by Perry Miller and Thomas H. Johnson. American Literature Series (New York: American Book Company, 1938), p. 687.

5. Lanier described Poe thus. Quoted by William Hayes Ward in his "Memorial" for the *Poems of Sidney Lanier,* ed. by Mary D. Lanier (New York: Charles Scribner's Sons, 1890), pp. xxxv–xxxvi.

sages in the *Magnalia,* I think, are those which describe the scholarly habits of the seventeenth-century New England divines. "The work of the study" is a constantly recurring phrase; a scholar's day was something to marvel at. "His library was vast," we are told of one famous divine, "and vast was his acquaintance with it." [6]

The tradition of learning persisted in the nineteenth century despite some appearances to the contrary. Emerson, to be sure, deprecated the tradition, as he deprecated traditions in general: "Books are for the scholar's idle times." [7] Yet Emerson's own reading list would be sufficiently impressive. Thoreau read enormously, notwithstanding the almost infinite leisure which he devoted to plants and brute neighbors. Special students of Thoreau have been at pains to point out his familiarity with the classics and the oriental scriptures. I have been particularly impressed, in a recent reading of some of this author's works, by his avid interest in colonial Americana. Surely no one, with the possible exception of some of our professional historians, has ever read so widely in colonial American literature. One finds, to mention only a few examples, repeated references to Bradford, Morton, Winthrop, Johnson, Wood, Josselyn, Hubbard, Gookin, Cotton Mather, the Jesuit Relations, the town histories, Smith, Byrd (he liked the "Great Dismal" in the *Dividing Line*), and Bartram, whose *Travels* he enjoyed long before the discovery of Coleridge's interest in the book gave it a special sanction for American readers. [8]

If the reading of Emerson and Thoreau is evident on every page of their writings, evidence of this sort is comparatively rare in the purer art of Hawthorne and Emily Dickinson. But

6. *Magnalia Christi Americana.* 2 vols. (New York: Russell & Russell, 1967), I, 274.

7. Entry dated July 29, 1837, *The Heart of Emerson's Journals,* ed. by Bliss Perry (Boston and New York: Houghton Mifflin Company, 1926), p. 112.

8. I know of no critic of Thoreau who has properly appraised his saturation in early Americana. [R. S.]

even for the work of these pure artists, we can be confident of a rich background of reading. A distinguished critic has said that Hawthorne "had no particular amount of reading";[9] yet Hawthorne's reconstruction of early Puritan New England, for example, required more "research" than one might guess from his transparent, unallusive prose. He was an "authority," one might say, on Puritan mores, the lore of witchcraft, the arcana of the Puritan mind. Much of this knowledge he had by instinct and by tradition. But the facts had to be right, too; and Hawthorne's facts—as the investigations of Professor Orians and others have shown—were right, unless he deliberately invented (as in "The Gray Champion") for his purpose. The historians have found little to object to in Hawthorne's historical fiction, except, perhaps, as Professor Morison has said, that his picture is too "somber." [10] His reading was perfectly assimilated, as the reading of the pure artist must be; it does not intrude itself on his page; but the extent of the reading can be seen in part in a list of the books borrowed from the Salem Athenaeum in the 1830s, in which his selections from colonial Americana are heavily on the side of history, theology, and witchcraft, as Thoreau's were preponderantly in nature lore and travel literature. Hawthorne and Thoreau, between them, could have conducted a quite respectable "seminar" in the life and letters of colonial New England.

In the case of Emily Dickinson, the word "learning" seems much too heavy. She had, nevertheless, the traditional New England reverence for books:

There is no Frigate like a Book. . . .[11]

9. For a contrary view which Mr. Stewart would heartily endorse, see Austin Warren, "Hawthorne's Reading," *New England Quarterly*, VIII (December 1935), 480–497. [Ed.]

10. Samuel Eliot Morison, *Builders of the Bay Colony* (Boston and New York: Houghton Mifflin Company, 1930), p. 135.

11. "There is no Frigate like a Book" (1263), *The Poems of Emily Dickinson*, ed. by Thomas H. Johnson (Cambridge: The Belknap Press of Harvard University Press, 1955), III, 879.

> And this Bequest of Wings
> Was but a Book. . . .[12]

She continued her reading, even though her father—all the while buying her "many books"—warned that they "joggle the Mind." And we may be certain that her reply to Higginson ("I have Keats—and Mr. and Mrs. Browning . . . and the Revelations" [13]) erred greatly on the side of understatement.

The New England mind, then, was a bookish mind, fed by countless books. In its most artistic literary expressions—in the works of Hawthorne and Emily Dickinson—the reading has been perfectly assimilated, leaving scarcely a trace behind. And if, in other writers, the learning is imperfectly assimilated, as in Emerson, or laid on too thick, as in the academic pedantries of Cotton Mather or the playful, exhibitional pendantries of James Russell Lowell, one may always have recourse to Mather's own defense, that "the real excellency of a book will never lie in saying of little." [14]

New England literature, in the second place, has been orderly and restrained. The order and the restraint are found in both thought and expression. One sees these qualities variously in Edward Taylor's "knot" of flowers, which are "disciplinde," [15] and in the tight structure of his poems, in the "plain style" of the early divines, in the close reasoning of Edwards, in the tales of Hawthorne, in the sentences of Thoreau, where "every stroke" is "husbanded." [16]

The fact is doubtless owing to several causes. Puritanism im-

---

12. "He ate and drank the precious words—" (1587), *Ibid.*, III, 1094.

13. Letter to T. W. Higginson dated 25 April 1862 (261), *The Letters of Emily Dickinson*, ed. by Thomas H. Johnson (Cambridge: The Belknap Press of Harvard University Press, 1958), II, 404.

14. "Of Poetry and Style," *The Puritans*, p. 687.

15. "The Glory of and Grace in the Church set out," *The Poetical Works of Edward Taylor*, ed. by Thomas H. Johnson (Princeton: Princeton University Press, 1943), p. 106.

16. *A Week on the Concord and Merrimack Rivers*, ed. by Walter Harding (New York: Holt, Rinehart & Winston, Inc., 1963), p. 84.

posed its restraints all along the line. In the social and political realm, true liberty, John Winthrop declared in his famous "little speech," "is a liberty to that only which is good, just and honest." [17] "Order," William Hubbard insisted in an election sermon, is the basic principle of the universe; it is, among other things, an aesthetic principle, manifested in the symmetry of the human body or in "a comely Building, while homogeneous bodyes (as the depths of waters in the Sea, and heaps of sand on the Shore) run into confused heaps, as bodyes uncapable to maintain an order in themselves." [18] In the psychological realm the same principle holds: "Faith," said John Cotton, "is like a poyse, it keeps the heart in an equal frame, whether matters fall out well or ill." [19] The curriculum of school and college also made for order and restraint. Recent historians have pointed out the emphasis upon logic and upon the Greek and Latin classics. The grand result may be called a "Puritan Humanism," which persisted well into the nineteenth century with almost undiminished strength.

As early as 1647 Nathaniel Ward in the *Simple Cobler of Aggawam* served notice that all "Enthusiasts shall have free liberty to keep away from us";[20] and the words "enthusiast" and "enthusiasm" were terms of reproach in Puritan usage. The excesses of the Great Awakening were comparatively short-lived in Massachusetts. Although Edwards gave a new and un-Puritan emphasis to the doctrine of the religious affections and approved of certain surprising conversions in Northampton, Charles Chauncy attributed the phenomena of the Great Awakening to "an overheated imagination," [21] and Edwards himself

17. Winthrop's Speech to the General Court, July 3, 1645, *The Puritans*, p. 207.
18. "The Happiness of a People," *The Puritans*, p. 247.
19. "Christian Calling," *The Puritans*, p. 324.
20. *The Puritans*, p. 227.
21. Cf. *Seasonable Thoughts on the State of Religion in New-England* (Boston: Rogers and Fowle, 1743), p. iv.

became more careful to distinguish between the "false affections" and the "true." [22]

The romanticism of the nineteenth century likewise may appear, at first glance, to have weakened the old restraints, particularly in Emerson. Emersonian individualism appears utterly unrestrained and lawless if one takes literally certain isolated statements: for example, "I would write on the lintels of the door-post, *Whim*." [23] But a closer study reveals, as Professor Norman Foerster has shown in his *American Criticism*, that "the main current of Emerson's mind was not the romantic but the classic." [24] Like Edwards, he was on his guard against "spurious intoxications" in himself and in others. He was as censorious of "know-nothing" America, which "disparaged books and cried up intuition," [25] as some of his recent critics (Mr. James Truslow Adams, for example[26]) who like to attribute this aspect of our national life, in part, to Emerson's influence.

New England literature, then, has been an orderly and restrained literature, and the vital infusions of Edwards and Emerson were kept under control. New England has never produced, it seems almost gratuitous to say, an unrestrained, romantic genius like Walt Whitman or Thomas Wolfe. The romantic impulses have been tempered and restrained.

The control of emotion ought not to be confused with its absence; and yet some of our ablest critics, I fear, have mistaken reticence and restraint for the lack of feeling. I have in mind

22. See *A Treatise Concerning Religious Affections* in *The Works of Jonathan Edwards*, Vol. II (New Haven: Yale University Press, 1959), pp. 121, 138.

23. "Self-Reliance," *Selections from Ralph Waldo Emerson*, ed. by Stephen E. Whicher. Riverside Edition (Boston: Houghton Mifflin Company, 1957), p. 150.

24. Boston and New York: Houghton Mifflin Company, 1928, p. 84.

25. *The Heart of Emerson's Journals*, p. 278.

26. See *The Epic of America* (New York: Blue Ribbon Books, Inc., 1931), pp. 197–199.

particularly the strictures of the late W. C. Brownell in a chapter in his *American Prose Masters* which has had a great influence upon academic judgments of Hawthorne during the last thirty years. Hawthorne "took great pains," Brownell says, "but with great placidity. . . . His own temperament was too little enthusiastic. . . . His stories do not touch him." [27] Brownell objects to the "neatness" of style "which is never discomposed by fervor or thrown into disarray by heat. . . . His writings from beginning to end do not contain an ardent or even a fervent passage." [28] And our critic goes on to quote a passage in Thackeray, full of what Mr. Carl Van Doren has called "Thackerayan whimper and sniffle," to show what he means by true feeling. A curious, romantic preference, certainly; and a curiously mistaken reading of Hawthorne and of the New England genius. One might well ask if "neatness" is quite the word for Hawthorne's firm-textured prose, or if feeling is any the less real for its being controlled. There is ardor enough in Hawthorne—beneath the surface. Mr. T. S. Eliot spoke more truly when he said that "Hawthorne had . . . the true coldness, the hard coldness of the genuine artist." [29] The "coldness" to which Mr. Eliot refers, I think one may safely add, is the result of a powerful restraint, and not of the absence of ardor. Similarly, several critics (among them, Arnold and Brownell), deceived by the Emersonian restraint, have supposed that Emerson "lacked energy" [30] or was "deficient in sentiment." [31] Students of New England literature would do well to remember Robert Frost's orchard, whose trees yield the sounder fruit for their having

27. *American Prose Masters,* ed. by Howard Mumford Jones (Cambridge: The Belknap Press of Harvard University Press, 1963), pp. 48, 70, 72.

28. *Ibid.,* p. 85.

29. From a review of *The Cambridge History of American Literature,* Vol. II, in *The Athenaeum,* April 25, 1919, p. 237.

30. "Emerson," *Discourses in America* (New York: The Macmillan Company, 1902), p. 154.

31. *American Prose Masters,* p. 102.

been set out on a northerly slope: "Keep cold, young orchard. Good-by and keep cold." [32]

Not only learning and restraint but also a religious point of view has characterized the literature of New England. New England could hardly have produced a Poe, whose writings were quite untouched by religious ideas and who accused the New England poets of his day of that (to him) worst of literary offenses, the "heresy of *The Didactic*." [33] The lower, less artistic manifestations of the religious point of view—the moral tag of Bryant or Longfellow, the didacticism of Dwight or Lowell— would seem, it is true, to warrant Poe's objection. But the higher expressions of the same general urgency, as seen in the best of Taylor, Emerson, Thoreau, Hawthorne, and Emily Dickinson, surely lie beyond the reach of aesthetic censure, even though Poe himself might have had—and did have in certain instances—his doubts. Poe's own writings have never been rightly appreciated in New England, a fact which may suggest one limitation of the New England mind. But be this as it may—for I have no intention of becoming involved in the moral-aesthetic question —it seems safe to say that the literature of no other region has been so consistently and pervasively religious in tone.

The most obvious explanation seems the correct one, namely, again, the Puritan tradition. The major writers of New England were Puritan, if not always literally so in creed, at least in temperament and attitude. The orthodoxy of seventeenth-century Massachusetts underwent many changes during the centuries which followed, and the intellectual historians very properly are concerned with defining those changes through their successive stages. But I am interested, for the moment, in similarities rather than in differences. And indeed, despite sharp differences in intellectual belief, there are some remarkable resemblances in

32. "Good-by and Keep Cold," *Complete Poems of Robert Frost 1949* (New York: Henry Holt and Company, 1949), p. 281.
33. "The Poetic Principle," *The Portable Poe*, ed. by Philip Van Doren Stern (New York: The Viking Press, 1945), p. 571.

spirit among the writers of New England from the beginning through the nineteenth century. Very possibly the literary historians have not sufficiently stressed the continuity of the native tradition. Seen in a long perspective, differences of creed or philosophy tend to flatten out, and we have a body of writing with this fundamental characteristic in common: namely, the assumption that spiritual values are paramount; the assumption —"the first and last lesson of religion," Emerson said—that " 'the things that are seen are temporal; the things that are unseen, are eternal.' " [34] Viewed in the long perspective, also, the various foreign influences of the Romantic period may be regarded as having to a certain extent supplied only new vehicles for the old ideas. [35]

A comparative study of Emerson and Edwards, for example, would reveal a good deal in common, although Emerson, curiously enough, seems not to have had a proper appreciation of Edwards. Both sought and experienced a mystical communion with the divine. Edwards wrote of the experience:

This I know not how to express otherwise, than by a calm, sweet abstraction of soul from all the concerns of this world; and sometimes a kind of vision, or fixed ideas and imaginations, of being alone in the mountains, or some solitary wilderness, far from all mankind, sweetly conversing with Christ, and wrapt and swallowed up in God. [36]

Emerson's account is as follows: "I became a transparent eyeball; I am nothing; I see all; the currents of the Universal Being circulate through me; I am part or parcel of God." [37] The spiritual aims and experiences of the two men appear to have been similar,

34. "Nature," *Selections*, p. 47.
35. The "unorthodox" transcendentalist may turn out to be not nearly as unorthodox as he seems. Consider in this connection, for example, Thoreau's treatment of the New Testament in *A Week*. [R. S.] (This passage appears in Harding's edition on pp. 111 ff. [Ed.])
36. "Personal Narrative," *Jonathan Edwards: Representative Selections*, ed. by Clarence H. Faust and Thomas H. Johnson. American Writers Series (New York: American Book Company, 1935), p. 60.
37. "Nature," *Selections*, p. 24.

though it may be observed in passing that Edwards's account has a greater vividness and immediacy.

To illustrate further the varieties of religious emphasis in New England literature and to show again the continuity of the nineteenth century with the Puritan period, a parallel may be suggested, with no intention of forcing the evidence, between Emily Dickinson and Edward Taylor. Both lived retired lives; both wrote poetry for their private satisfaction and not at all for publication; both lived lives which were a religious ecstasy. "All pity for Miss Dickinson's 'starved life,' " observes Mr. Allen Tate, "is misdirected. Her life was one of the richest and deepest ever lived on this continent." [38] Miss Dickinson, of course, did not go to church, while Taylor was the faithful pastor of the parish at Westfield; but this formal difference seems unimportant.

> Some keep the Sabbath going to Church;
> I keep it, staying at Home,
> With a Bobolink for a Chorister,
> And an Orchard, for a Dome—
>
> Some keep the Sabbath in Surplice—
> I just wear my Wings—
> And instead of tolling the Bell, for Church,
> Our little Sexton—sings.
>
> God preaches, a noted Clergyman—
> And the sermon is never long,
> So instead of getting to Heaven, at last—
> I'm going, all along! [39]

Taylor, too, was "going all along"—and in a coach! Earnest souls might travel afoot, like Bunyan's Pilgrim, but Taylor is

38. "Emily Dickinson," *Collected Essays* (Denver: Alan Swallow, 1959), p. 202.
39. "Some Keep the Sabbath going to Church—" (324), *Poems*, I, 254–255.

"*encoacht* for Heaven." It is a triumphant progress, with the music of voices and stringed instruments:

> Oh! joyous hearts! Enfir'de with holy Flame!
>   Is speech thus tasseled with praise?
> Will not your inward fire of Joy contain,
>   That it in open flames doth blaze?
>   For in Christs Coach Saints sweetly sing,
>   As they to Glory ride therein.

> And if a string do slip by Chance, they soon
>   Do screw it up again; whereby
> They set it in a more melodious Tune
>   And a Diviner Harmony.
>   For in Christs Coach they sweetly sing,
>   As they to Glory ride therein.[40]

In both poets there is an easy familiarity with sacred things. Symbols are drawn from the commonplace objects of daily life because the religious experience is such an intimate part of that life.

The emphasis in Hawthorne—to take one other example—is on the darker side of religious experience, upon "secret sin, and those sad mysteries which we hide from our nearest and dearest, and would fain conceal from our own consciousness, even forgetting that the Omniscient can detect them." [41] Hawthorne went to school to the Puritan divines; the reading-list already referred to indicates an extensive study during his formative years of seventeenth-century Puritan sermons. Professor Perry Miller writes:

Puritanism would make every man an expert psychologist, to detect all makeshift "rationalizations," to shatter without pity the sweet

40. "The Joy of Church Fellowship rightly attended," *Poetical Works*, p. 109.
41. "The Minister's Black Veil," *The Novels and Tales of Nathaniel Hawthorne*, ed. by Norman Holmes Pearson (New York: The Modern Library, 1937), p. 874.

dreams of self-enhancement in which the ego takes refuge from reality. A large number of Puritan sermons were devoted to exquisite analyses of the differences between "hypocrites" and saints, and between one kind of hypocrite and another, to exposing not merely the conscious duplicity of evil men, but the abysmal tricks which the subconscious can play upon the best of men. The duty of the Puritan in this world was to know himself—without sparing himself one bit, without flattering himself in the slightest, without concealing from himself a single unpleasant fact about himself.[42]

A discourse by Thomas Hooker illustrates Professor Miller's analysis with such sharpness and clarity that I wish to quote several sentences from it:

When men have found a mine or a veyn of Silver, they do not content themselves, to take that which is uppermost and next at hand within sight which offers itself upon the surface of the Earth, but they dig further as hoping to find more, because they see somewhat. So meditation rests not in what presents itself to our consideration, but digs deeper, gathers in upon the truth, and gaynes more of it than did easily appear at the first. . . . Meditation is as it were the register and remembrancer, that looks over the records of our daily corruptions, and keeps them upon file, and brings them into court and fresh consideration. . . . By recounting and recalling our corruptions to mind, by serious meditation, we sew them all up together, we look back to the lineage and pedigree of our lists, and track the abominations of our lives, step by step, until we come to the very nest where they are hatched and bred, even of our original corruption, and body of death, where they had their first breath and being, links al our distempers together from our infancy to our youth, from youth to riper age, from thence to our declining daies. . . . Look as the Searcher at the Sea-Port, or Custom-House, or Ships, satisfies himself not to over-look carelessly in a sudden view, but unlocks every Chest, romages every corner, takes a light to discover the darkest passages. So it is with meditation, it observes the woof and web of wickedness, the ful frame of it, the very utmost Selvage and out-side of it, takes into consideration all the secret conveyances, cunning contrivements, all bordering circumstances

42. *The Puritans*, p. 284.

that attend the thing, the consequences of it, the nature of the causes that work it, the several occasions and provocations that lead to it, together with the end and issue that in reason is like to come of it. . . . Meditation goes upon discovery, toucheth at every coast, observes every creek, maps out the daily course of a man's conversation and disposition. . . . Hence it is Meditation laies siege unto the soul, and cuts off al carnal pretences that a wretched self-deceiving hypocrite would relieve himself by; and stil lies at the soul . . . so that the soul is held fast prisoner, and cannot make an escape.[43]

In such a passage, it seems to me, we have Hawthorne's ultimate "source." Hawthorne was a psychologist of sin, an analyst of what the Puritans liked to call "soul cases" or "cases of conscience." In an early sketch he posed the question: "What is Guilt?" [44] And in story after story he answered the question with a wealth of examples, or case histories, employing the inexorable method prescribed by Hooker—unlocking every chest, "romaging" every corner, taking a light to discover the darkest passages. The sin of concealment and hypocrisy; the sin of egotism and pride; the sin of evil thoughts which are not realized in act; the Unpardonable Sin, "the hard and stony heart" (which reappears after Hawthorne notably in *The Country of the Pointed Firs*); imaginary sins even (one of the devices of Satan, the Puritans thought, was to cause the saint to despair through an illusion of sin)—these were his favorite themes. They are elaborated with a Puritan thoroughness and a psychological truth which transcends Puritan theology.

A fourth and final generalization which I venture to make is that the classic New England literature is indigenous: it is of native growth; it could not have been written elsewhere; it is a provincial literature.

New England writers have always felt a great pride in their native region. "God sifted a whole Nation," William Stoughton wrote in 1668, "that he might send choice Grain over into this

---

43. "Meditation," *The Puritans*, pp. 302–306 *passim*.
44. This is the first sentence of "Fancy's Show Box" (1837).

Wilderness." [45] Colonial New Englanders considered themselves the objects of God's special providences, and their confidence in the divine regard was not shaken—was confirmed rather—by adversities, "for whom the Lord loveth He chasteneth, and scourgeth every son whom He receiveth." [46] In "God's Controversy with New-England," composed in the time of the great drought of 1662, Michael Wigglesworth wrote poignantly:

> Ah dear New-England! dearest land to me;
>   Which unto God hast hitherto been dear,
> And mayst be still more dear than formerlie,
>   If to his voice thou wilt incline thine ear.[47]

The loyalty and devotion of New England writers to their native region did not diminish in later times. "I have never got over my surprise," Thoreau said, "that I should have been born into the most estimable place in all the world. . . .[48] This is my home, my native soil; and I am a New-Englander." [49] "New England," Hawthorne declared, "is quite as large a lump of this earth as my heart can really take in." [50] Emerson's statement is characteristically general and aphoristic: "The wise man stays at home." "I have no churlish objection," he adds, "to the circumnavigation of the globe for the purposes of art, of study, and benevolence, so that the man is first domesticated, or does not go abroad with the hope of finding somewhat greater than he knows." [51] Emily Dickinson's devotion to New England, latent

45. "New-Englands True Interest," *The Puritans*, p. 244.

46. Hebrews 12:6.

47. *The Puritans*, p. 616.

48. Entry dated December 5, 1856, *The Heart of Thoreau's Journals*, ed. by Odell Shepard (Boston and New York: Houghton Mifflin Company, 1927), p. 256.

49. Entry dated November 7, 1851, *Ibid.*, p. 96.

50. Letter to Horatio Bridge dated Liverpool, January 15, 1857, in his *Personal Recollections of Hawthorne* (London: James R. Osgood, McIlvaine & Co., 1893), p. 173.

51. "Self-Reliance," *Selections*, p. 164.

everywhere in her poetry, is particularly explicit in the following lines:

> The Robin's my Criterion for Tune—
> Because I grow—where Robins do—
> But, were I Cuckoo born—
> I'd swear by him—
> The ode familiar—rules the Noon—
> The Buttercup's, my Whim for Bloom—
> Because, we're Orchard sprung—
> But, were I Britain born,
> I'd Daisies spurn—
> None but the Nut—October fit—
> Because, through dropping it,
> The Seasons flit—I'm taught—
> Without the Snow's Tableau
> Winter, were lie—to me—
> Because I see—New Englandly—
> The Queen, discerns like me—
> Provincially—[52]

There is a good deal to be said for seeing provincially. Thoreau stated the case better than anyone else:

I cannot but regard it as a kindness in those who have the steering of me that, by the want of pecuniary wealth, I have been nailed down to this my native region so long and steadily, and made to study and love this spot of earth more and more. What would signify in comparison a thin and diffused love and knowledge of the whole earth instead, got by wandering? [53] . . . When it is proposed to me to go abroad, rub off some rust, and *better my condition* in a worldly sense, I fear lest my life will lose some of its homeliness. If these fields and streams and woods, the phenomena of nature here, and the simple occupations of the inhabitants should cease to interest and inspire me, no culture or wealth would atone for the loss. I fear the dissipation that travelling, going into society, even the best, the enjoyment of

52. "The Robin's my Criterion for Tune—" (285), *Poems*, I, 204.
53. Entry dated November 12, 1853, *The Heart of Thoreau's Journals*, p. 188.

intellectual luxuries, imply. If Paris is much in your mind, if it is more and more to you, Concord is less and less, and yet it would be a wretched bargain to accept the proudest Paris in exchange for my native village.[54]

A cosmopolitan culture, Thoreau believed, was in danger of spreading itself pretty thin; an indigenous culture would more than compensate in its depth for its lack of breadth; and from Thoreau's point of view an indigenous culture was the creative artist's chief, if not indeed his only, resource.

Our cosmopolitan historians and critics, it seems to me, have done less than justice to the provincial virtue. Professor Parrington could admire in New England literature only those things which seemed to him to show the influence of certain liberal European or Jeffersonian currents of thought.[55] A recent writer on Jonathan Edwards, while appreciating Edwards's greatness, regrets that he was so "narrow," that his mind was cast so "strictly in the New England mold." [56] If only he had not been a Calvinist, if he could somehow have been *broadened* either during his brief stay in New York or perchance through a dinner conversation with Benjamin Franklin, he would almost certainly have been even greater than he was! The instinctive popular view of Emily Dickinson—a view which can be traced to the cosmopolitan ideal so stressed in the books about American literature—is that the regional restriction was a serious handicap. Henry James, as everyone knows, deplored the fact that Hawthorne had lived the best years of his life in an environment destitute of those "items of high civilization" [57] which one found

54. Entry dated March 11, 1856, *Ibid.*, pp. 236–237.

55. A thesis which appears through the three volumes of his *Main Currents in American Thought* (New York: Harcourt, Brace and Company, 1927, 1930).

56. Ola Elizabeth Winslow, *Jonathan Edwards, 1703–1758* (New York: The Macmillan Company, 1940), p. 327.

57. *Hawthorne.* English Men of Letters series (New York: Harper and Brothers, 1879), p. 42.

in England and in France, and much criticism of Hawthorne and of other American writers has taken its tone from James's book. A recent academic critic repeats the Jamesean lament: Hawthorne "never really assimilated Europe," "the European journey came several years too late." (Curiously enough, it would never have occurred to such a critic to deprecate the provincialism of a British writer, to think it a pity that Burns had not enjoyed the advantages of an Oxford education or that Wordsworth "saw Westmorelandly.")

It seems to me very doubtful if an earlier European journey, a less provincial experience, would have worked to the advantage of the *Twice-Told Tales* and *The Scarlet Letter*. The virtue, moreover, of *The Marble Faun,* which came after the European journey, is still its New Englandism, presented now in a new relationship—the Italian setting—which proves to be a very dubious asset. If Hawthorne never really assimilated Europe, he did assimilate New England—which was a good deal. New England was his proper milieu, and the literary result would seem to show that New England and Hawthorne did rather well by each other.

I hope that I shall not be accused of taking a cheap advantage of the present international situation to advocate a cultural isolationism. Cultural isolationism is neither possible nor desirable, either for the laity or for the creative artist. It would be a gross error to underestimate the importance of the fertilizing influences from Europe upon New England literature. But it may not be an error to say that in our historical and critical studies we have been impressed too much by the pollen from abroad and too little by the native plant. Moreover, the traditional literary judgments need a careful re-examination lest we be misled into admiring works of borrowed splendor and despising those of native integrity.

Thoreau believed that the first duty of the man who would write something that was worth the writing was to be "expert in home-cosmography," [58] and Emerson said, "So that the man is first domesticated." [59] From the point of view of the present day the history of New England literature seems to attest to the enormous advantage which domestication gives to the writer. For if one asks, What are the New England books most likely to endure?, the titles which can be named most confidently are titles by those authors who were most thoroughly domesticated: the *Sacramental Meditations* of Edward Taylor (already a classic, though published only within the year), the *Journals* of Thoreau and *Walden,* the *Twice-Told Tales* and *The Scarlet Letter,* the *Poems* of Emily Dickinson, and, less confidently, the *Essays* of Emerson. Less confidently, because Emerson himself was not so well domesticated as the others; he was rather too hospitable to philosophies drawn from many lands and ages. Consequently, his work lacks a perfect integrity; conflicting elements remain imperfectly resolved.[60] Much of the work of more cosmopolitan writers like Longfellow and Lowell seems to illustrate well enough the thinness and diffuseness which Thoreau was anxious to guard against. In our own day the poems of Robert Frost demonstrate once more the virtue for the New England poet in seeing New Englandly.

It would appear, then, that the best New England writers have stayed at home and that their knowledge of the cultures of other lands and ages has been of value to them chiefly as it has helped them to understand their own inheritance and has sharpened their perceptions of the home-bred virtues and the home-felt scenes. The paradox of such a provincialism is that it achieves, without deliberately setting out to do so, the real thing in universality.

58. *Walden and Civil Disobedience,* ed. by Sherman Paul. Riverside Edition (Boston: Houghton Mifflin Company, 1957), p. 218.

59. "Self-Reliance," *Selections,* p. 164.

60. He is variously Platonist, Neo-Platonist, Berkeleyan idealist, Kantian idealist, Lamarckian evolutionist, Hindu philosopher, Unitarian divine, and Concord Yankee. [R. S.]

THREE VIEWS OF THE INDIVIDUAL
AS REFLECTED
IN AMERICAN LITERATURE [1]

B ROADLY speaking, one may discover in American literature three different views of the individual.[2] I shall endeavor to name and describe these views (taking them up in their historical order), to illustrate them from American writers, and to consider some of their ethical and social implications.

I

The first is the Puritan view. Puritan thought, though comprising many shades of opinion, was in agreement on one basic belief, namely, the doctrine of original sin, the belief in the innate sinfulness of man. The classic expression of this doctrine is found in the writings of Jonathan Edwards. "By Original Sin," wrote Edwards in a discourse entitled *The Great Christian Doctrine of Original Sin Defended,* "is meant the innate, sinful depravity of the heart." [3] In defending the doctrine, Edwards relied not only upon scriptural authority and metaphysical argument but also upon the evidence of fact, for the Puritans were realists. "It signifies nothing," he declared, "to exclaim against plain *fact*. Such is the *fact*, most evident and acknowledged *fact*, with respect to the state of all mankind." [4] Man was not only

1. Read before a meeting of the English Club of Wellesley College.
2. In a short paper of the present scope over-simplification is inevitable. I have attempted to present only what have seemed to be the dominant trends of thought. [R. S.]
3. *Jonathan Edwards: Representative Selections,* ed. by Clarence H. Faust and Thomas H. Johnson. American Writers Series (New York: American Book Company, 1935), p. 316.
4. *Ibid.,* p. 328.

innately sinful, according to Edwards, but also predestined by the sovereignty of God. The divine predestination, however, did not relieve man of responsibility. The great need was for man's redemption through divine grace, and everlasting diligence was necessary "to make your calling and election sure." [5]

Views similar to Edwards's were held by many people in colonial America. But these views lost ground in the eighteenth century with the rise of deistical thought, and they continued to lose ground in the nineteenth century with the advance of romantic thought. The Puritan attitude, however, had an able and sympathetic interpreter in the nineteenth century in Nathaniel Hawthorne, who set himself pretty stubbornly against the romantic current. Hawthorne was, in many ways, an incorrigible reactionary.

The romantic view very generally superseded the Puritan view in nineteenth-century America. Despite the many shades of romantic opinion, the romantics agreed in rejecting the Edwardsian doctrines. Man was not predestined but free; he was not innately sinful but innately good. This last point is so crucial that the distinguished critic T. E. Hulme has defined "romantics" as "all who do not believe in the Fall of Man." [6]

I shall not attempt to trace the origin and development of the familiar romantic doctrines: the goodness of man, his essential freedom, his infinite perfectibility. Suffice it to say that first Emerson, and later Whitman, were the most eloquent interpreters of the romantic doctrines in nineteenth-century America. The new doctrines were certainly expansive and encouraging. God reveals himself to every man, Emerson believed; and, since this is so, every man should trust his own high intuitions. (Emerson apparently made an exception to this fundamental belief when he wrote in his journal: "It is not in the power of God to make a communication of his will to a

5. 2 Peter 1:10.
6. *Speculations*, ed. by Herbert Read (New York: Harcourt, Brace and Company, 1924), p. 256.

Calvinist." [7]) Whitman urged upon the individual an appreciation of himself:

I celebrate myself, and sing myself. . . .

. . . .

Nor do I understand who there can be more wonderful than myself.[8]

The self that was being celebrated, the reader will note, was what Edwards would have called the natural man, the unregenerate self. Whitman certainly went as far as possible in the opposite direction from Edwards. He even celebrated, somewhat irrelevantly, the animals, because

> They do not lie awake in the dark and weep for their sins;
> They do not make me sick discussing their duty to God.[9]

Emerson and Whitman, in short, deified the individual. He no longer stood in need of regeneration because he was excellent as he was. "Yourself a new-born bard of the Holy Ghost . . ." [10] said Emerson. And Whitman declared: "Now on this spot I stand with my robust soul." [11]

If, according to the Puritan view, man is bad and requires a radical regeneration, and according to the romantic view, he is good and needs only an opportunity for his latent goodness to develop, according to the third view, which we may call the modern or scientific or mechanistic, man is neither good nor bad but the result of certain inexorable forces of heredity and environment. This view obviously bears the mark first of biological science and second—a somewhat later influence—of

7. *The Heart of Emerson's Journals,* ed. by Bliss Perry (Boston and New York: Houghton Mifflin Company, 1926), p. 196.

8. *Whitman's "Song of Myself"—Origin, Growth, Meaning,* ed. by James E. Miller, Jr. (New York: Dodd, Mead & Company, 1964), p. 3, 1, 1; p. 91, 48, 1282.

9. *Ibid.,* p. 49, 32, 687–688.

10. "Divinity School Address," *Selections from Ralph Waldo Emerson,* ed. by Stephen E. Whicher. Riverside Edition (Boston: Houghton Mifflin Company, 1957), p. 113.

11. *Whitman's "Song of Myself,"* p. 83, 44, 1169.

sociological investigation. Even Emerson, in an essay on "Fate" in 1860, recognized biological inheritance as imposing a limitation upon the individual, though he asserted again the transcendency of man's spiritual capacities: "For though Fate is immense, so is Power." [12] Whitman, needless to say, never thought of biology as limitation.

The mechanistic view became dominant in American literature with Dreiser and has continued the dominant view down to the present time, particularly in our prose fiction. The characters in *Sister Carrie*, published in 1900, have no will, no responsibility, no liability to praise or blame. They are neither good nor bad. They are the products, willy-nilly, of certain chemical forces and of certain social forces. One might plot their courses infallibly if one were scientist enough to discover the chemical formulas of their bodies and the formulas of their environments. "Among the forces," wrote Dreiser, "which sweep and play through the universe, untutored man is but a wisp in the wind." [13] From Dreiser to Steinbeck, the individual tends to lose his importance as an individual. He becomes interesting, rather, for a certain representative value, and he becomes interesting as a study in behavior. There have been, to be sure, dissenting opinions: the humanism of Babbitt and Foerster, the classicism of Eliot, the romanticism of Thomas Wolfe. But the dominant attitude of the last forty years—the attitude not only of our most influential writers, the novelists, but also of the educated laity generally— has been the mechanistic attitude.

II

Having identified and described the three principal views of the individual, we may now consider some of their ethical and social implications. These implications may be of value not only in the interpretation of our past but in the recognition of some

12. *Selections*, p. 339.
13. *Sister Carrie*, ed. by Claude Simpson. Riverside Edition (Boston: Houghton Mifflin Company, 1959), p. 67.

of our present difficulties. Perhaps the best approach to the problem is to inquire what was gained and what was lost when the first view was superseded by the second and the second by the third—for, with each step of what used to be called "progress," there has been both gain and loss.

There were all sorts of gains, of course, when the romantic view of the individual took the place of the Puritan view. There was a new hopefulness and cheerfulness in the air. The romantic doctrines were enormously stimulating. The young men, after listening to a lecture by Emerson, "walked homeward with prouder strides over the creaking snow." Much of our best literature from Emerson down to Thomas Wolfe reflects this exalted conception of human nature. The stimulus was productive in America not only of literature, but of action, action which was confident and aggressive, if not always intelligent and ethical.

Perhaps the greatest single gain is to be found in the advance of democracy. I shall not attempt to say whether democracy would have come at all without the romantic philosophy. Lowell, to be sure, once said that "Puritanism . . . laid . . . the egg of democracy";[14] and one might argue that there was nothing in Puritan theology to preclude democracy. Indeed, Puritan theology seemed to begin with a kind of equalitarian premise: that all men are sinners, and all souls are precious, in God's sight. But the fact remains that the early Puritans were hostile to the democratic idea: "Democracy," said John Cotton, "I do not conceive that ever God did ordain as a fit government either for church or commonwealth. If the people be governors, who shall be governed?" [15] Moreover, it can hardly have been an accident that a late Puritan like President Timothy Dwight

14. "New England Two Centuries Ago," *James Russell Lowell: Representative Selections,* ed. by Harry Hayden Clark and Norman Foerster. American Writers Series (New York: American Book Company, 1947), p. 322.

15. Copy of a Letter from Mr. Cotton to Lord Say and Seal in the Year 1636, *The Puritans,* ed. by Perry Miller and Thomas H. Johnson (New York: American Book Company, 1938), pp. 209–210.

of Yale was the staunchest of political conservatives, an extreme Federalist who looked upon the people with profound distrust and who predicted in 1800 that if Jefferson were elected, "we may see our wives and daughters the victims of legal prostitution." [16] The conclusion seems inescapable that the Puritan idea retarded, and the romantic idea greatly accelerated, the growth of democracy. If men were innately good, obviously they could be trusted with the responsibility of self-government. Emerson and Whitman of course—Emerson sometimes with a touch of Puritan reluctance and Whitman with scarcely any reluctance at all—were champions of democracy. Let us grant, then, that the great contribution in America of the romantic view was American democracy.

That was a great gain. But there was an attendant loss. The loss may be described as a relaxation. Now there was nothing relaxed about Emerson, thanks to his Puritan inheritance. His doctrines had a Puritan austerity. His self-reliance presupposed a disciplined intuition. The good life according to Emerson was no doubt almost as difficult as the good life according to Edwards. But Emerson did not sufficiently advertise the difficulty; to the casual reader, the Emersonian plan looked easy. In Whitman, the relaxation was more than apparent:

I loafe and invite my soul,
I lean and loafe at my ease observing a spear of summer grass.[17]

Hawthorne sensed the danger when he wrote that brilliant satire, "The Celestial Railroad." It is an adaptation of *Pilgrim's Progress* with modern improvements. Instead of going to the Celestial City on foot like Bunyan's pilgrim, Hawthorne's characters ride comfortably on the railroad train. Burdens are

---

16. Fourth of July Sermon of 1798. The relevant passage is quoted in Samuel Eliot Morison and Henry Steele Commager, *The Growth of the American Republic, 1763–1865,* 2nd ed. (New York: Oxford University Press, 1937), p. 267n.

17. *Whitman's "Song of Myself,"* p. 31, 1, 4–5.

no longer carried on the back but checked in the baggage car. A bridge spans the Slough of Despond; a tunnel leads through the Hill Difficulty; modern gas lamps illuminate the Valley of the Shadow of Death. But the train stops short of the Celestial City, owing to a limitation of franchise. Bunyan's way, Hawthorne thought, was still the best.

The doctrine of original sin makes an important difference. If a man cries out, "God be merciful to me, a sinner," then we have at once a recognition of a state of affairs which requires amendment. He may be expected to put himself through a course of discipline. By fasting and prayer and meditation on holy things, he may attain unto salvation. But if he says with Whitman, I am good already, I "stand cool and composed [the original reading was "cool and supercilious"] before a million universes," [18] It is difficult to find in such an attitude a motivation for discipline. We lost with the eclipse of the Puritan view a powerful disciplinary force; we became comparatively relaxed, ethically speaking.

Once more, what did we gain and lose when the scientific or mechanistic view superseded the romantic? Man now becomes, the reader will recall, neither good nor bad, but the unmoral product of physiological and social forces over which he has little if any control.

There has been an immense gain in tolerance, in human sympathy, in social consciousness. A man was formerly thought in some degree reprehensible if he committed a crime. This is hardly true any longer. His heredity or his environment or both are to blame. Possibly the glandular secretions are to blame; possibly an unfortunate incident in childhood has given him a distorted outlook on life. It becomes the obligation of society to provide the instruments by which these distortions and maladjustments may be corrected. The physician, the psychoanalyst,

18. *Ibid.*, p. 91, 48, 1277.

the social worker are these instruments, and their position in modern society has assumed enormous and constantly increasing importance. We have never been so socially minded, so tolerant, as now. This is a very great gain and I should not wish to be construed as minimizing its value.

But there has been a loss. The individual as individual has withered—so much so that the terms "individual," "individual-istic," "individualism," at least in some quarters, are no longer quite respectable. (I was a little shocked to read in a recent book by a distinguished professor of English a reference to "the Philistine dogma of self-help." It had never occurred to me to apply the term "Philistine" to Emerson and Edwards and the many other representatives of the humane tradition.)

Under the Puritan dispensation, the individual was disciplined and responsible. He also had a peculiar importance: there was more joy in heaven over one sinner who repented than over ninety and nine just persons who needed no repentance. Under the romantic dispensation, the individual, though undisciplined, was still important and responsible—more important, at least in an egoistic sense, and more responsible, if social freedom is the measure of responsibility. Moreover, Puritan and romantic were agreed in this: that the good society was a society composed of good individuals. Improvement could be made, not in the mass, but only one individual at a time. "As for Doing-good," Thoreau wrote in *Walden*,

it does not agree with my constitution. . . . If I were to preach at all in this strain, I should say rather, Set about being good. As if the sun should stop when he had kindled his fires up to the splendor of a moon or a star of the sixth magnitude, and go about like a Robin Goodfellow, peeping in at every cottage window, inspiring lunatics, tainting meats, and making darkness visible, instead of steadily increasing his genial heat and beneficence till he is of such brightness that no mortal can look him in the face, and then, and in the meanwhile too, going about the world in his own orbit, doing it good, or rather, as a truer philosophy has discovered, the world going about him getting good.[19]

Under the mechanistic dispensation, the individual has deteriorated into an automaton. He has been deprived of the Puritan discipline and the Puritan responsibility to God; he has also been deprived of the romantic sense of his high nature, his freedom, his obligation to hitch his wagon to a star. I am inclined to attribute the present reduced status of the individual to the influence of scientific thought and procedures. The individual is important today—indifferently with other individuals —only as a subject of a vast scientific experiment. Physiologically, if the thyroid doesn't get you, then the pituitary must. Psychologically, you are a congeries of responses to stimuli. Sociologically, you must "adjust" (the verb no longer requires, in common scientific usage, the reflexive pronoun). The greatest of American individualists was not interested primarily in adjustment: "Whoso would be a man," Emerson said, "must be a non-conformist." [20]

It is no profound observation to suggest a connection between the present state of the individual and the present state of the world. If in the romantic period the individual was somewhat relaxed, in the mechanistic period he is practically paralyzed. And the ethical paralysis of the individual is at once a cause and a result of totalitarianism. Archibald MacLeish in *The Fall of the City* portrays these helpless individuals of the modern scientific world and the political consequences of their helplessness:

They don't see! They lie on the paving. They lie in the
Burnt spears: the ashes of arrows. They lie there . . .
They don't see or they won't see. They are silent. . . .

19. *Walden and Civil Disobedience*, ed. by Sherman Paul. Riverside Edition (Boston: Houghton Mifflin Company, 1957), pp. 50–51.
20. "Self-Reliance," *Selections*, p. 149.

The people invent their oppressors; they wish to believe in them.
They wish to be free of their freedom: released from their liberty—
The long labor of liberty ended! . . .

The city of masterless men has found a master!
The city has fallen! [21]

Well, the American city has not fallen. Americans have not
been reduced to such apathy that they wish to be free of their
freedom, to be released from their liberty, because they have not
completely lost their inheritance from the great Puritan period
and from the great romantic period. The mechanistic view and its
concomitant, political totalitarianism, have not been able utterly
to abolish or destroy the belief in the individual's importance, his
responsibilities, his powers under divine guidance. We still believe, despite what we have been told for a generation, that man
is something more than a chemical combination of secretions, or a
collection of responses to stimuli, or a product of social and
economic forces. There are already signs of a revitalized individualism, an individualism which defies and transcends the modern
determinisms.

The Puritan individual was often bigoted and grim. The
romantic individual was often unscrupulous. I am not advocating a return to either the bigotry and grimness or the un-
scrupulousness. But while retaining the modern tolerance and
social sense, we need to recapture something of the discipline of
the Puritan view and something of the positive faith, the
Emersonian self-reliance, of the romantic view. If the question
is asked, How can one hold beliefs derived from conflicting
premises?, the answer must be that we are all eclectics: undeterred
by origins and premises, we select beliefs which we find neces-
ary. And in any event, there can be little doubt that the special
virtues inherent in each of the three views are necessary to our
well-being today.

21. New York and Toronto: Farrar & Rinehart, Inc., 1937, pp. 32–33.

THE SOCIAL SCHOOL
OF AMERICAN CRITICISM

T HE social approach in American literary criticism has become increasingly popular in recent years. Vernon Parrington's *Main Currents in American Thought,* published in three volumes between 1927 and 1930, was the first comprehensive work to employ social and economic criteria in the interpretation of American literature. A Jeffersonian liberal with strong socialist leanings, Parrington may be said to have introduced to the generality of students this kind of literary study. More doctrinaire works by critics whose position is considerably farther to the left than Parrington's have greatly reinforced the social approach, the chief of these being Granville Hicks's *The Great Tradition,* published in 1933 and with added material in 1935, and Bernard Smith's *Forces in American Criticism,* published in 1939. Although Parrington, Hicks, and Smith hold by no means identical views, they are agreed in the exclusive employment of social criteria in estimating the value of a literary work. There is a widespread and constantly growing acceptance of this approach at the present time.

The social critics have explored new areas in literary history and criticism. They have placed literature in its milieu, and have shown the relation of literature to developing political and economic forces. But despite this valuable contribution, the school, in my judgment, is open to serious objections. To draw attention to some of these is the purpose of this paper.

I

My first objection is the neglect of aesthetic values. This neglect is best seen, perhaps, in the treatment of Poe, Hawthorne, and James, the three among our older writers whose works best exemplify such values. Parrington's indifferent, brief dismissal of Poe is well known: "The problem of Poe, fascinating as it is, lies quite outside the main current of American thought, and it may be left with the psychologist and the belletrist with whom it belongs." [1] Hicks does not mention Poe at all in his introductory survey of the post-Civil War "heritage." Smith devotes a fair amount of space to Poe, only to reject him contemptuously because he held "the Virginia view of life," that is, the aristocratic view. [2]

Parrington's treatment of Hawthorne is deprecatory: "He was the extreme and finest expression of the refined alienation from reality that in the end palsied the creative mind of New England." [3] Hicks is equally disparaging: "When Hawthorne was a representative American, he was not an artist; when he was an artist, he was not a representative American." [4] And the social critics evince even less admiration for James. Parrington dismisses him with Philistine bluntness: "In his subtle psychological inquiries, he remained shut up within his own skullpan." [5] Hicks treats James with more respect. Unlike Parrington, he is aware of James's general importance; but he is compelled to give him a low rating, chiefly, one feels, because "we are seldom shown by what [financial] means James's characters are supported." [6] Smith, in an extended treatment, rings the changes upon "aristocrat," "tory," and "snob." [7]

Such are the attitudes of the social critics toward the three indisputable artists of our literature! Indeed, from the social

1. *Main Currents in American Thought*, 1-vol. ed. (New York: Harcourt, Brace & World, Inc., 1958), II, 58.
2. *Forces in American Criticism* (New York: Harcourt, Brace and Company, 1939), p. 191.
3. *Main Currents*, II, 450.
4. *The Great Tradition* (New York: The Macmillan Company, 1933), p. 6.
5. *Main Currents*, III, 241.
6. *The Great Tradition*, p. 122.
7. *Forces in American Criticism*, pp. 210–212 *passim*.

point of view, a serious concern with literary form is reprehensible because it is the mark of an aristocratic trifler. This is not the place to attempt a vindication of the artist and his art. Quite effectively, time has accomplished and will continue to accomplish just that, while social philosophies rise and fall. It is arguable that the works of Poe, Hawthorne, and James will outlast all other works of their century in America (however forward-looking those other works may have been) because of their superior artistry. And in any case, a critical system so completely indifferent to aesthetic values must be regarded as less than satisfactory.

II

The social critics not only neglect aesthetic values; they reject all conservative literature. It is their assumption that, in the socialist state of the future, only those literary works of the past which were harbingers of socialism will survive: those only will constitute the "usable past." Accordingly, the social critics consistently regard with disapproval those writers whose sympathies are with traditional values. Among the many available examples, a few will suffice to illustrate this bias.

Parrington's treatment of Timothy Dwight does that great Calvinist and Federalist less than justice: ". . . a steadfast friend of truth in whatever garb it might appear . . . he assuredly was not." [8] To Smith, Dwight is "laughable," or, in another connection, "literally painful." [9] Now Dwight was not a great writer, but his *Greenfield Hill* and *Travels in New England and New York* are pleasant and instructive works. He believed in original sin; he distrusted the excesses of the French Revolution: attitudes neither laughable nor painful to readers with historical perspective.

If Dwight was sympathetic with the traditions of Connecticut, Ellen Glasgow has been sympathetic with, though also critical

8. *Main Currents*, I, 363.
9. *Forces in American Criticism*, p. 12.

of, the traditions of Virginia, and for Hicks her work is vitiated by the sympathy. "She becomes one more apologist," he says, "for a way of life that is rapidly vanishing." At bottom, he cannot forgive her preference for "the well-bred person." [10] By a similar token, Hicks condemns T. S. Eliot's return to tradition in words which betray animus and an incomplete view of the matter: "We need not ask how so melodramatic a skeptic can accept the dogmas of Anglicanism, or what so intelligent an observer can expect from the King of England, or why so resolute an experimenter should affirm his allegiance to the laws of ancient art. The need for security was too strong to pay any attention to common sense or logic." [11] To the social critics, any conservative position in any time or place—whether it be New England Congregationalism or the well-bred school of Virginia manners or Anglo-Catholicism and metaphysical poetry—is intrinsically bad.

Again, it is not within the scope of this paper to attempt a vindication of conservatism. But it is arguable that in the development of human society the conservative and progressive principles are of equal importance, that indeed without the conservation of traditional values no development at all, properly speaking, is possible.

III

The social critics limit the scope of literature, not only by excluding all conservatism, but also (and this is particularly true of Hicks, though the tendency is present in the others) by restricting the writer to the treatment of contemporary political, economic, and social problems.

Mark Twain's greatest fault, according to Hicks, is that he wrote only once concerning the public questions of his own time: "Except *The Gilded Age* . . . not one of his major fictions concerns itself with the movements and events of American life

10. *The Great Tradition*, p. 226.
11. *Ibid.*, p. 270.

in the latter half of the nineteenth century." [12] *Huckleberry Finn* is unsatisfactory because it is a nostalgic re-creation of the author's boyhood (though, oddly enough, the only specific fault Hicks finds in the book—"the tedious and labored account of the rescue of Jim" [13]—should be attributed not to the choice of subject but to its handling). Similarly, Mrs. Wharton, baffled by the New York of 1920, turned with nostalgia to the New York of 1870 in *The Age of Innocence*. It was a fatal retreat which Hicks finds repeated many times in the history of American literature.

The social critics are vaguely aware that in restricting the writer's scope to contemporary social phenomena they are faced with the problem of appraising admittedly great writers whose works transcend the limitations of milieu. What of Emily Dickinson, who wrote of eternity more than of time? Hicks is uneasy in his treatment of this unsocial poet. "The discovery of her work is, for any sensitive reader," he admits, "an exciting event." But her *life,* he adds, warily shifting his ground, touches the lives of her readers "at very few points"; and, at any rate, she was unable to come "to terms with her own age." [14] What of Shakespeare? Bernard Smith concedes, though the concession would seem to damage the central thesis, that there are "values in Shakespeare that are permanent for all classes." [15]

Let us grant that the writer should deal with reality. But reality is not confined to the public issues of the day. There is, after all, the reality of the private life.

IV

My final objection to the social critics is that they set up a philosophy of materialistic determinism.

One recalls, for example, the frequency with which the phrase

12. *Ibid.,* p. 45.
13. *Ibid.,* p. 44.
14. *Ibid.,* p. 130.
15. *Forces in American Criticism,* p. 291.

"economic determinism" recurs in *Main Currents*. The economic interpretation has doubtless been an important contribution to the study of history. But there are still those who believe that all history cannot be brought within economic confines, that life does not exactly equal economics, that, for example, religious as well as economic motives played a part in the first settlements of New England.

Marxian critics like Hicks and Smith go farther than Parrington, who remained something of an idealist, and frankly advocate a philosophy of scientific materialism. Religion is taboo. "Religion," declares Smith, "flourishes in a hierarchical society"; "the materialists are partisans of democracy." [16] The Marxian is convinced that religion is hostile to democracy; I am not. The New Testament has always seemed to me a gospel of the common man. But it is an individual gospel, and to the social critics the individual is also taboo. The words "individual," "individualistic," "individualism" are terms of reproach in the social lexicon. In approved social fiction—in Dos Passos's *U. S. A.*, for example, which Hicks regards as a model—the individual character is reduced to a social specimen and a product of natural forces.

The social approach has its uses if intelligently employed; but when applied exclusively and in doctrinaire fashion, it becomes narrow and impoverishing. I am unwilling to accept the disparagement of literary art as such, the rejection of conservative values in literature, the restriction of literature to social phenomena, and the establishment of scientific materialism as an "over-all" philosophy. I am unwilling, moreover, to believe that the health and prosperity of democracy are contingent upon this body of doctrine, for such a belief excludes from a democratic society art and religion, traditions and manners, and a proper respect for the individual life.

16. *Ibid.*, p. 386.

THE MORAL ASPECT
OF HENRY JAMES'S
"INTERNATIONAL SITUATION"

THE impression persists that in his comparative studies of America and Europe Henry James did less than justice to America, that indeed he was incapable of "appreciating" America. This impression has been confirmed by the literary historians who like to emphasize James's Europeanism and who point to certain obvious and incontrovertible facts in support of their interpretation: his residence in England and his eventual naturalization as a British subject, his insistence upon the "cultural" deficiencies of America and Americans, the removal of his Americans to Europe. These and other items in the case for James's Europeanism are of course not to be gainsaid. It is my purpose, not to gainsay them, but rather to see what can be said for a somewhat different view of the matter: if in James's works America is "culturally" inferior to Europe, Europe is morally inferior to America; and although "cultural" values were of great importance to our author, moral values were of even greater importance. It will be instructive to look at some of the Americans in the major novels who are exposed to European influences and to note the results of the exposure. These characters may be divided into two groups: the Europeanized Americans and the Americans uncorrupted by Europe.

Among the Europeanized Americans—those who have repudiated America and have resided in Europe for a considerable period—four of particular prominence require our attention: Gilbert Osmond, Madame Merle, Charlotte Stant, and Chad Newsome. We freely admit of course their remarkable sophistication and social poise. We must believe that their European experience has stimulated their intellectual interest, developed their aesthetic sense, enlivened their conversation, and given polish to their manners, as a residence in America could never have done. All of these things are presented in James's account for our admiration. But his account does not stop here: his stories compel us to consider the question of manners in relation to morals.

The four splendid persons just named are far from impeccable morally. The first three display selfishness and guile of extraordinary proportions. Madame Merle and Charlotte Stant are mistresses: the former is, or was, the mistress of Gilbert Osmond; the latter is the mistress of Prince Amerigo. Since James omits extenuation and apology, we are led to infer that these sophisticated American ladies have merely adopted a European code. Osmond, who might have competed with Count Urbain de Bellegarde for the distinction of having the finest manners in Europe, is the villain of *The Portrait of a Lady*. Not the least among his villainies is his recommending to his wife an extra-marital freedom with Lord Warburton as part of a plot to bring about the marriage of his daughter to the noble lord.

Compared with others, Chad Newsome is still in the novitiate. He is in process of refinement—and corruption. Looking through Strether's eyes, we applaud the "improvement" of the young man from Wollett, Massachusetts, as he stands at a balcony window, or enters a box at the theatre, or moves among the guests at a garden party. Keeping pace with Strether's expanding tolerance, moreover, we accept the connection with Madame de Vionnet: it is a beautiful relationship. Toward the end of *The Ambassadors*, however, we are disturbed—as Strether is disturbed—by the discovery that Chad's attitude toward the lady is not the fine devotion which we have supposed:

"I give you my word of honor," Chad frankly rang out, "that I'm not a bit tired of her." Strether at this only gave him a stare: the way youth could express itself was again and again a wonder. He meant no harm, though he might after all be capable of much; yet he spoke of being "tired" of her almost as he might have spoken of being tired of roast mutton for dinner.[1]

We are chagrined to learn that already Chad's interest has deviated to an unnamed inamorata in England:

"And is your idea," Miss Gostrey asked, "that there was some other woman in London?"

"Yes. No," Strether replied. "That is, I *have* no ideas, I'm afraid of them. I've done with them." [2]

The conclusion of the matter is that Chad's luster is visibly tarnished. After having embellished with loving care the theme of Chad's improvement in manners, James reveals at the end of the story an attendant corruption in morals.

In a passage which James doubtless remembered, Hawthorne wrote: "Taste seems to be a department of the moral sense; and yet it is so little identical with it, and so little implies conscience, that some of the worst men in the world have been the most refined." [3] Hawthorne's statement, though James made his own discovery of its truth, fits perfectly the evidence before us, and takes us to the center of the conflict in James's writings.

The characters in the major "international" novels to whom the appellation "hero" or "heroine" may be properly applied are Americans who are uncorrupted by Europe: Christopher Newman, Lambert Strether, Isabel Archer, Milly Theale, and the Ververs.

Christopher Newman is the least "cultured" of this group; but with all of his American deficiencies heavy on his head, he is an inspiring "hero." James gives the "essence" of *The American* in his Preface as follows:

I recall that I was seated in an American "horse-car" when I found

1. New York Edition (New York: Charles Scribner's Sons, 1909), II, 312–313. All references to James's novels and his Prefaces are from this edition.

2. II, 325.

3. *The Ancestral Footstep*. Riverside Edition (Boston and New York, 1883), p. 507.

myself, of a sudden, considering with enthusiasm, as the theme of a
"story," the situation, in another country and an aristocratic society,
of some robust but insidiously beguiled and betrayed, some cruelly
wronged, compatriot: the point being in especial that he should suffer
at the hands of persons pretending to represent the highest possible
civilization and to be of an order in every way superior to his own.
What would he "do" in that predicament . . . ? He would behave in
the most interesting manner—it would all depend on that: stricken,
smarting, sore, he would arrive at his just vindication and then would
fail of all triumphantly and all vulgarly enjoying it. He would hold his
revenge and cherish it and feel its sweetness, and then in the very act
of forcing it home would sacrifice it in disgust. He would let them
go, in short, his haughty contemners, even while feeling them, with
joy, in his power, and he would obey, in so doing, one of the large and
easy impulses *generally* characteristic of his type. He wouldn't "forgive"
—that would have, in the case, no application; he would simply turn, at
the supreme moment, away, the bitterness of his personal loss yielding
to the very force of his aversion. All that he would have at the end
would be therefore just the moral convenience, indeed the moral
necessity, of his practical, but quite unappreciated, magnanimity; and
one's last view of him would be that of a strong man indifferent to his
strength and too wrapped in fine, too wrapped above all in *other* and
intenser reflexions for the assertion of his "rights." [4]

The evidence seems to show clearly enough not only that the
untutored American won a moral victory but that a moral victory counted for most, in the long run, to James himself.

Lambert Strether, like Newman, is patient, high-minded, and
generous, and is capable of renunciation; he has a finer intelligence than Newman and is more susceptible of European
cultivation. The case of Strether is especially useful. He ap-
preciates to the full the advantages of Europe, to which he has
come belatedly; he wishes that he might have come earlier; he
frankly envies Chad Newsome his opportunities. "Live all you
can," he tells little Bilham; "it's a mistake not to." [5] Before a

4. Pages vi–vii.
5. *The Ambassadors*, I, 217. See also the Preface, pp. v–vi.

great while, the bottom has fallen out of his mission to reclaim
Chad, so happy has been his initiation into European society.
Near the end of *The Ambassadors,* however, a moral problem
emerges which for Strether overshadows considerations of
"culture." He has discovered Madame de Vionnet's passionate
attachment to Chad and her fear of losing him; he has discovered
also Chad's lack of steadfastness. He accordingly urges Chad to
remain in Paris, not because of the superior "cultural" advantages to be enjoyed there, but because of the young man's
obligations to his charming benefactor:

"You'll be a brute, you know—you'll be guilty of the last infamy—if
you ever forsake her. . . . You owe her everything—very much more
than she can ever owe you. You've in other words duties to her of the
most positive sort; and I don't see what other duties—as the others are
presented to you—can be held to go before them." [6]

Though Strether's approval of an irregular relationship gives us
the measure of his "emancipation" from Puritan morality under
Parisian influences, his final insistence upon Chad's "duties,"
upon the prime necessity of personal integrity, strikes the moral
note.

The moral note is repeated, again and again, in the stories of
the American Young Woman, whose "indestructible innocence"
(to quote from Howells's encomium on *Daisy Miller*) "had
never been so delicately appreciated." [7]

The Portrait of a Lady had its origin in "the conception of a
certain young woman affronting her destiny";[8] *The Wings of
the Dove,* in the idea of "a young person conscious of a great
capacity for life, but early stricken and doomed . . . aware moreover of the condemnation and passionately desiring to 'put in'
before extinction as many of the finer vibrations as possible." [9]

6. *Ibid.,* II, 308, 313.
7. William Dean Howells, "Henry James, Jr.," *Century Magazine,* III, n. s.
(November 1882), 24.
8. Preface, p. xii.
9. Preface, p. v.

Both Isabel Archer and Milly Theale are remarkable for their freshness and spontaneity, their zest for life, their high-mindedness and fineness of grain, their innocence and inexperience, and their naiveté. Both are victims of artful deception. Isabel is lured into an unfortunate marriage by the stratagems practised upon her by Gilbert Osmond and Madame Merle. Milly is the victim of a nefarious scheme devised by Kate Croy and carried out with the aid of the reluctant Densher. The death of Milly rescues her from further injury; but Isabel at the end has apparently resolved to stick to her bad bargain. Both exemplify a fine, if misdirected, loyalty: Milly leaves her money to Densher, and Isabel returns to Osmond. In both cases, American innocence is the dupe of European guile.

In his last great novel, James redresses the balance by giving a modicum of guile to his innocent Americans. Naive and unwary, the Ververs from American City have fallen into an ugly trap laid by two Europeanized Americans and an Italian nobleman, with the result that Maggie Verver's husband, the Prince, and Mr. Verver's wife, Charlotte Stant, have renewed a liaison which antedates their marriages. Throughout the first half of *The Golden Bowl*, father and daughter are delightfully domestic and unsuspecting. In the second half, however—as if James were weary of having his high-minded Americans forever imposed upon—the Ververs become shrewd and artful and prove to be more than a match for the intriguers. The Prince gains a new appreciation of Maggie; Charlotte, though still "splendid" as always, responds to the gentlest pull of Mr. Verver's "string." We applaud the victory of the Ververs. At the same time, we may regret the price of victory when we compare Maggie with her predecessors; for Maggie is a less attractive figure than Isabel or Milly. With the addition of worldly wisdom and cunning, the brightness—the "divine innocence" which Howells rightly admired—has been dimmed. Possibly James meant to suggest, with mixed emotions, that it was time for Americans to "come of age." The Ververs, at any rate, learned to play the game.

In his essay on Emerson, James said: "The genius itself it seems to me impossible to contest—I mean the genius for seeing character is a real and supreme thing." [10] This statement gives us an important and neglected clue to the moral significance of many of James's works. James, like Emerson, believed that character is "a real and supreme thing." The resolution of a novel tells us a good deal about the author's intention, and the resolutions of the five major "international" novels turn upon the high moral principles of the American protagonists: [11] Newman's magnanimity; Isabel Archer's faithfulness to duty as she saw it; Strether's clear perception of the only right course in a tangled situation; Milly Theale's purity and benevolence, shaming the conspirators; the Ververs' patient and successful effort toward the righting of an old wrong. In all of these instances James stands revealed as a moralist.

In stressing the moral aspect, I have no intention of discounting other important aspects of James. He became more and more engrossed, as everyone knows, in matters of form and technique. He never relinquished his belief that "it takes an old civilization to set a novelist in motion." [12] But while cultivating the art of the novel and maintaining his devotion to the "highly civilized," he did not neglect moral values. It is not an exaggeration to say that he attached an almost Puritan importance to them. In the moral conflicts on his international stage, moreover, James represented Europe as productive of evil, and America, of good. He had an exalted opinion of the American character at its best. Indeed, where, outside of Emerson and Whitman, does one find such confidence in the high moral capacities of the American?

10. "Emerson," reprinted in F. O. Matthiessen, *The James Family* (New York: Alfred A. Knopf, 1947), p. 442.

11. With the exception of *The Spoils of Poynton,* moral issues are not so decisive in the "English" novels of the middle period. [R. S.]

12. Letter to William Dean Howells dated London, June 1879, *The James Family,* p. 502.

MORAL CRISIS
AS STRUCTURAL PRINCIPLE IN FICTION
A Few American Examples

I CLAIM no originality for the principle; it has doubtless been used many times. But I haven't seen it applied with any consistency or continuity to the American novel where in several cases, at least, it seems applicable. And its application in these several cases seems to me to throw light on both structure and, more important, meaning. Moreover, the interpretations so arrived at are at variance in certain instances with those rather widely held: so much so that one sometimes wonders what kind of "insight" some of our most accomplished readers bring to these works. The novels which I propose to deal with from this standpoint are *The Scarlet Letter, Billy Budd, The American, Huckleberry Finn,* and *Sister Carrie.*

Arthur Dimmesdale's problem is whether or not to confess. The crisis extends from his acquiescence in the forest scene in Hester's plan to run away and his public confession on the scaffold. Hawthorne doesn't give a full account of what intervened, but he gives a good deal. He tells of Dimmesdale's being tempted on his way back to commit various blasphemies and obscenities. (Dimmesdale might have exclaimed with Cotton Mather, "Was ever man so tempted as I? Was ever man so completely given over to the Devil?" [1]) And he tells us that as soon as he reached his study, he tore up the sermon he had written and began furiously to write a new one. And this is about all Hawthorne does to fill in the gap. Perhaps he didn't want to run the risk of weakening his climax, of lessening the

1. Cf. *Diary of Cotton Mather: Part I, 1681–1708. Massachusetts Historical Society Collections.* 7th ser., Vol. VII (Boston, 1911), pp. 475, 578, 585.

shock of surprise when the minister mounts the scaffold. But the reader understands a few basic things: that Arthur has been reduced to utter despair, that out of his dire extremity he has called upon God, and that he has done this only after a life-and-death struggle with the flesh. In general, in Hawthorne's view of things, virtue, if it comes at all, comes only after a life-and-death struggle.

If Hawthorne were writing *The Scarlet Letter* today, I believe he would end the story with Arthur's confession. The rest is largely by way of epilogue, a concession to the sort of reader who wants to know what happened to Chillingworth, to Hester, to little Pearl. Chillingworth's death (especially the manner of it) and Hester's return, it is true, have a certain relevance to the action, but Pearl's subsequent career is quite irrelevant.

The moral crisis is Arthur's and only Arthur's. Hester had none because her mind was not divided. She had no understanding of Arthur's problem. She proposed a solution which was fine for her: a change of residence to a more congenial community would remove her difficulties because they were largely external. But Arthur's divided soul warred within him, and his civil war would have continued with little if any abatement in any part of the world. Arthur's confession resolved his difficulty; the decision was his, and it was made without Hester's knowledge or consent. It came with as much surprise to her as to the other members of the congregation. The resolution then is made through Arthur's moral agency; Hester is a contributing force, though one working in a contrary direction.

If Dimmesdale's confession is the high point of *The Scarlet Letter*, an event even more startling is the high point of *Billy Budd*: Billy's crying out in clarion tones from the yardarm, "God bless Captain Vere." [2] The preparatory stages by which Billy arrives at this super-human eminence are even less clearly

2. *The Portable Melville*, ed. by Jay Leyda (New York: The Viking Press, 1952), p. 729.

set forth than the corresponding portion of *The Scarlet Letter*. For it *is* a super-human eminence at which Billy arrives: "Love your enemies . . . pray for them which despitefully use you." [3] Of course Captain Vere is not Billy's "enemy" and does not "despitefully use" him: but he is responsible for the death sentence, and Billy knows this. To the "natural" man he would appear in the guise of enemy. That Billy blesses him is the spiritual miracle of the story.

The preparatory scene is the interview between the Captain and Billy after the verdict has been reached. Billy's blow struck at Claggart had been an act of defiance; the scene with the Captain is one of reconciliation. The narrative, told conjecturally, opens up almost unlimited possibilities: Vere "may in the end have caught Billy to his heart even as Abraham may have caught young Isaac"; "there is no telling the sacrament." [4] But that there has been a change in Billy, a transformation, a new insight, is shown symbolically by the disappearance of the speech impediment as he spoke the last words and by the author's description of Billy's "personal beauty" at this last moment as "spiritualized now through late experiences so poignantly profound." [5]

Melville's epilogue is more integral than Hawthorne's. The captain's deathbed murmur "Billy Budd, Billy Budd" [6] (recalling the elder Pierre's "My daughter, my daughter," [7] and emphasizing as in *Pierre* the parental relation) is significant, and so is the sailors' reverence for the yardarm, even pieces of it, as if it were the Cross of Christ. They both refer back meaningfully to the main action, which is Billy's, the Captain, like Hester (though more understanding than Hester), playing an ancillary role.

3. Matthew 5:44.
4. *The Portable Melville*, p. 720.
5. *Ibid.*, p. 729.
6. *Ibid.*, p. 736.
7. *Pierre*, ed. by Henry A. Murray (New York: Hendricks House, 1949), p. 82.

If the moral crisis is incompletely described in *The Scarlet Letter* and only hinted at in *Billy Budd* (perhaps because both authors after the manner of the old-fashioned romance or melodrama wished to preserve the impact of surprise), Christopher Newman's moral crisis is described in detail, James being a "realist" who (as Coleridge said of Shakespeare) preferred expectation to surprise. Newman's problem is what to do with the letter—to use it or not to use it—and the crisis is a prolonged affair which begins with his getting possession of the incriminating document and ends with his burning it. The reader knows that he won't use it because James has prepared us so thoroughly for the outcome ("What is character but the determination of incident? What is incident but the illustration of character?" [8]). The early incident of the dash to Wall Street in a hack is almost too obviously "planted." But Newman doesn't know he won't use it, for a long time, and the stages by which he arrives at his final decision are related with the meticulous detail of the new realism.

"Crisis" is primarily a medical word and means in dictionary terms the change in a disease which indicates whether the result is to be recovery or death. Newman's crisis is prolonged over weeks and months. He visits the convent and hears the wail of the Carmelite nuns; he confronts, accuses, makes his demand upon the intransigent Bellegardes ("Give me back Madame de Cintré") [9]; he calls on the Duchess and realizes the futility of any appeal in that quarter; he travels in England, returns to the United States, returns to Paris. He visits Mrs. Tristram, still in a defiant mood: "Good God! Do you expect me to forgive?" He revisits the convent: "It told him that the woman within was lost beyond recall." He goes to Notre Dame: "this was the best place he could be in . . . a great cathedral offers a very various

8. "The Art of Fiction," *The Future of the Novel,* ed. by Leon Edel (New York: Vintage Books, 1956), pp. 15–16.

9. *The American* (New York: Holt, Rinehart and Winston, 1949), p. 334. (This is the text of the original 1877 edition.)

hospitality." He didn't pray: he didn't kneel. Instead "he leaned his head for a long time on the chair in front of him." James's account of what happens in these crucial minutes is as follows:

When he took his head up he felt that he was himself again. Some-where in his mind, a tight knot seemed to have loosened. He thought of the Bellegardes; he had almost forgotten them. He remembered them as people he had meant to do something to. He gave a groan as he remembered what he had meant to do; he was annoyed at having meant to do it; the bottom, suddenly, had fallen out of his revenge. Whether it was Christian charity or unregenerate good nature—what it was, in the background of his soul—I don't pretend to say; but Newman's last thought was that of course he would let the Bellegardes go. If he had spoken it aloud, he would have said that he didn't want to hurt them. They had hurt him, but such things were really not his game. At last, he got up and came out of the darkening church; not with the elastic step of a man who has won a victory or taken a re-solve, but strolling soberly, like a good-natured man who is still a little ashamed.[10]

The account is a little equivocal. "Whether it was Christian charity or unregenerate good nature" is a theological straddle. "Unregenerate good nature" presupposes the romantic doctrine of innate goodness. "Christian charity" presupposes the Christian doctrine of original sin, for Christian forgiveness starts from a recognition of one's own sins ("Forgive us our trespasses as we forgive those who trespass against us"). But the scales are turned in favor of the Christian view of the matter toward the end of the passage: Newman is "ashamed," and at the very end he "is still a little ashamed." [11] That is, he is conscious chiefly of his own guilt, the guilt of having entertained thoughts of revenge. He realizes in effect that vengeance is the Lord's.

The book ends with the burning of the letter. There is no epilogue. "What becomes of Christopher Newman?" the con-ventional reader asks. "Did he stay on in Paris, stretching his

10. *Ibid.*, pp. 355, 356, 357.
11. *Ibid.*, p. 357.

legs on Mrs. Tristram's balcony?" "Did he return to America, make more money, marry an American heiress?" James the artist is adamant against the temptation to indulge the reader's idle curiosity (as Hawthorne was not when he told of Pearl's later career). Any aftermath must be supplied by the reader's own imagination; because Newman's moral crisis is resolved, the proper action of the book is finished.

James, who had a consummate sense of structure, stands at the opposite pole to Mark Twain, who has no sense of structure at all, or almost none. Huck's problem of course is whether to stick to Jim or turn him in. It is a moral crisis of the first magnitude, and Mark Twain describes it very well. On the one side was the societal pressure, the custom of the country, and Huck—outcast that he was—felt the pressure acutely. According to the Southern antebellum mores, the lowest-down thing a white man could do was to help a Negro slave escape, and understandably so because slaves were property, they represented a substantial expenditure of money. The more Huck thought about this side of the question, the more his "conscience went to grinding" [12] him. After he had written the letter to Miss Watson, he began to think how good Jim had been to him and how he was the only friend Jim had in the world. "It was a close place," this famous account continues; "I took it up, and held it in my hand. I was a-trembling, because I'd got to decide, forever, betwixt two things, and I knowed it. I studied a minute, sort of holding my breath, and then says to myself: 'All right then, I'll go to hell'—and tore it up." [13] Here is one of the supreme examples in literature of moral agency at work.

Mark Twain's use of the word "conscience" is interesting. He uses it to mean not the still small voice, the voice of God, but a socially conditioned response, and the hell to which Huck is

12. *Adventures of Huckleberry Finn*, ed. by Henry Nash Smith. Riverside Edition (Boston: Houghton Mifflin Company, 1958), p. 178.
13. *Ibid.*, pp. 179–180.

willing to go is the hell to which his society consigned all such malefactors. One wonders if the author had not been reading William Graham Sumner, the Yale sociologist. One wonders too if Huck's conscience wasn't grinding him also while he was thinking of Jim's side of the debate, and if it wasn't conscience, then by what name one would call it. The reader who is unwilling to accept such a sociological definition of "conscience" may resent for a moment the sly trick, but he forgets this offense against language in his admiration for the magnificent demonstration of Huck's ability to resist the social pressures, realizing full well that the sociologists who provided Mark Twain with his concept of "conscience" would have allowed Huck no such ability.

If James had been writing the story (if one could imagine James writing *Huckleberry Finn*), he would have ended it here. The moral crisis is resolved; the story proper is finished; anything added is another story. Mark Twain himself must have felt that way about it, for he shifted his center from Huck to Tom, and the rest is Tom's doings. I have never seen a convincing defense of the Tom Sawyer business; most readers dislike it, and even those who enjoy it regard it as a structural fault. After his famous encomium of the book, Hemingway called the Tom Sawyer part "just cheating." [14] It *was* a hard book to end, for the farther the raft travelled down the river the more difficult the freeing of Jim became. Many a writer today would leave the story unended. But the acceptability of the indeterminate ending, the unfinished story, dates in American literature from Sherwood Anderson. The fact remains that Mark Twain had a great moral crisis, but he wasn't artist enough to utilize it properly as a structural principle. He tried to continue the story after the crisis had been resolved, and his book falls to pieces.

When we come to our fifth illustration, *Sister Carrie*, we are

14. *The Green Hills of Africa* (New York: Charles Scribner's Sons, 1935), p. 22.

confronted by the question, How does a writer fare when there is no moral crisis at all? For by the tenets of naturalism, man is not a moral agent and so cannot experience a moral crisis. Dreiser's books are in effect a tremendous, massive attempt to exculpate his characters, to relieve them of all responsibility. He says in effect, "If you knew all the facts, you would see that Carrie could not have acted otherwise under the circumstances." Dreiser is in short an amoralist.

There are three places in the story at any one of which we should have had a quite satisfactory moral crisis if the story had been written by a moralist: where Carrie goes to live with Drouet, where Carrie allows herself to be abducted by Hurstwood, and where Carrie deserts Hurstwood. One can hardly say, where Carrie "decides," because the word implies moral choice, and Carrie makes no decisions, no moral choices. She is carried along by circumstances, and the author is at great pains to slide over these rough places, to smooth them out, to remove any possible feeling of crisis. He succeeds fairly well in the first two places but gets into difficulty, I think, in the third. The account of the disintegration of Hurstwood is done so thoroughly that Hurstwood steals the show: and as our interest in Hurstwood increases, the problem of making us sympathize with Carrie's desertion of him becomes more difficult. Dreiser's aim in his overelaborate documentation here seems to be to demonstrate beyond any possible doubt that Hurstwood is *through*, that he will never get on his feet again, and that Carrie therefore is quite justified in deserting him. It is the ethic of social Darwinism: Dreiser had been reading Herbert Spencer. But it was surely myopic of him to think that the ethic of survival—the principle on which Carrie operated from first to last—would be acceptable to readers, most of whom could be supposed to have a certain amount of human or even Christian indoctrination.

Most people I know think *Sister Carrie* is inferior *as a novel* to the other novels examined in this paper. Might the absence of moral crisis be a reason? A passage in Eliot's *After Strange Gods* is pertinent at this point:

With the disappearance of the idea of Original Sin, with the disappearance of the idea of intense moral struggle, the human beings presented to us both in poetry and prose fiction today . . . tend to become less and less real. It is in fact in moments of moral and spiritual struggle depending upon spiritual sanctions, rather than in those "bewildering minutes" in which we are all very much alike, that men and women come nearest to being real. If you do away with this struggle, and maintain that by tolerance, benevolence, inoffensiveness, and a redistribution or increase of purchasing power, combined with a devotion, on the part of an elite, to Art, the world will be as good as anyone could require, then you must expect human beings to become more and more vaporous.[15]

Possibly this is the answer. Carrie is certainly "vaporous." Nothing happens to her, really. There is no resolution, because there is nothing to resolve. She is less real than the other characters we have considered because there is no "intense moral struggle." And she is unreal despite the mass of documentation by which the author intends to make her real.

And that must be why naturalism never succeeded, why it has been given up for the most part. Those who continue in that vein are not so highly regarded any longer, I believe. The most highly regarded writers today—Faulkner and Warren, for example—have gone back to the older concept of moral crisis. One would find, beyond doubt, such a concept operative as a structural principle in *All the King's Men* and in an extraordinarily complex way in *The Sound and the Fury*. To trace its operation in recent fiction—particularly in Southern fiction— would be a rewarding task which lies outside the intention of this paper. Suffice it to say here that the firmness of the principle in Hawthorne, Melville, and James, its weakening in Mark Twain, its abandonment in Dreiser, and its recovery in Faulkner and Warren are a sequence which seems to throw some light on our literary history and our spiritual history too.

15. New York: Harcourt, Brace and Company, 1934, pp. 45–46.

THE OLD COST OF
THE HUMAN REDEMPTION

T H E modern conservative movement has come about as a
reaction against nineteenth-century liberalism. What was
nineteenth-century liberalism? It had several facets.

It was, in part, what Matthew Arnold called "faith in
machinery." [1] It was belief in progress. The evolutionary theory
seemed to give the assurance that continuous improvement was
inevitable. (One recalls Emerson's "Melioration is the law." [2])
The growth of democracy gave a similar assurance: the spread of
the franchise seemed in itself a guarantee of progress. (I remember hearing it argued, when I was a boy in Middle Tennessee
early in the century, that if women were given the vote, there
would be no more consumption of alcoholic beverages in the
United States.) It was believed, too, that the advance of science
and technology would bring about a Utopian world. Emerson
reflected the progressive spirit when he said late in life that, if
he were a young man, he would enroll in the college with the
best courses in science and engineering. Whitman went along
with this view when he exclaimed, in "Song of Myself," "Hurrah
for positive science!" [3]

It was believed that the set-up was foolproof—that it couldn't
fail. Add to all this the belief that man is innately good and sin

1. "Sweetness and Light," *The Portable Matthew Arnold,* ed. by Lionel
Trilling (New York: The Viking Press, 1949), p. 478.

2. "The Sovereignty of Ethics," *The Complete Works of Ralph Waldo
Emerson,* ed. by Edward Waldo Emerson. Centenary Edition (Boston and
New York: Houghton Mifflin Company, 1903–1904), X, 188.

3. *Whitman's "Song of Myself"—Origin, Growth, Meaning,* ed. by James
E. Miller, Jr. (New York: Dodd, Mead & Company, 1964), p. 37, 23, 485.

only a name, and you have a fair picture of the liberal milieu. Since this milieu was so pervasive and so dominant in the nineteenth century and after, it is no wonder that the sequence of world events dating from August 1914 produced a good deal of acute pain. For there is no disillusionment quite so painful as that of a disillusioned liberal. The "lost generation" of the 1920s were the unprepared and unwarned inheritors of a progressivism which had backfired in their faces.

William Ellery Channing, one of the great early liberals, declared in 1820 that "Calvinism is giving place to better views." [4] It gave place to more benign, more flattering views, but whether they were better views is open to serious doubt. We are concerned here, of course (as we have been concerned throughout this discussion), with the most fundamental of all questions, *What is the nature of man?* A corollary to this question might be, What have we a right to expect? The view which asserts man's intrinsic goodness, denies original sin, effaces the cross from the human horizon, may be supposed to be an inadequate preparation for "life" in any age. The opposition between Hawthorne and Emerson continues to be of use. Hawthorne was saddened by the American Civil War, but he was not disillusioned by it. Emerson's reaction to the war (the war being so out of keeping with his metaphysical calculations) was the rather insane one of prescribing a policy more extreme even than that of the extreme Reconstructionists.[5] The mental state of the "liberal" who discovers that the world is imperfect, and is likely to continue so for a long time, is not an enviable one. Your Calvinist, on the other hand, may be a bit grim, but he can grin and bear it. He is never too much surprised at the behavior of the *natural* man.

It would be an interesting semantic inquiry to determine to

4. "The Moral Argument against Calvinism," *The Works of William E. Channing, D. D.* (Boston: American Unitarian Association, 1886), p. 468.
5. That the slaves themselves be paid in the amount of their market value. (See "The Boston Hymn.") [R. S.] (*Works*, IX, 204. [Ed.])

what extent the word "liberal" in a religious context is used favorably today and to what extent, unfavorably. A generation or two ago its connotation was certainly favorable in many, perhaps most, quarters; today it is a pejorative in many. Emily Dickinson was probably in a small minority in the Unitarian New England of her day when she satirized the clergyman who preached upon "breadth." [6] Today she finds a growing number on her side. In 1936 when Allen Tate named a collection of his pieces *Reactionary Essays,* he was flaunting a sign. Thinking it time for a reaction against a number of impracticable, if not undesirable, progressivisms, he called himself *reactionary,* a word which had been used only in a pejorative sense for a good while. It is still very generally a pejorative, I suppose, so ingrained in America is the progressive idea. "Reactionary" is likely to remain for some time an epithet with which progressives enjoy damning the conservative or orthodox party.

It was used by many progressives, no doubt, to condemn T. S. Eliot when he announced in the late 1920s that he had become an Anglo-Catholic. A return to the Middle Ages, they said, was an impossible solution. But if we substitute for "Middle Ages" "orthodox Christian belief," wherein is the solution impossible? In the last two or three decades an increasing number of thoughtful people have sided with Eliot at least to this extent: they believe a return to Christian fundamentals (whether within the Anglo-Catholic fold, or some other) is the chief need of our time. These people (I reject the name "intellectual," used substantively, as by and large an unfortunate usage) are the ones whom I mean to designate as "neo-orthodox." They were probably brought up in the Christian faith, whether Catholic or Protestant. They almost necessarily fell into various kinds of agnosticisms and infidelities. And after having suffered from

6. "He preached upon 'Breadth' till it argued him narrow—" (1207), *The Poems of Emily Dickinson,* ed. by Thomas H. Johnson (Cambridge: The Belknap Press of Harvard University Press, 1955), III, 839.

spiritual famine, like the prodigal son in a far country, they have at length undertaken to arise and return to their Father. They have undertaken to return to Christian fundamentals, though the position to which one returns can never be quite the position from which one fell away.

Eliot's poetry shows a steady progression toward religious belief. It is the tortuous progress of the modern intellectual man who recognizes the necessity of religion, but for whom a spontaneous, simple faith is difficult, if not impossible. The poems are an honest record. There are no easy affirmations. What the poems give, instead, is something more valuable: a dramatic and symbolical description of the complex consciousness of a modern intellectual mind.

"The Love Song of J. Alfred Prufrock" is a picture of ineffectualness. Prufrock's condition is symbolized by the comparison between the evening and a patient etherized upon a table. His condition is one of distress and restlessness (for the patient under ether is not really quiet, but infinitely restless) and, at the same time, of paralysis. He is unable to answer questions, either great or small, or to arrive at a decision. He is incapable of action. He is bored by the petty round of tea parties and social calls. He lacks motivation because he is without conviction or belief. Contrasts are suggested with heroic figures of the past: with Hamlet, who, though greatly perturbed by the task thrust upon him, was nevertheless a passionate, heroic figure; with Michelangelo, who epitomizes the creative energy of the Italian Renaissance; with John the Baptist, the first Christian martyr. The presence of allusions like these gives the poem a religious implication: Hamlet, Michelangelo, and John the Baptist were energized by a passionate belief; Prufrock is separated from them by the distance between health and neurosis.

The ironic futility of "Prufrock" is continued in *The Waste Land*, but the despair is greater, and the religious implications correspondingly more emphatic. It is as if the poet meant to suggest that man must be reduced to utter despair before there can be a conscious striving toward religious faith, that God's opportunity must wait upon man's extremity. Many passages in *The Waste Land* point to a religious interpretation. The desert passages recall the Old Testament in both tone and language. Eliot's "Son of man,/ You cannot say, or guess, for you know only/ A heap of broken images" [7] is reminiscent of Ezekiel's "Son of man, can these bones live? And I answered, O Lord God, thou knowest." [8] Ecclesiastes describes a waste land similar to Eliot's: ". . . and the grasshopper shall be a burden, and desire shall fail. . . ." [9] The allusion to Christ's agony and death ("After the torchlight red on sweaty faces/ After the frosty silence in the garden/ After the agony . . ." [10]) suggests the Christian solution.

Ash Wednesday is perhaps the chief Christian poem of our time. It describes the progress of the soul from despair to hope, from unbelief to belief. The hopelessness of the opening lines seems as profound as that of *The Waste Land*, and more apathetic:

> Because I do not hope to turn again
> Because I do not hope
> Because I do not hope to turn. . . .
> Because I do not hope to know again
> The infirm glory of the positive hour
> Because I do not think
> Because I know I shall not know. . . .[11]

Prufrock's uncertainty was not greater than that of the "I" of these lines. But the ending is very different from Prufrock's. Prufrock ended with a sensation of drowning; his inadequacy is

---

7. *The Complete Poems and Plays 1909–1950* (New York: Harcourt, Brace and Company, 1952), p. 38, I, 20–22. All references to Eliot's poetry are from this text which is cited hereafter as *Poems and Plays*.

8. 37:3.

9. 12:5.

10. *Poems and Plays*, p. 47, V, 322–325.

11. *Ibid.*, p. 60.

such that he is overwhelmed by the demands of life. *Ash Wednesday* ends with a prayer which is not the soliloquy of a beholding and jubilant soul, but a petition for grace to subject the individual will to the divine will:

> Teach us to care and not to care
> Teach us to sit still
> Even among these rocks,
> Our peace in His will. . . .[12]

"Teach us to care and not to care" well expresses the central Christian paradox, the apparent contradiction between individual responsibility and divine sovereignty. The Christian faith posits the active, responsible, even militant individual, the individual who has put on the whole armor of God, ready to do battle against principalities and powers and the rulers of darkness. This is an individual who "cares" intensely. Over against this is set reliance upon and submission to an overruling Providence. The two concepts operate on entirely different "levels." One concept counsels vigilance, effort; the other, faith, submission.

Between *Ash Wednesday* and *Four Quartets* Eliot developed in the direction of a more philosophic religious attitude. *Four Quartets* is a series of religious meditations. The series reaches its culmination in "Little Gidding," which takes its name from a famous Anglican shrine in Huntingdonshire, where Nicholas Ferrar and his family, in 1625, retired to lead a life of religious devotion, and where Charles I, "a broken king," came to pray. It is a place, the poem says, "where prayer has been valid." The protagonist of the poem visits Little Gidding to pray, or at least to assume the attitude of prayer: "You are here to kneel." But true prayer is not easy, for "prayer is more/ Than an order of words, the conscious occupation/ Of the praying mind, or the sound of the voice praying." The modern intellectual man is

12. *Ibid.*, p. 67.

different from the seventeenth-century worshippers at Little
Gidding. To the modern intellectual visitor, even with the best
of intentions, this shrine or any other shrine is likely to be only
"a shell, a husk of meaning." [13]

Man is capable of moments of illumination when the timeless
touches or intersects the temporal ("the intersection of the
timeless moment," "this intersection time"). The meeting with
the "dead master" during the bombing of London is such a
moment. Experience, the poem seems to say, is a preparation for
the "intersection time," the moment of insight or revelation. The
preparation is a purification by fire. Fire, indeed, seems the
dominant symbol of the poem. In Part I, the sun shines with
"pentecostal fire." In Part II, fire appears as "the flickering
tongue" of a bomber, shockingly contrasted with the "cloven
tongues" of Pentecost. Part IV repeats the fire motif, particularly
in "the intolerable shirt of flame," the Nessus shirt of Hercules.
But in whatever manifestation, the fire is for man's behoof; it is
"refining" (this is the lesson of the dead master); it is "devised"
by "Love." [14]

More than any other twentieth-century poet writing in
English, Eliot takes us into the heart of the devotional, the
liturgical, the sacramental aspects of Christianity. Many of his
poems can be regarded as prayers and liturgies. The liturgical
tone is often definitely suggested by quoted phrases from the
Anglican or Catholic service, as, for example, by these lines in
Ash Wednesday from the "Hail Mary": "Pray for us sinners
now and at the hour of our death,/ Pray for us now and at the
hour of our death." [15]

To Eliot the Christian faith and worship are a discipline, in
the practice of which, forms and ceremonies are important, even
necessary aids. In "The Dry Salvages," he speaks of "hints and
guesses," by which he means the imperfect insights to which we

13. *Ibid.*, pp. 138, 139.
14. *Ibid.*, pp. 139–144 *passim.*
15. *Ibid.*, p. 61.

as human beings are limited, and then goes on to say, "The rest is prayer, observance, discipline, thought, and action." [16] Always Eliot's emphasis is upon the disciplined personality. In his "Thoughts After Lambeth," he says that Christianity is "difficult both to the disorderly mind and to the unruly passions." [17] And always Eliot is concerned with the great question of salvation. "Where shall the word be found?" [18] he asks repeatedly, referring back to St. John's "In the beginning was the word." [19]

If *Ash Wednesday* (1930) is perhaps the outstanding explicitly Christian poem of our century, *Death Comes for the Archbishop* (1927) is perhaps the outstanding explicitly Christian novel. Eliot belongs to that branch of the Anglican Church which would like to see the ancient breach with Rome healed, while at the same time finding certain Roman doctrines—papal infallibility is one—an obstacle. Willa Cather, though not technically a convert to Rome, could hardly have written of Catholicism with greater warmth and sympathy had she been one. Her novel is the inspiring story of the missionary labors of two Catholic priests in the old Spanish Southwest. These labors culminated in the building of the Cathedral in Sante Fe. "Where there is great love," Father Latour said, "there are always miracles. . . . The miracles of the Church seem to me to rest not so much upon faces or voices or healing power coming suddenly near to us from afar off, but upon our perceptions being made finer, so that for a moment our eyes can see and our ears can hear what there is about us always." [20] A Catholic commentator has spoken of what he calls "Miss Cather's perfect assimilation of Catholic usage" in *Death Comes for the Archbishop*.[21]

16. *Ibid.*, p. 136.

17. *Selected Essays* (New York: Harcourt, Brace and Company, 1950), p. 329.

18. *Ash Wednesday, Poems and Plays*, p. 65.

19. 1:1.

20. New York: Alfred A. Knopf, 1927, p. 50.

21. For a discussion of this and related matters, see Edward A. Bloom and Lillian D. Bloom, "The Genesis of *Death Comes for the Archbishop*," XXVI (January 1955), 479–506.

It is not easy to say how influential the religious examples of Eliot and Cather have been upon American writers or how prognostic their religious histories may be of future trends in our literature. One has the feeling that the religious trend in literature is becoming more marked, without at the moment being able to offer a large documentation. The conversion of Allen Tate to Rome is worthy of mention, especially since Catholicism has not been known to flourish particularly in his part of the South —Kentucky-Tennessee. Readers of his future works will probably be on the lookout for evidence of Catholic influence. John Henry Newman, who more than a century ago traveled the churchly road from Oxford to Rome, declared in his *Apologia* that "there was no medium, in true philosophy, between Atheism and Catholicity, and that a perfectly consistent mind, under those circumstances in which it finds itself here below, must embrace either the one or the other." [22] The Cardinal's dictum is of course unacceptable to the great world of Protestantism, but it has the merit, at least, of pointing to the dissatisfaction which the seeker after belief today is likely to feel, more and more, in various sorts of "middle ground."

The virtue of ritualistic discipline (so much emphasized in the Anglican and Catholic Churches), which appealed to Eliot and Willa Cather, has been made much of by some writers whom one might hesitate to designate, technically, as Christians. I have in mind, particularly, Ernest Hemingway, of whom Carlos Baker has said, "The consciousness of God is in his books, and the Book of Common Prayer is seldom far out of his reach." [23] The ritualistic aspect is seen throughout Hemingway but best perhaps in some of his shorter pieces. One might almost substitute "sacramental" for "ritualistic," remembering the "Catechism" of the *Book of Common Prayer,* where "sacrament" is defined as

22. *Apologia Pro Vita Sua,* ed. by A. Dwight Culler. Riverside Edition (Boston: Houghton Mifflin Company, 1956), p. 193.
23. *Hemingway: The Writer as Artist,* 2nd ed. (Princeton: Princeton University Press, 1956), p. 328.

"an outward and visible sign of an inward and spiritual grace."

"A Clean, Well-Lighted Place" tells about a café and two waiters, and an elderly customer who stays on after all the other customers have left, drinking his brandy meticulously and deliberately. The elderly gentleman is there every night, and he is obviously reluctant to leave this clean, well-lighted place. Past eighty, he must have been a rather special person in former years (he still is): his strong head for brandy (a liquor for heroes, Dr. Johnson said [24]), his ability, though a little drunk, to drink without spilling, and at last to walk away "with dignity," though a bit unsteadily—these connote a certain distinction of character. Care and precision mark the manner in which the waiter serves his customer: "He put down the saucer and poured the glass full of brandy. . . . The old man motioned with his finger. 'A little more,' he said. The waiter poured on into the glass so that the brandy slopped over and ran down the stem into the top saucer of the pile." [25] One can be sure that in the first instance the glass was filled in exactly the right amount, and in the second, the excess was exactly measured, also. Bartenders (a favorite symbolic character in Hemingway) are careful and precise. They are, in the present story, ministering priests, as it were, at this ritual.

The café becomes a symbol, too. It is a lighted area surrounded by darkness. The lighted area seems pitifully small in comparison with the enveloping darkness. If the darkness stands for the disorder and chaos of an evil world, and the spot of light for the small amount of order and discipline and civilization which the individual has been able to wrest out of the surrounding chaos and old night, then, the story seems to say, the small lighted area

24. "Claret is the liquor for boys; port, for men; but he who aspires to be a hero . . . must drink brandy" (Boswell's *Life of Johnson*). [R. S.] (See the conversation of Wednesday, April 7, 1779, which appears in the Oxford Standard Authors edition, London, 1953, on page 1016. [Ed.])

25. *The Short Stories of Ernest Hemingway* (New York: Charles Scribner's Sons, 1953), pp. 381, 380.

is enough, or, at any rate, must be made to do. Not to be over-looked, also, is the advantage of human sympathy. The café is a place where congenial souls may meet. The older waiter, par-ticularly, has a sympathetic understanding of the elderly gentle-man's problem. Living in a clean, well-lighted place does not mean solitary withdrawal so long as there are others who also prefer such a place. One can belong to a communion of saints, however small.

In "Big Two-Hearted River," the feeling of ritual is even more emphasized. The story gives an account of Nick Adams's fishing expedition in the Michigan woods. We are told of his hike with a heavy pack after leaving the train (one recalls Christian's burden in *Pilgrim's Progress*), the selection of the campsite, pitching tent, cooking the evening meal, the night's sleep, the fishing next day, the throwing back into the water of the trout too small to keep, the avoidance of a place farther downstream which presents special difficulties, and which Nick is not yet spiritually prepared to enter. The whole account has a ceremonial air. It is not a novitiate, for Nick has been there before. But further trial and cleansing are necessary before Nick can fish in the most hazardous waters.

"Big Two-Hearted River" is a religious symbolism. It tells of purgation and preparation. When Nick Adams goes into the woods, he is a sick soul. The spiritual therapy is not the old romantic communing with Nature. (A fisherman's "nature" is different from a romantic poet's.) There is, on the contrary, an exacting procedure which Nick must follow, a course of action which calls out his own powers. Eliot's line quoted above—"The rest is prayer, observance, discipline, thought, and action" [26]—is, interestingly enough, rather applicable to Nick's conduct in "Big Two-Hearted River." The story becomes, at last, a symbol of sacramental living.

It is an easy and inviting transition from Nick Adams of

26. *Poems and Plays,* p. 136.

Hemingway's "Big Two-Hearted River" to Ike McCaslin of Faulkner's *The Bear*. Both stories have to do with boys who undergo a certain spiritual preparation, and both stories have the aura of ritual and sacrament.[27] One difference worth noting is that Nick goes on his expedition alone, while Ike goes in the company of his elders. Nick is on his own; Ike is a learner. But both, it should be observed, are following a traditional procedure, a long-established ritual. It would be a mistake, I think, to infer from Nick's aloneness that he is not part of a traditional society. He has learned from his father before him. Fishermen as well as hunters belong to a noble company. But it is also true that the social and traditional aspects are more prominent in Faulkner's story than in Hemingway's, and this greater prominence would perhaps justify the inference that a stable, traditional society is more important to Faulkner than to Hemingway.

Faulkner glorifies the old hunters. Their talk was "the best of all talking." [28] Sam Fathers, the son of a Negro slave and a Chickasaw chief, was the boy's principal mentor, though he learned, too, from Boon Hogganbeck (who was also part Indian), from the educated leaders—Major de Spain, General Compson, and cousin McCaslin—from Ash, the Negro cook, and even from Tennie's Jim. The animals also were his instructors— the lesser ones as well as Old Ben and Lion. In such a school the boy learned humility and patience and the conquest of fear. Fathers told the boy, "Be scared. You can't help that. But don't be afraid. Ain't nothing in the woods going to hurt you if you don't corner it, or it don't smell that you are afraid." [29] The crowning spiritual grace was a kind of surrender, which was

27. It would be interesting and perhaps fruitful to compare Eliot, Hemingway, and Faulkner in this matter of ritualistic observance. All three might be discovered to possess the essential quality about equally, the difference being that Eliot is explicitly ecclesiastical and liturgical, while the others are not. [R. S.]

28. *The Faulkner Reader* (New York: Random House, 1954), p. 253.

29. *Ibid.*, p. 264.

achieved when the boy, his novitiate completed, entered the forest alone, and without gun, watch, or compass.

(Here then—to recur to the earlier comparison—Ike was alone, after all, like Nick. Perhaps Nick's aloneness was preceded by a social preparation; perhaps the kind of healing Nick was seeking was something which one can win only by oneself. In any case, the two stories encompass both the social and the individual phases and seem to say that the very last steps to salvation must be taken alone.)

Faulkner's hunting world is a world of noble qualities. The men observe a long-established ritual. It is a society where every man has his place and knows it, where rank is respected, and merit too, where rank is likely to have a solid basis in merit, and where the idea of responsibility, of *noblesse oblige*, is operative. The boy's attitude toward this society of hunters is one of respect and admiration, and he feels great satisfaction in their recognition of his worthiness.

The contrast between the hunting story (in Parts 1, 2, and 3) and the story of the "old ledgers" in Part 4 (which gives the history of the McCaslin family from Ike's grandfather down), is a shocking one, for one story is heroic, and the other sordid. The sordidness derives chiefly from the evils of slavery. The plantation economy, Faulkner emphasizes, was founded upon injustice, the injustice of Negro slavery. "This whole land, the whole South," Ike McCaslin cries out, and the author seems to be crying out with him, "is cursed, and all of us who derive from it, whom it ever suckled, white and black both, lie under the curse." [30]

If one asks which story is true, the heroic one of the hunters or the sordid one of the dealers in slaves, the answer must be that both are true. Man is both sordid and heroic. Man—as Captain Peleg said of Captain Ahab—is both ungodly and Godlike. The special advantage of Faulkner's technique, by which he com-

30. *Ibid.*, p. 315.

bined two stories into one, is that he can in this way suggest
the fundamental ambiguity, the basic duality, of man's nature.
Man is the child of God, made a little lower than the angels. He
is also fallen man, born in sin and conceived in iniquity. Both
sides are intensified in Faulkner, elevated to high tragedy. The
tragedy of man grows out of the conflict between the high
impulses and the low, grows out of the coexistence of potentialities for good and for evil. Faulkner likes to juxtapose, shockingly,
the two potentialities. Hawthorne (whom Faulkner resembles in
many ways[31]) juxtaposed them effectively in the portrait of
Arthur Dimmesdale.

The particular symbolisms in *The Bear* are probably best left
to the individual reader. Faulkner's great hunt recalls Melville's,
but with important differences as well as similarities. The Bear,
like the Whale, takes on a mythical supernatural quality. But
the Bear, unlike the Whale, seems more benign than sinister,
and the hunt of the Bear, unlike the hunt of the Whale, is
conducted reverently, not blasphemously. The aid called in, in
the hunt of the Whale, is the Devil's agent, Fedallah; the aid,
and an effective aid he proves to be, in the hunt of the Bear is
the dog Lion. It may be stretching a point to suggest that Lion
is symbolically "the Lion of the tribe of Judah" of the Book of
Revelation.[32] But it is not too much to say that Ahab is Devil-
inspired in his quest, and Ike and his associates are God-inspired.
There is an aura of piety (in the best, older sense) in *The Bear*
which is absent from *Moby-Dick*.

The Lion of Judah I take to be a type of Christ, and the point
recalls Faulkner's fondness for the Christ-symbol. He likes to

31. The reader is referred to a brief elaboration of the resemblance in an
article by the present writer, "Hawthorne and Faulkner," *College English*,
XVII (February 1956), 258–262, and a fuller treatment by William Van
O'Connor, "Hawthorne and Faulkner: Some Common Ground," *Virginia
Quarterly Review*, XXXII (Winter 1957), 105–123. [R. S.] (Mr. Stewart's
essay appears in this volume. [Ed.])
    32. 5:5.

create characters who resemble Christ, not at all in their totality, but in a few particulars. One such character is Benjy in *The Sound and the Fury*, who recalls Christ in his innocence and his sorrowfulness. Benjy's sorrowful wail seems nothing less than a lament over a lost world; he seems the Spirit itself making intercession for us with groanings which cannot be uttered. Another is Joe Christmas, in *Light in August*, who is a kind of scapegoat, on whose head have been heaped all the sins since the race began, and who suffers a bitter agony, and death at last, at the hands of "soldiers" not unlike those who crucified Christ. Ike McCaslin in *The Bear* is another who, after his long novitiate, renounced his landed inheritance (tainted as it was with the curse of slavery) and took up the carpenter's trade, "because," he said, "if the Nazarene had found carpentering good for the life and ends He had assumed and elected to serve, it would be all right, too, for Isaac McCaslin." [33] And still another is the Corporal, in *A Fable*, whose history parallels Christ's at several points. Faulkner is definitely fascinated by this kind of symbolism. The effect is at least threefold: first, the reader is shocked by the recognition of similarities to Christ in a character who, in other respects, is so un-Christlike; second, the character is deepened and enriched by this added dimension; and third, the idea is conveyed, gradually and firmly, that Christian meanings can have a surprising ubiquity.

Faulkner is still, I fear, a much misunderstood author. He is still read by some as a sociologist. But he is not a sociologist at all. He is, rather, a great imaginative, symbolical writer, a moral allegorist. We do not read Faulkner to learn about Mississippi in a sociological sense, any more than we read Hawthorne to learn about Massachusetts, or Melville to learn about maritime practices, or Shakespeare to discover economic and social conditions in sixteenth-century England. Let not the Mississippians suppose that Faulkner is writing about them in an exclusive sense, and

33. *The Faulkner Reader*, p. 337.

let not the New Englanders or the Middle Westerners or the Californians, even, suppose that he is *not* writing about them, because he is. Faulkner is not reporting on "conditions"; he is reporting on the human condition. He is reporting on original sin, which is—there are good reasons to believe—in widest commonalty spread.

Faulkner is an elemental writer like Melville and Shakespeare. He writes in his own powerful idiom; he is not concerned with surface pleasantries; he is not a "polite" author; he is concerned with profundities; he is concerned with the soul of man laid bare. To the prudish objection which one critic has made to *The Sound and the Fury*, that it is "about ugly people in an ugly land," the answer might well be, So is *King Lear*. The London *Times Literary Supplement* (in that historic number devoted to American writing today) had this to say about Faulkner: "Faulkner is all true—he is poetically the most accurate man alive; he has looked straight into the heart of the matter, and got it down for good." [34] The matter which he has looked straight into the heart of, we may be sure, is not peculiar to Mississippi. It is peculiar only to the human race.

Faulkner said in the Stockholm speech, "I believe that man will not only endure: he will prevail." [35] A writer for one of the magazines professed to be puzzled by the word *prevail,* and decided that it is vague and meaningless. I would suggest, however, that it might be helpful to look up the word in Cruden's *Concordance* to the Bible, and then read the passages (there are sixty-five) in which it occurs. In general, *prevail* occurs in contexts where a victory is won with God's help. *Prevail,* as Faulkner uses it, has nothing to do with modern technology. It is a Biblical word and has a religious connotation.

Prevailing in Faulkner is never an easy matter. The Christian

34. September 17, 1954. [R. S.] (Reprinted in *American Writing Today,* ed. by Allan Angoff [New York: New York University Press, 1957], pp. 214–215. [Ed.])

35. *The Faulkner Reader,* p. 4.

view has never underestimated human tribulation. "Nobody knows the trouble I've seen, nobody knows but Jesus," is the old spiritual's way of saying that suffering has a central and necessary place in Christian doctrine. Well, Faulkner's protagonists are nearly always up to their ears in trouble, are nearly always surrounded by hell and high water. They may find release only in a martyr's death. But they always tower. They always enhance our conception of the human potential.

Faulkner's most heroic character is his most Christian character: Dilsey "closed the door and returned to the kitchen. The stove was almost cold. . . . 'Ise seed de first en de last,' she said, looking at the cold stove, 'I seed de first en de last.' She set out some cold food on the table. As she moved back and forth she sang a hymn. She sang the first two lines over and over to the complete tune." [36] Above the ruins of the House of Compson, Dilsey, the old Negro servant, towers. Dilsey's towering strength is founded on Christian faith. It is a rugged faith, from which she refuses to be separated by death, or life, or angels, or principalities, or powers, or things present, or things to come, or height, or depth, or any other creature.

Faulkner embodies and dramatizes the basic Christian concepts so effectively that he can with justice be regarded as one of the most profoundly Christian writers in our time. There is everywhere in his writings the basic premise of original sin, everywhere the conflict between the flesh and the spirit. One finds also the necessity of discipline, of trial by fire in the furnace of affliction, of sacrifice and the sacrificial death, of redemption through sacrifice. Man in Faulkner is a heroic, tragic figure. He may on occasion rise to spiritual greatness. The greatness is measured by the distance between the heights he attains and the depths to which he descends, or, but for the grace of God, might have descended.

Robert Penn Warren's fiction resembles Faulkner's in several

36. *The Sound and the Fury, The Faulkner Reader*, p. 223.

ways—in a vigorous handling of Southern subject matter, in a philosophical and religious position rooted in Southern tradition, in technical virtuosity, in symbolical intensity. Warren's work, too (again like Faulkner's), is infused with a kind of neo-Calvinism. But Warren is no mere disciple. He strikes out on his own.

In *All the King's Men*, Boss Willie Stark, "the man of fact," explains to Dr. Adam Stanton, "the man of idea," [37] that there is no such thing as natural goodness, and goes on to give his pragmatic version of how "good" and "bad" jostle each other in this imperfect world:

"Yeah," the Boss said, "he was one of those guys wants everything and wants everything two ways at once. You know the kind, Doc?"

He flicked a look over at Adam, like a man flicking a fly over by the willows in the trout stream. But there wasn't any strike.

"Yeah, old Hugh—he never learned that you can't have everything. That you can have mighty little. And you never have anything you don't make. Just because he inherited a little money and the name Miller he thought you could have everything. Yeah, and he wanted the one last damned thing you can't inherit. And you know what it is?" He stared at Adam's face.

"What?" Adam said, after a long pause.

"Goodness. Yeah, just plain, simple goodness. Well, you can't inherit that from anybody. You got to make it, Doc. If you want it. And you got to make it out of badness. Badness. And you know why, Doc?" He raised his bulk up in the broken-down wreck of an overstuffed chair he was in, and leaned forward, his hands on his knees, his elbows cocked out, his head outthrust and the hair coming down to his eyes, and stared into Adam's face. "Out of badness," he repeated. "And you know why? Because there isn't anything else to make it out of." [38]

The passage is a down-to-earth statement of original sin. Not natural goodness but natural badness is what we have to work with.

37. *All the King's Men* (New York: Harcourt, Brace and Company, 1946), p. 462.

38. *Ibid.*, p. 272.

Human nature is corrupt and corruptible. Percy Munn in *Night Rider* is one of Warren's more memorable characters. A tobacco raiser and country-town lawyer, educated in Philadelphia and highly respected in his community, Munn is a kind of modern Southern Brutus, an honorable man who is seduced by conspirators or organizers who are also honorable men for the most part, and who set out quite honorably and justifiably to redress a great wrong, namely, the cheating of the tobacco growers by the Tobacco Trust. But the conspirators go down hill, and Munn goes down hill with them. He joins the night riders. He sets fire to barns; he commits murder; he becomes bestial sexually. Natural badness is triumphant. And there is an inexorableness (reminding one of Hawthorne) about it all. Having taken the first step almost involuntarily, Munn goes inevitably, step by step, to his doom.

Warren's "Original Sin: A Short Story" (it is a short poem) gives another (quite different) account of a lost innocence. If *Night Rider* shows a man, Percy Munn, sinking into a depravity which is astonishing to those who behold him, and most of all perhaps to Munn himself, "Original Sin: A Short Story" shows, through symbolic images, a process of growth and maturation (ostensibly an "upward" rather than a "downward" course), in which there is involved necessarily an unhappy conflict between the new and the old, maturity and childhood, experience and innocence. The narrator's country boyhood (suggested by such images as "the old hound that used to snuffle your door and moan," "an old horse cold in the pasture") is contrasted with an intellectually distinguished maturity (suggested by such images as "Harvard Yard," "the quantum glare of the sun"). The narrator is haunted by childhood ghosts, which he equates with a lost innocence. Perhaps the narrator, somewhat in the manner of Hawthorne's Ethan Brand, left the simple life of his youth behind in quest of some high abstraction. He cries, "There must be a new innocence for us to be stayed by." [39] It is the cry everywhere of the modern intellectual man. Where is this new innocence? Where shall the word be found?

Warren's book-length poem, *Brother to Dragons,* which has been used in an earlier connection, contains some fairly explicit statements which perhaps can be regarded as giving an "answer," or a part of an answer, to questions like these. The poem is one of the most impressive treatments in modern American literature of the problem presented by the human condition.

The human condition, in the first place, is (as we study its dramatizations in the poem) one of extremity. There can be no hope so long as the recognition of this basic fact is absent. It is to a realization of man's extremity that Jefferson, in this post-humous inquiry, has come painfully and by degrees. Man learns only through suffering. Near the end of the poem, a changed Jefferson speaks:

> Now I should hope to find the courage to say
> That the dream of the future is not
> Better than the fact of the past, no matter how terrible.
> For without the fact of the past we cannot dream the future.
> I think I begin to see the forging of the future.
> It will be forged beneath the hammer of truth
> On the anvil of anguish. We shall be forged
> Beneath the hammer of truth on the anvil of anguish.[40]

And Jefferson's sister, Lucy, says:

> But my dear Brother, if your dream
> Was noble, there's a nobler yet to dream.
> It will be nobler because more difficult and cold
> In the face of the old cost of the human redemption,
> And the knowledge of that cost is, in itself, a kind of redemption.[41]

39. *Selected Poems 1923–1943* (New York: Harcourt, Brace and Company, 1944), pp. 23, 24.
40. *Brother to Dragons* (New York: Random House, 1953), pp. 193–194.
41. *Ibid.*, p. 193.

"The old cost of the human redemption!" That, of course, is the great Christian thesis: man's need of redemption—and its great cost.

The human condition, secondly, is one of paradox. Paradox is at the heart of Christian doctrine. "He that is greatest among you shall be your servant." [42] "Many that are first shall be last; and the last shall be first." [43] "Whosoever will save his life shall lose it; but whosoever will lose his life for my sake, the same shall save it." [44] In the last speech of the poem the author attempts to sum up in a series of paradoxes the wisdom, the Christian wisdom, which the poem has wrung out of this tragic tale:

The recognition of complicity is the beginning of innocence,
The recognition of necessity is the beginning of freedom.
The recognition of the direction of fulfillment is the death of the self,
And the death of the self is the beginning of selfhood.[45]

The human condition, imperfect and predestined in the high religious sense as it is, is, once more, a condition of responsibility. The idea of responsibility is included, indeed, in the word "complicity" in the passage just quoted; we are all, in a profound sense, accomplices, and complicity is inevitable. At the very end of *Brother to Dragons*, the author visited the grave of Jefferson's nephew, Lilburn Lewis, the murderer. "Why am I here?" he asks, and answers, "Some need has drawn me." [46] And then, in the poem's last lines, the author says,

And so I stood on the headland and stared at the river,
In the last light of December's, and the day's, declension.
And the river declared its cold gleam beyond the flat land. . . .
I went down the bluff, and crossed the evening barn-lot,

42. Matthew 23:1.
43. Matthew 19:30.
44. Matthew 16:25.
45. *Brother to Dragons*, pp. 214–215.
46. *Ibid.*, p. 207.

> I opened the sagging gate, and was prepared
> To go into the world of action and liability.[47]

The last word in the quotation, *liability*, should be noted especially. "Liable" has two complementary meanings: (1) obligated by or answerable to law (as in "liable for military service"), and (2) exposed to danger or risk (as in "liable to err"). "Liability" is, therefore, a particularly happy word choice, for it comprises two paradoxical aspects of the human condition: man's responsibility and his fallibility. Christian doctrine insists to the last that man is fallible *and* responsible, that he is responsible though fallen.

47. *Ibid.*, p. 215.

PART III   *Southern Literature in Outline and Perspective*

TIDEWATER AND FRONTIER [1]

S OUTHERN literature from the beginning has been more diverse, more varied, than the literature of New England or of the Middle West. There have been greater extremes in Southern literature, and the basic difference is that which separates two traditions, which one may call the Tidewater tradition and the Frontier tradition. There is no such division in New England literature, for the frontier in New England was never very pronounced or articulate; nor in the literature of the Middle West, because that region has been more homogeneously democratic. But in the South the contrast has been marked, indeed. It would be difficult to find writers more different than William Byrd of Westover and George Washington Harris, the author of the *Sut Lovingood Yarns*; or, to take more recent examples, Ellen Glasgow of Richmond and Jesse Stuart of W-Hollow in the Kentucky mountains. It is a remarkable fact about Southern literature that both traditions have had a great deal of vitality, and have flourished side by side.

In modern times, the Tidewater tradition is represented by (among others) the Virginians, Ellen Glasgow and James Branch Cabell; by John Crowe Ransom and Allen Tate of the Nashville school; by Mississippians like Stark Young and Eudora Welty. These writers stem spiritually and culturally from William Byrd's Tidewater: they are courtly, sophisticated, intellectual; they cultivate "wit" in the older sense and a fine irony; they address an inner circle; they possess restraint, dignity, a sense of form; they are classicists.

1. This article was originally a lecture given by Mr. Stewart while he was Walker-Ames Professor of English at the University of Washington in Seattle.

The Frontier first found expression in the early nineteenth century. This was a full one hundred years after Byrd's *History of the Dividing Line,* but it is remarkable that the Frontier should have been represented in literature at all, let alone so early. The Frontiersman—whether in the mountains of East Tennessee or the canebrakes of Arkansas—was a pretty lively fellow, and he has his niche—and a secure one it is turning out to be—in such writings as Longstreet's *Georgia Scenes, The Autobiography of David Crockett,* Harris's *Sut Lovingood Yarns,* Hooper's *Adventures of Captain Simon Suggs,* Baldwin's *Flush Times in Alabama and Mississippi,* Thorpe's "Big Bear of Arkansas." In modern times the tradition is represented by such literary descendants as Erksine Caldwell and Jesse Stuart. Thomas Wolfe, who came from the same mountain region as George Washington Harris, belongs with the members of this Frontier school in some respects, though he lacked their sense of humor and their mastery of the vernacular.

The two traditions—Tidewater and Frontier—have maintained a good deal of separateness from each other down to our time, though Faulkner and Warren, as I shall suggest presently, have combined elements from both. You will find, as a general thing, little truck between writers of the two schools. I shouldn't expect Ransom to have a high opinion of Wolfe, and I shouldn't expect Jesse Stuart to think very well of James Branch Cabell. (I mean, of course, of their writings.) I doubt if Tate admires Caldwell, and I should be surprised if Caldwell reads Tate. Tidewater and Frontier are still Tidewater and Frontier.

William Byrd, of course, is the grand prototype in literature of the Tidewater, and he is best seen in his delightful *A Progress to the Mines* (1732). The journey was undertaken to investigate the state of the mining industry in Virginia, and the account shows that Byrd was a most painstaking investigator, but the more lively parts of the narrative concern the social entertainment along the way. *A Progress to the Mines* was indeed a royal progress, for Byrd was most hospitably received by the neighboring gentry. The account of his visit with the Spotswoods is revealing:

Here I arrived about three o'clock and found only Mrs. Spotswood at home, who received her old acquaintance with many a gracious smile. I was carried into a room elegantly set off with pier glasses, the largest of which came soon after to an odd misfortune. . . . A brace of tame deer ran familiarly about the house, and one of them came to stare at me as a stranger; but, unluckily spying his own figure in the glass, he made a spring over the tea table that stood under it, and shattered the glass to pieces, and falling back upon the tea table, made a terrible fracas among the china. This exploit was so sudden, and accompanied with such a noise, that it surprised me and perfectly frightened Mrs. Spotswood. But 'twas worth all the damage to show the moderation and good humor with which she bore this disaster.[2]

The moderation and good humor with which Mrs. Spotswood bore the disaster is clearly the point to underscore. She was, as Alexander Pope put it in that most elegant of all compliments to a gentlewoman, "mistress of herself though China fall." [3]

Colonel Spotswood, whom Byrd called the "Tubal-cain of Virginia," and who modestly substituted for "Virginia" in the appellation, "North America," [4] was generous with his knowledge of the mining and smelting of iron ore; like many a Southerner after him, he was a great talker. After business, which was not scanted, came the social hour with the ladies, Mrs. Spotswood and her spinster sister, Miss Theky. "The conversation with the ladies" (Byrd recorded in this private narrative; the *Progress* was not published until after his death) was "like whip sillabub, was very pretty but had nothing in it." [5] Southern gallantry, it would seem, was not incompatible with a certain amount of masculine condescension toward the ladies.

2. *The Prose Works of William Byrd of Westover,* ed. by Louis B. Wright (Cambridge: The Belknap Press of Harvard University Press, 1966), pp. 355–356.

3. "Epistle II. To a Lady," 1. 268.

4. *Prose Works,* pp. 356–357.

5. *Ibid.,* p. 359.

At the home of the Chiswells, Byrd was shocked to discover that the twenty-four years which had passed since he last saw Mrs. Chiswell

had made great havoc with her pretty face and plowed very deep furrows in her fair skin. It was impossible to know her again, so much the flower was faded. However, though she was grown an old woman, yet she was one of those absolute rarities, a very good old woman.[6]

Of Colonel Jones's plantations, situated nearby, Byrd recorded:

The poor negroes are a kind of Adamites, very scantily supplied with clothes and other necessaries; nevertheless (which is a little incomprehensible), they continue in perfect health and none of them die except it be of old age. However, they are even with their master and make him but indifferent crops, so that he gets nothing by his injustice but the scandal of it.[7]

During his visit at the Flemings, the company were confined indoors all day by rainy weather, and Byrd, always the agreeable guest, "began to talk of plays," and he goes on to say,

finding her [Mrs. Fleming's] taste lay most towards comedy, I offered my service to read one to her, which she kindly accepted. She produced the second part of The Beggar's Opera [Polly, 1729], which had diverted the town [London Town] for forty nights successively, and gained £4000 to the author. . . . After having acquainted my company with the history of the play, I read three acts of it, and left Mrs. Fleming and Mr. Randolph to finish it, who read as well as most actors do at a rehearsal. Thus we killed the time and triumphed over the bad weather.[8]

I resist with difficulty the temptation to quote further from this classic of the colonial South. A Progress to the Mines contains most of the essential elements which will recur, with modifications of course, as we attempt to trace the history of the Tidewater tradition: the good manners, the decorum, the

6. Ibid., pp. 346–347.
7. Ibid., pp. 349–350.
8. Ibid., pp. 345–346.

sense of community, the sense of justice, the interest in polite literature, the gallantry, the wit. Byrd has never had justice done him as a writer. His taste and style were formed under Restoration and early Augustan auspices, and his writing as writing compares favorably with some of the best in contemporary London. Particularly noteworthy is the wit, which illustrates well enough Addison's definition in *Spectator* No. 62. Wit, Addison says, involves a turn of surprise, as in the statement, "My mistress' bosom is as white as snow, *and as cold.*" Byrd has similar turns of surprise: "Though she was grown an old woman, yet she was one of those absolute rarities, *a very good old woman*"; "so that he gets nothing by his injustice *but the scandal of it*" [italics mine].

If we divide the nineteenth-century South into two periods— the antebellum and the postbellum—we find that the best book in each period to illustrate the Tidewater tradition is still, appropriately enough, a product of Virginia: I refer to John Pendleton Kennedy's *Swallow Barn* (1832) and Thomas Nelson Page's *In Ole Virginia* (1884).

Kennedy was a Baltimorean, but his mother's family were Virginians, and Kennedy, like his narrator Mark Littleton, was a welcome guest in the Old Dominion. In writing *Swallow Barn*, the author therefore enjoyed the double advantage of detachment and sympathy. His picture is faithfully drawn. Kennedy is less witty than Byrd; his closest literary affinity seems to have been with Irving. But (like Irving) he is a good observer, he has a sense of humor, and he can be, and often is, amusing.

"Swallow Barn," he says, "is an aristocratic old edifice which sits, like a brooding hen, on the Southern bank of the James River." It gives "the idea of comfort." [9] Frank Meriwether, "the master of this lordly domain," is "a very model of landed gentleman." He is most hospitable: "A guest is one of his daily

9. *Swallow Barn*, rev. ed. (New York: Hurd and Houghton, 1866), pp. 27, 28.

wants." [10] He is a good citizen and attends to business, but contrary to the expectation and desire of his friends, "he has never set up for Congress." [11] "Meriwether is not much of a traveller. He has never been in New England, and very seldom beyond the confines of Virginia. He makes now and then a winter excursion to Richmond, which he considers the center of civilization" [12] (matching Dr. Holmes's view of Boston as the hub of the solar system). He is a Jeffersonian Agrarian, thinking "lightly of the mercantile interest," and believing that those who live in large cities are "hollow-hearted and insincere." [13] He opposed the re-election of John Quincy Adams to the Presidency in 1829, and voted for Andrew Jackson, without, I imagine, being an ardent Jacksonian. "He piques himself upon being a high churchman, but is not the most diligent frequenter of places of worship, and very seldom permits himself to get into a dispute upon points of faith." "He is somewhat distinguished as a breeder of blooded horses." [14] These are some of the main points in Kennedy's "character" of the Virginia planter of the 1830s.

There is less elegance at Swallow Barn than at Westover, a hundred years earlier. The life seems homespun in comparison. A self-contained provincialism has taken the place of the cosmopolitanism of Byrd, who was as much at home in London Town as in Williamsburg. There is an even greater emphasis on neighborliness and family life: Swallow Barn fairly swarms with relatives and neighbors. There are dinner parties, and the drinking of toasts. There is still the practice of polite learning: interlocutors quote Virgil and Horace. Negro slavery has become a controversial question by 1832 (though not so much so as it was soon to become, after the Abolitionists took over), and

10. *Ibid.*, pp. 31, 33.
11. *Ibid.*, p. 33.
12. *Ibid.*, p. 34.
13. *Ibid.*, p. 35.
14. *Ibid.*, p. 36.

Kennedy's book contains a statement on the subject which seems more judicious than propagandistic. "No tribe of people," says Mark Littleton, "have ever passed from barbarism to civilization whose middle stage of progress has been more secure from harm, more genial to their character, or better supplied with mild and beneficent guardianship, adapted to the actual state of their intellectual feebleness, than the Negroes of Swallow Barn." [15] We recall that Byrd spoke of the "scandal" attached to mis-treatment of Negroes in the Tidewater of his time, and it is interesting to see the same view expressed a hundred years later in Kennedy's book: "Public opinion . . . is stronger than law," Meriwether declares, "and no man can hold up his head in this community who is chargeable with mal-treatment of his slaves." [16] As if to prove the point, one of the more prominent characters in *Swallow Barn* is Old Carey, the much-indulged, crotchety, loyal family retainer, whose progeny in Southern fiction was to be legion.

If *Swallow Barn* was realistic and objective, though sympa-thetic with the life described, *In Ole Virginia* was romantic and propagandistic. The war had come between, and Thomas Nelson Page wrote out of a profound nostalgia for the antebellum days. "Dem wuz good ole times, marster—de bes' Sam ever see! Dey wuz, in fac!" [17] Page's hero, Marse Chan, is a paragon of all the virtues: "de peartes scholar ole Mr. Hall hed," and at the same time, "de head in all debilment dat went on." [18] He is the soul of chivalry, fighting for his lady fair and for his father's good name. There is just one false touch in the portrait of this manly young knight, namely, his statement to the heroine that he has kept himself "pure" for her sake. There is nothing objectionable in the "purity," but it is the kind of statement which a young man doesn't ordinarily make to a young woman, for fear (if for

15. *Ibid.*, p. 453.
16. *Ibid.*, p. 457.
17. *In Ole Virginia* (New York: Charles Scribner's Sons, 1926), p. 10.
18. *Ibid.*, p. 8.

no other reason) that she may think the less of his manhood. Page knew this, of course, as does every man, but he was willing to sacrifice verisimilitude to propaganda, willing to go to this extreme length in an attempt (useless though it was) to refute the stock accusation of miscegenation.

The narrator is the faithful darkey, Sam, Marse Chan's "body-servant." I am not at all disposed to deprecate Carey, Sam, and the others. The relationship which they represent would be anachronistic today, but it was a lovely one in its time and place. It was based upon personal loyalty, and the loyalty was reciprocal. Mutuality and irrevocableness (that is, permanence) are the important characteristics. Nothing of the sort exists in the modern world, such relationships having long ago been superseded by what Carlyle, long ago, called the "cash-nexus."

I am not at all disposed, either, to deprecate chivalry. I am not willing to dismiss the literature of chivalry as nonsense merely because the age of chivalry is gone, and that of sophists, economists, and calculators has succeeded. And still less am I disposed to deprecate a sense of honor. Allen Tate raised the question some years ago as to whether there is any such thing in the modern world as a sense of honor. It is a serious question.

The literary work of the modern period which best embodies the Tidewater tradition is Stark Young's *So Red the Rose* (1934). It would be interesting to examine the relation of this work to the earlier works which I have been discussing. A few observations must suffice here. We note the presence of wit, Augustan wit, a quality conspicuous in Byrd, but not much emphasized in Kennedy and absent from Page, where the Tidewater tradition is thoroughly sentimentalized. The remark, for example, in *So Red the Rose*, by Cynthia Eppes, a cousin from New Orleans, "I get my hats and my absolutions in Paris," [19] recalls the wit of *The Rape of the Lock*: "Dost sometimes counsel take and sometimes tea"; "Or stain her honour, or her new

19. *So Red the Rose*, with an Introduction by Donald Davidson. Modern Standard Authors Edition (New York: Charles Scribner's Sons, 1953), p. 161.

brocade." [20] The recovery of wit was a valuable recovery. Page's sentimentality was a debasing of the tradition. The true aristocrats were not sentimentalists.

The prominence given to family ties, neighborliness, community life recalls *Swallow Barn*. The Bedfords and the Mc-Gehees resemble in their neighborly rivalry (though "rivalry" may be too strong a word—there is no envy between them) the Meriwethers and the Traceys of Swallow Barn. Nearly everybody is somebody's cousin. Young Duncan Bedford has some of Marse Chan's chivalry, and William Veal, the family butler at Montrose, resembles Marse Chan's Sam. Agnes McGehee, who journeyed in a wagon to the battlefield of Shiloh, accompanied only by William Veal, to recover and bring home the body of her dead son, recalls in her heroic, quiet firmness the poised Mrs. Fleming of Byrd's narrative; the unobtrusive, efficient mistress of Swallow Barn, Lucy Meriwether; and the heroine, though sentimentalized, of Page's story. The Southern gentlewoman was not a clinging vine, a weak sister. On the contrary.

Hugh McGehee, who regards the changing world with a philosophic mind (he had been opposed to secession), is an ampler and wiser Frank Meriwether. "The way I've been obliged to see it is this," he says to his son: "Our ideas and instincts work upon our memory of these people who have lived before us, and so they take on some clarity of outline. It's not to our credit to think we began today, and it's not to our glory to think we end today. All through time, we keep coming in to the shore like waves—like waves. You stick to your blood, son; there's a certain fierceness in blood that can bind you up with a long community of life." "And think with passion," he added: "it's the only kind of thought that's worth anything." [21] "In Hugh McGehee," says the book's best interpreter, Donald Davidson, "Southern society has produced a fine example of the unified

20. III. 8; II. 107.
21. *So Red the Rose*, pp. 150–151.

personality, in tune with its environment, while also commanding it." [22] Davidson comments also on the oral quality in *So
Red the Rose.* "The tones of the speaking voice," he says, "ring
throughout the book as in few other novels." Young has caught,
he thinks, "the characteristic tone of Southern speech, its variation in pitch, its rhythms, as well as the idioms, the vocabulary,
the occasional archaisms and small oddities of pronunciation." [23]
The naturalness, the leisureliness and desultoriness of good talk
are found not only in Young's novel, but also in the works
(though perhaps to a less degree) which I have taken to be the
principal antecedents of *So Red the Rose.* There is also, in these
works, an anecdotal quality, which reflects the Southern habit
of telling stories—stories which, for the most part, have come
out of the community life.

We must look now at the other tradition—the tradition of
the Frontier.

The Frontier referred to is, first of all, that of the Old
Southwest, which comprised the states now known as the South,
if we exclude Virginia and the Carolinas. The literature which
flourished in this region between 1830 and the Civil War is the
opposite, in most respects, of the literature which we have been
considering. Instead of courtliness, sophistication, restraint, there
is uninhibited nature. Instead of chivalry, gallantry, polite learning, there is rough-and-tumble. Instead of wit, there is slapstick.
The region in this period specialized in the tall tale. The liveliest
and most amusing of the frontier humorists is George Washington Harris, author of *Sut Lovingood Yarns,* published in 1867.

The 1867 edition is long since out of print and now difficult
to come by. A new edition has been recently published, but the
editor committed the unpardonable error of revising the language and orthography. The intention was to make the tales
more intelligible to the general reader. The original work *is*

22. *Ibid.,* pp. xix-xx.
23. *Ibid.,* p. xxix.

difficult for many educated Northerners, but the difficulty is not insuperable (not greater, for example, than in Chaucer), and to revise a Sut Lovingood tale is to destroy it.

On the occasion of the appearance of the "revised" edition, Mr. Edmund Wilson wrote a long article in the *New Yorker* on the Sut Lovingood yarns in which he deals so harshly with his subject that one suspects he does not rightly understand what is going on. The work is, he says, "by far the most repellent book of any real merit in American literature." He objects to the "crude and brutal humor." Sut, he says, "avenges his inferiority by tormenting other people; his impulse is avowedly sadistic." [24] He quotes as an example of the sadism the following statement by Sut about "universal onregenerit human nater":

Ef enything happens to some feller, I don't keer ef he's yure bes' frien, an I don't keer how sorry yu is fur him, thar's a streak ove satisfackshun 'bout like a sowin thread a-runnin all thru yer sorrer. Yu may be shamed ov hit, but durn me ef hit aint thar.[25]

Can it be that Mr. Wilson is so unaware of "universal onregenerit human nater"—possesses indeed so little of it himself— that this is a shockingly new thought to him? If so, he needs a course in original sin, and I suggest that he read, as a starter, Robert Penn Warren's poem entitled "Original Sin: A Short Story" where he will find the accusing line: "You hear of the deaths of friends with sly pleasure." [26]

The truth is that the Lovingood yarns are rowdy slapstick fun, the most hilarious, uninhibited compositions in American literature, and the broadest humor written in nineteenth-century America; and if time permitted I would prove it to you by reading one—I should like nothing better. They were not printed in the *Atlantic Monthly*, but in a sub-literary journal, the *Spirit of*

24. " 'Poisoned,' " *The New Yorker*, XXXI (May 7, 1955), 150.
25. *Ibid.*, p. 151.
26. *Selected Poems 1923–1943* (New York: Harcourt, Brace and Company, 1944), p. 26.

the Times (published in New York), whose importance has only recently been discovered by the historians. The fun is often rough, but we read these yarns, if we read them correctly, with the willing suspension of the sentimental-humanitarian attitude, which is as inappropriate here as a Puritan-moralistic attitude toward a comedy by Congreve or Noel Coward. As for sadism and taking pleasure in spoiling other people's fun, Sut is himself as often as not the butt. Many of the funniest things, moreover, do not involve physical pain at all. "Rare Ripe Garden Seed" might easily be mistaken for a Chaucerian fabliau, and the discourse on the "points" of young widows is hardly surpassed anywhere for its appreciation of sexual pleasures.

Mr. Wilson's crowning error is the statement that Sut is a direct ancestor of Flem Snopes. Faulkner, as I shall suggest presently, does owe a good deal to Harris, but Sut and Flem are as unlike as two human temperaments can very well be. Did Flem Snopes ever go to a party, get drunk, spark the girls? Flem never had any good healthy fun in his life—he was mercenary, calculating, and impotent. Sut, on the other hand— indiscreet, fun-loving, practical joker extraordinary—wasn't exactly the kind to get himself elected president of a bank.

Bernard DeVoto pointed out twenty-five years ago, in his *Mark Twain's America,* Mark Twain's debt to the Old Southwest humorists. Sut belonged in the East Tennessee mountains, in the neighborhood where Mark Twain's parents lived before they moved to Missouri. Mark Twain was almost certainly *conceived* in Sut's neighborhood, and if he had been born there and had not gone East and come under the dispiriting influence of Livy, Howells, and the Reverend Mr. Twitchell, he might have become the great Rabelaisian author whom Van Wyck Brooks, with a good deal of insight, thought him capable of being.

One must recognize the bearing of Southern topography on these matters, and the age-old distinction between the highlands and the lowlands: between the Shenandoah and the Tidewater, the up-country and the low-country in South Carolina, the

Kentucky mountains and the Blue Grass, East Tennessee and Middle Tennessee. The Southern Appalachians—comprising Eastern Kentucky, East Tennessee, and Western North Carolina —are a homogeneous region—and a kind of modern Frontier. This region was Union in sympathies during the Civil War, and is still Republican. There were no plantations in these mountains and few slaves. The Clemenses had one Negro slave, a girl, who accompanied the family to Missouri, and today there are in this region comparatively few Negroes. The mountain people are, or have been, less restrained than their neighbors in the lowlands. They are, or have been, characterized by a special kind of wildness, and it is worth noting in this connection that Tom Wolfe's Altamont is just over the range from the Sut Lovingood country. Wolfe, of course, attended Chapel Hill, studied drama in Professor George Pierce Baker's 47 Workshop at Harvard, taught English in N.Y.U., Washington Square, lived in Brooklyn, read Shelley and Walt Whitman, and came under other "corrupting" influences, but he was a Southern mountaineer, and the mountain wildness is the most autochthonous fact about him. There is a particularly interesting passage in *Of Time and the River*, where Eugene and his cronies go for an automobile ride, drinking as they ride, careering from the hills to the plains, and landing in jail after a wildly drunken time of it. The passage, except for the somewhat Shelleyan treatment of landscape, recalls Lovingood.

It must have been, in part at least, Faulkner's admiration for the mountain wildness which led him to rank Wolfe first among the American novelists of the twentieth century (placing himself second). For this wildness—whether of the mountains or the plains—is an important part of Faulkner's inheritance, and it comes out in some of his best writing. Perhaps the best example is the story "Spotted Horses" (later incorporated in *The Hamlet*). Complete pandemonium can be carried no further than in Faulkner's account of what happens after the Texas ponies (the liveliest ever created by God or man) break out of the corral, and run pell-mell down the country roads, upsetting many a cart, wagon, and surrey, and trampling their occupants under foot. For a sheer all-hell-broke-loose narrative, it has no equal unless in one of Sut Lovingood's farmyard escapades. Faulkner's yarn, like many of Sut's, is hilariously funny, despite the fact that several people get hurt, and I don't quite see how Mr. Wilson can escape his old difficulty here. But the difficulty, in fact, is quite common. Non-Southerners often react to the Southern wildness in the wrong way.

If I may be permitted the pedantry of a note on Southern folklore in general, and in particular the special kinship of Faulkner and Wolfe, I should like to quote from each author (from *Of Time and the River,* and from *Sartoris*) a description of the proper way to drink moonshine out of a jug. It is an important subject, and the correct technique is a matter of importance. Each author is obviously proud of this bit of connoisseurship. Wolfe says: "They hooked their thumbs into the handle of the jug, and brought the stuff across their shoulders with a free-hand motion, they let the wide neck pour into their tilted throats with a fat thick gurgle. . . ." [27] Faulkner says: "Bayard was already drinking, with the jug tilted across his horizontal forearm and the mouth held to his lips by the same hand, as it should be done." [28] The methods are not quite identical, but basically similar. An allowance can be made for a small variation between North Carolina and Mississippi. (Young Sartoris, at the time, is hobnobbing with the neighboring farm boys, and one of them is saying to another, "I knowed he was all right.") In each case, it is a ritual—and not being familiar with it marks one as lacking the proper initiation into good Frontier society.

We have been considering two traditions in the literature of the South—the Tidewater and the Frontier—and we have seen that they have flourished side by side, and somewhat separate from each other. There is just one more point which I wish to

27. *Of Time and the River* (New York: Charles Scribner's Sons, 1935), pp. 364–365.
28. *Sartoris* (New York: Harcourt, Brace and Company, 1929), p. 139.

suggest: it is that the two traditions are united in the works of the writer who, all agree, is the greatest in the South today, and possibly this is one important reason why he *is* the greatest. For like Shakespeare, Faulkner embraces the high and the low, the aristocratic and the plebeian, the courtly and the uncouth, the educated and the illiterate, the literary and the vernacular, the traditional and the modern. I have already glanced at his affinity with the Frontier tradition. His sympathetic interest, on the other hand, in the Sartorises, the Compsons, and other aristocrats (Faulkner's treatment of these people can rise to the high-tragic mode) allies him with the Tidewater. It is this comprehensiveness, among other things, which sets Faulkner apart from his contemporaries in the South, though I should add that Robert Penn Warren has some of this same comprehensiveness.

I hope these remarks have at least suggested a genetic relationship (I believe not much appreciated) between the new literature of the South and the old. However important various influences from outside the South may have been in the present century (and it has not been my intention to deal with these), modern Southern literature—both Tidewater and Frontier—has had a long background in Southern writing.

THE RELATION BETWEEN
FUGITIVES AND AGRARIANS

I WANT to say a word about the constitution of the
English Department at Vanderbilt at the time of Fugitive
beginnings. Between 1922 and 1925, when the Fugitives were
holding their meetings, where the members, as Warren said,
"were tough on each other critically," the Department (a small
one) consisted of three major professors: Edwin Mims, Walter
Clyde Curry, and John Crowe Ransom. The interesting thing
about this situation is that each man stood autonomously for
something quite different from what either of the others stood
for. Mims, a post-Victorian, was an appreciator, an inspirational
oral interpreter of the literature of the nineteenth century,
especially the poetry. He was also a progressive Southerner (consistently enough, since belief in "progress" was one of the basic
tenets of the nineteenth century) who supported the "New
South" movement, which was based upon the view that the
South should get into economic and social step with the North.
Curry was the new-type graduate school scholar, and a very
good one. His *Chaucer and the Mediaeval Sciences*, published in
1926, is among the half-dozen most durable scholarly works in
its field. And Ransom, of course, was the poet. It is interesting,
and I think unique at that time, and very much to the credit of
Mims, the department head, that he advanced Curry and
Ransom, *pari passu*, through the various grades; that is, he allowed equal "credit" for a scholarly article in *PMLA*, and a
poem, for "The Horoscope of the Wife of Bath" and "Antique
Harvesters." This was indeed a remarkable situation at a time
when George Lyman Kittredge dominated practically every
English department in the country. That domination, incidental-

ly, may very well explain the absence of literary creativeness on so many college campuses. The so-called great departments simply were not interested in that sort of thing. My point is that the students at Vanderbilt were exposed *equally* to three stimuli, not just one: the stimulus of the romantic nineteenth-century school, the stimulus of modern scholarship, and the stimulus of literary creation (and of the new criticism). The first had become a little old-fashioned by 1925; the second was strictly *au courant*; the third was, or proved to be, the wave of the future. If this situation, with its tri-partite balance, existed in any other English department of the 1920s, I have yet to hear of it.

From what did the Fugitives flee? There are a good many answers to that question. Like their contemporaries elsewhere, of course, they reacted against the nineteenth century: against romanticism, progressivism, and sentimentalism. So did Eliot. But the Fugitives had at least this advantage over Eliot: of the three *isms*, the greatest irritant of all—sentimentalism—was probably more prominent in their immediate environment than in his. And that is why, I suppose, they declared at the very outset: "The Fugitives flee from nothing faster than from the high-caste Brahmins of the Old South," [1] with whom they identified a particularly noxious kind of sentimentalism, the moonlight and magnolia of a Thomas Nelson Page. (*So Red the Rose*, by Stark Young, whom the Nashville writers greatly admire, does not belong to the literature of sentimentalism, needless to say.) Fugitive poetry was for the most part intellectual poetry; it employed wit and irony; it partook of the world literary movement to a degree that had scarcely been true of Southern writing for a century.

A question which provoked a particularly interesting discussion at the Fugitive reunion was the connection, if any, between the Fugitive and Agrarian movements. Merrill Moore, who was not an Agrarian, insisted upon the complete separateness of the

1. *The Fugitive*, I (April 1922), 1.

two, but the weight of opinion was heavily in support of the view that there was a connection, and an important one. The problem became how to define the connection.

It seems that the Fugitives felt by 1925 that they had written themselves out as poets for the time being, or at least had utilized to the fullest, for the time being, the benefits of close mutual criticism. And yet there was among them the feeling that there were other fields to conquer. Their poetry has been a peculiarly autochthonous product. It had presupposed, without their being conscious of the fact, Southern traditions, manners, viewpoints. It seems generally agreed that the Dayton Trial in 1925 converted them from unconscious to conscious Southerners. Louise Cowan, the chief scholarly authority on the Nashville writers, says: "As in all cultural crises, the turmoil issuing from the trial brought into the foreground ideas and attitudes that had been taken for granted in the past, but were now no longer generally accepted. An event which caused many intelligent Southerners to reject their native land propelled the Fugitive poets into a careful study of Southern history. . . . From an understanding of the deeply religious structure of life in the Tennessee hills, a structure which had its expression in Fundamentalism, grew the conviction which led these poets to their first overt defense of the South." [2]

It was a laughable and ridiculous thing to the Northern and Western observer, no doubt, when Tennessee in the 1920s passed a law against the teaching of evolution in the public schools, but it showed at least this, which seems to me rather commendable, namely, that the Tennesseans were not going to give up their religion without a struggle. There used to be a good deal of talk about Moses *versus* Darwin, and I can remember when learned men from the University of Chicago used to come down to

2. "The Fugitive Poets in Relation to the South" in "The Southern Literary Renascence: A Symposium," *Shenandoah*, VI (Summer 1955), 6. See also *The Fugitive Group* (Baton Rouge: Louisiana State University Press, 1959), pp. 208, 240. [R. S.]

Nashville and give us scolding lectures on the superiority of Darwin over Moses. If I may speak for myself (I was not a member of the Fugitive-Agrarian group, but I find myself in sympathy with their attitudes) today, if absolutely forced to choose, I'm not so sure I wouldn't string along with Moses. I should hate to give up the burning bush, the gushing of the water from the rock, the dividing of the Red Sea, the thunder on Mt. Sinai, the vision of the Promised Land, and all the rest of this wonderful Myth, and it may very well be that the Pentateuch adds up to more "truth" (vague, slippery word) than the writings of Darwin, as important as they doubtless are in the history of biological science. For Myth is truer than Fact.

Actually, of course, there was, and is, no conflict between Moses and Darwin, the literal scientific truth of Darwin being on one plane, and the symbolic religious truth of Moses being on quite another, and higher, plane. But the issue was falsely presented in 1925 at Dayton, where Dayton and Tennessee and the world-at-large were told, by the Darrows as well as the Bryans, that *a choice had to be made!* An unwillingness, under such circumstances, to reject Moses seems to me quite understandable —he *was* a little better known to most of us. At least, that is the way some Southerners used to think about it. And some such attitude as this may have been in the background of the great manifesto, *I'll Take My Stand*.

Donald Davidson has said of the Southern reaction to the Dayton Trial: it was "a fierce clinging to poetic supernaturalism against the encroachments of cold logic." [3] And Andrew Nelson Lytle has summed up the matter as follows: "The issue at the Dayton trial was between the old god and the new, the supernatural and the natural, the irreducible mystery and matter conquered and controlled by science." [4] What the whole business

3. "The Artist as Southerner," *Saturday Review of Literature*, II (May 15, 1926), 783.
4. "A Summing Up" in "The Southern Literary Renascence: A Symposium," p. 30.

seems to have amounted to is that the Tennesseans in 1925 were not quite ready to make a religion of science.

I'll Take My Stand was not an economic blueprint, which many of its critics have mistaken it for, but a philosophy of a way of life. It recalls in some respects Thoreau's *Walden*. The South was about as far along industrially in 1930 as New England had been in 1854, the date of Thoreau's book. And if *Walden* was the chief criticism of industrial America written in the nineteenth century, *I'll Take My Stand* is the chief criticism of the same subject to appear in this century (the Southerners did not grapple with the problem until it arrived at their own doorstep). It is difficult to see how one can praise one book and dispraise the other, they have so much virtue in common. The fame of *Walden* was almost a century in coming (it dates from the 1930s), and oddly enough, while *Walden* was enjoying its first considerable fame, *I'll Take My Stand* was being pretty roundly damned both at home and abroad. Progressive Southerners (the "New South" men) accused the authors of wanting to turn back the clock of progress, and Northerners called the authors by such pejoratives as "aristocrats," "neo-Confederates," and the like, all of which were wide of the mark.

There are signs today of a fresh recognition of the importance of *I'll Take My Stand* (it has been recently reprinted), and I have noticed these indications particularly in New England. The book is indeed probably more read today in New England than in the South. Well, the economy of New England is, I believe, what the economists call "mature," while the South's is still in the expanding phase, which means that most Southerners are not yet in the proper frame of mind to appreciate *I'll Take My Stand*, just as most New Englanders, when New England was in *its* expanding phase, were not in the proper frame of mind to appreciate *Walden*. (I don't think there is a very large number of people anywhere in this country, now, capable of appreciating either *I'll Take My Stand* or *Walden*. Our belief in progress through improved machinery has become too much of a national religion, now, for that.)

Frank Owsley, the Southern historian, and one of the contributors to *I'll Take My Stand,* said at the reunion meeting that the symposium grew out of the feeling shared by the group

that the people of America were losing the basic values of civilization, that we were going as a nation into materialism, that money value had become the real basic value, that the sense of community was disappearing, that the common courtesies of life were disappearing. . . . [*I'll Take My Stand*] was a revolt against something and a revolt for something. . . . And this was, in a way, not just a defense; if it was, it was one of Robert E. Lee's defenses—it was an offensive defense. We became, I think, in our writings very deliberately provocative. . . . The turn to the Old South was simply the seeking of . . . an example in which at least many of these qualities that we thought were the basic qualities of civilization were embodied. We advocated . . . an agrarian way of life as at least being the only example in history where civilization had developed. And also a belief that the high-powered modern industrialization and materialism would either develop or maintain a civilization very long. . . . [*I'll Take My Stand*] was a philosophy, not an economy.[5]

Owsley thought the "Agrarian" tag was probably unfortunate, because, he said, "everybody thought we ought to go out and plow." [6] Other members of the group, it transpired in the reunion discussion, had questioned the rightness of "Agrarian." Tate had wanted, at one time, to call the movement, or philosophy, "religious humanism." Warren had suggested, at one time, the title "Tracts Against Communism." Ransom held that "the sort of economy we represented and the view of the Republic we represented was decidedly the Jeffersonian." [7] There are interesting shades of opinion here, but clearly a broad base of agreement.

5. *Fugitives' Reunion,* ed. by Rob Roy Purdy (Nashville: Vanderbilt University Press, 1959), pp. 204, 205, and 206.
6. *Ibid.,* p. 206.
7. *Ibid.,* p. 207.

Owsley was one of the chief driving forces (Davidson, of course, was another) behind *I'll Take My Stand,* and enough has been said to show the direction which his influence took. The so-called Agrarians had no notion of reviving the Confederacy. These men were, and are, about the hardest-headed realists in modern America; they are closer to bedrock fact than any writers I know. The attachment to them of the epithet "Fascist" by Robert Gorham Davis and others, one must charitably pass over with Dr. Johnson's remark, "Ignorance, sheer ignorance" —ignorance (so often encountered in the North) of these men and their world.

The Agrarians—it seems we must continue to call them by that name—were, and are, interested in values, and they are making converts to those values every day. They saw, or thought they saw, these values embodied in the agrarian South, but the agrarian South was not an end but an illustration and symbol of values which they regarded as important: courtesy, neighborliness, a sense of honor, a public spirit, a sense of personal responsibility, leisure for conversation, a recognition of the need for treating people as people and not as things. Being realists, they were willing to accept and use the products of modern technology, but they did not believe—and this is the crucial point—they knew better than to believe that people will be made better by these products, will forsooth be saved by them. They flatly rejected, in short, the modern American gospel of salvation through technology.

I will conclude with an interesting comment made by Ransom at the Fugitives' reunion: "We've got now the most exquisite problems that rest on any country that's at peace. And I could wish that we had great literary men engaging in it. It might be the difference between making a civilization and just going along with a shabby culture. I wish we could now start all over." [8]

8. *Ibid.,* p. 60.

DONALD DAVIDSON

D ONALD D AVIDSON is best known for his social criticism, which is a trenchant criticism of the modern notion of industrial "progress," the most trenchant and fearless we have had since Thoreau. For Thoreau, too, was skeptical of industrial progress. "Where is this division of labour to end?" [1] he cried out in *Walden*. He was regarded as an eccentric, a crank, in the New England of his time, that region being then full of industry and progress. A hundred years later, he is a diagnostician and prophet, the region's economy having changed meanwhile from "young" to "mature." By the same token, Davidson has been regarded as a bit "out of step" by many Southerners since the South has begun to hum industrially. He is today, I imagine, more widely and sympathetically read in New England than in his native South. But the whirligig of Time will continue to bring in his revenges.

Davidson was one of the chief figures in the neo-Agrarian movement which dates from the publication in 1930 of *I'll Take My Stand* by Twelve Southerners. In the chapter which he contributed to that volume, "A Mirror for Artists," he regarded industrialism as the foe of art. "The making of an industrialized society," he said:

will extinguish the meaning of the arts, as humanity has known them in the past, by changing the conditions of life that has given art a meaning. For they have been produced in societies which were for the most part stable, religious, and agrarian; where the goodness of life was measured by a scale of values having little to do with the material

1. *Walden and Civil Disobedience*, ed. by Sherman Paul. Riverside Edition (Boston: Houghton Mifflin Company, 1957), p. 31.

values of industrialism; where men were never too far removed from nature to forget that the chief subject of art, in the final sense, is nature.[2]

"The kind of leisure provided by industrialism," he said, "is a dubious benefit." "Mass-production, if applied to the arts," he maintained, "must invariably sacrifice quality to quantity." He saw, with industrial progress, "a gradual corruption of integrity and good taste." [3]

In 1952, in response to a questionnaire sent by the *Shenandoah* magazine to the contributors to *I'll Take My Stand*, Davidson reiterated his indictment of industrialism.

Industrialism has increased its sway. . . . It has provided more and better automobiles, airplanes, refrigerators, and weapons of war—including the atomic bomb. And it has also become a party to the infliction of war, death, and destruction on an unprecedented scale. It has wasted our resources to the point of danger. It has degraded society, perverted education, and undermined religion. It has invaded, abridged, and all but destroyed our constitutional liberties, and now threatens to convert our government into a totalitarian regime. It has spread confusion and suspicion; it has begotten corruption and treason; it has reduced millions to a state of groveling servility and fear.[4]

The only qualifying criticism of *I'll Take My Stand* which Davidson would make twenty-two years later was that "the term 'agrarian' was too narrow a description of the society that the 'Agrarians' were advocating." "The emphasis," he said, "should have been put, more firmly, upon religion." [5] The question came up during the Fugitives' reunion, held at Vanderbilt in May 1956. There seemed to be general agreement as to the inadequacy of the "agrarian" tag. As Frank Owsley put it,

2. *I'll Take My Stand* (New York: Harper and Brothers, 1962), p. 29.
3. *Ibid.*, pp. 34, 35, 36.
4. "A Symposium: The Agrarians Today," *Shenandoah*, III (Summer 1952), pp. 17–18.
5. *Ibid.*, p. 19.

"Everybody thought we ought to go out and plow." [6] (The same sort of symbolic misreading occurred in Thoreau's case when genteel readers objected to living in a cabin with only a pumpkin to sit on.) Reviewing the matter once more, in the Lamar Lectures in 1957, Davidson said, "I believe we would now be justified in defining the so-called Agrarian Movement not only in terms of its first gropings and tentative beginning, but also in terms of its ultimate broader direction and general fruitfulness of application. For brevity, I might call it the cause of civilized society, as we have known it in the Western World, against the new barbarism of science and technology controlled and directed by the modern power state." [7]

Davidson said in the *Shenandoah,* "There can hardly be such a thing as a 'society,' in any true sense, without religion as the all-pervasive arbiter of value." [8] And in religion, he prefers, I think, the Christian salvational religion—not the social gospel, which is secondary and organizational, and still less the "religion of science." Granted that the machine is here to stay (or until total destruction, which appears to be something more than a possibility), does it follow that one should fall down and worship it? Our *attitude* toward the machine is perhaps the crux of the whole matter. Henry Adams was tempted to pray to the Dynamo. The mass of lesser men in our time have succumbed to that temptation, indeed looking to the Dynamo and its surrogates for salvation.

A special objection by Davidson to industrialism is that its spread tends to make the whole country uniform, whereas he cherishes the local peculiarities. He argues that these persist hardily, despite the strong trend to national uniformity. He insists upon the necessity of our "recognizing the principle of

6. *Fugitives' Reunion,* ed. by Rob Roy Purdy (Nashville: Vanderbilt University Press, 1959), p. 206.

7. *Southern Writers in the Modern World* (Athens: University of Georgia Press, 1958), p. 45.

8. "The Agrarians Today," p. 20.

diversity in American life," and goes on (in his essay "Still Rebels, Still Yankees") to give two illustrations of diversity—Brother Jonathan of Vermont and Cousin Roderick of Georgia. Both portraits are drawn from life (the author has lived in both communities), and engagingly drawn. They contain just the right balance between the classic and the romantic, the general and the particular, the representative and the idiosyncratic. Although it must be confessed that Davidson seems a little more at home in Georgia (despite many summers' residence in Vermont), both portraits are sympathetic, and almost equally so. The author's thesis is simply that "the unity of America must rest, first of all, on a decent respect for sectional differences." [9]

The good writer must give to airy nothing a local habitation and a name. He cannot escape the urgency of place; if he does, he vanishes in sheer vapidity. In his essay "Why the Modern South Has a Great Literature," Davidson points out the importance to a writer like Faulkner or Warren of the Southern inheritance, of places as places, people as people.

Thus it is that in the moment of self-consciousness the Southern writer is able to bring to bear, not only his personal view, but also the total metaphysic of his society. He is therefore unlikely to indulge in the exaggerations and oversimplifications that are the mark of a divided sensibility. For him the people in the bend of the creek are not only sharecroppers representing a certain economic function. They are complete persons with significant personal histories. In fact, they are Joe and Emma, who used to work on old man Brown's place, but left him for reasons well known. The banker is not merely a banker. He is Mr. Jim, whose wife's mother was somebody's grandmother's double first cousin.[10]

And the author goes on to speculate on the ways *All the King's Men* would be different if it had been written by, say, Sinclair Lewis. Confidence in one's inheritance, belief in one's instinctive

9. *Still Rebels, Still Yankees and Other Essays* (Baton Rouge: Louisiana State University Press, 1957), pp. 233, 236.

10. *Ibid.*, p. 177.

knowledge ("knowledge carried to the heart," Davidson says, quoting Tate's *Ode to the Confederate Dead*), faithfulness to one's artistic vision—these are the qualities which distinguish the good writers of the modern South, the author believes—and indeed, one could add, good writers of any time, any place.

The love of old places, old customs, old histories is found everywhere in Davidson's writings (recalling Thoreau's love of the local histories of eastern Massachusetts). Take the meticulous, detailed reconstruction of the history of the Tennessee Valley (his unfriendliness to TVA was owing to the sacrifice by inundation of hundreds of homesteads and thousands of acres of rich bottomland—it *was* quite a sacrifice!—to the erection of a vast electric power plant). Or take this account of such a rural homestead in "The Two Old Wests" as Davidson himself may have known as a boy in Lincoln County, Middle Tennessee.

Let there be a fence around the grove, with a gate that opens upon a boxwood walk leading to a high-columned porch. And between fence and road let there be a pasture for the horses, with a creek flowing in it, and limestone outcroppings, and iron-weed scattered about (who cares?) and blackberries in the fence corners. Let there be fields of corn to left and right, and beyond them a high hill, well forested, a range for turkeys only half tame, and for 'possum and 'coon that are wholly wild.[11]

Or take the folk operetta *Singin' Billy* (Davidson wrote the words, Charles Bryan the music), which has an authenticity and a poignance lacking in most attempts of this kind. Or take his moving account of the white spirituals in "The Sacred Harp in the Land of Eden." From scenes like these, he seems to say, our country's grandeur springs.

Davidson, obviously, is a traditionalist, and the oldest literary tradition, he emphasizes, is the oral: the ancient epics were recited for many generations before they were written down;

11. *Attack on Leviathan* (Chapel Hill: University of North Carolina Press, 1938), p. 179.

Shakespeare's plays were composed to be spoken. "The admission of modern poetry to the textbooks of school and college classes," he says in "Poetry as Tradition," "may be in a sense as much an entombment as a triumph. This is for poetry a kind of death-in-life, to exist only on the printed page, not on the lips of men, not carried by their voices, and therefore almost never in their memories, rarely in their hearts." [12] Poetry is doomed to ultimate extinction, he believes, unless a way is found to restore something of its former oral character. "That is a problem for our civilization," he adds, "no less than for our poetry. . . . No civilization of the past has ever lived without poetry, and ours can hardly be an exception." [13]

Davidson is enamored of ballads (the South has been especially rich in this field), and his special understanding of balladry and folklore enables him to contribute important new insights. In his essay, "The Traditional Basis of Thomas Hardy's Fiction," for example, the author focuses attention on the folk element; seen from this viewpoint, Hardy was a ballad maker turned novelist, and it is just as much beside the point to call a Hardy novel "pessimistic" as it would be to apply that adjective to "Edward" or "Johnny Armstrong." In the literary essays in *Still Rebels, Still Yankees and Other Essays*, the author is always looking closely at backgrounds, traditions, the inherited ways of the folk. He likes "the nuances of tone" in Stark Young's *So Red the Rose* and "the unified personality" [14] of Hugh McGehee, contrasting with the modern fragmented world, where men are incomplete with the terrible division of their age. He discounts the blueprints of the sociologists, which can't explain Faulkner, or Shakespeare either—for both, he reminds us, were country boys from "backward" regions, and both belong among "the world's incomparable originals." [15]

12. *Still Rebels*, p. 20.
13. *Ibid.*, p. 22.
14. "Theme and Method in *So Red the Rose*," *Still Rebels*, pp. 92, 100.
15. *Still Rebels*, p. 174.

Davidson's prose, as searching as it is, should not be allowed to obscure his verse. For it was as a poet that he began, and it may very well be (as so often happens to a good poet) that he will be longest remembered for his verse—poetry, generally speaking, being literature's immortal part.

He began with the Fugitives. (Davidson himself has given a charming, idyllic account of the beginnings in "The Thankless Muse and Her Fugitive Poets.") He was not a "minor" Fugitive, as Mr. John Bradbury seems to think,[16] but a "major" one, as Mrs. Cowan abundantly shows in her book on the Fugitive group.[17] He was not as "modern" as the others. He seems to have escaped almost completely Eliot's influence and Pound's. He lacks the metaphysical density of Tate, the starkness of Warren, the nuanced ambiguity of Ransom. Miss Gamble quotes Ransom as saying that "the direct approach is perilous to the artist," and goes on to speak of Ransom's "oblique style," which "fends off the assaults of sentiment inherent in the direct approach." [18] Well, Davidson is comparatively direct, and isn't afraid of sentiment. There is sentiment aplenty (but not sentimentality, which is properly defined, I think, as feeling in excess of clear cause).

I should like to mention (without attempting much more) some of the characteristics of the verse, as it strikes me.

First, there is the classical influence. Davidson, like the other Fugitives, is grounded in the Greek and Roman classics. This influence comes out not only in quotation and allusion but in purity of language and in the severe, astringent imposition of restraint upon emotion.

---

16. *The Fugitives, A Critical Account* (Chapel Hill: University of North Carolina Press, 1958).

17. Louise Cowan, *The Fugitive Group* (Baton Rouge: Louisiana State University Press, 1959).

18. Isabel Gamble, "Ceremonies of Bravery: John Crowe Ransom," *Southern Renascence*, ed. by Louis D. Rubin, Jr. and Robert D. Jacobs (Baltimore: The Johns Hopkins Press, 1953), pp. 342, 350.

Second, there is a pervasive sense of the past, an ancestral past. This past is not merely a Southern, or even American experience; it goes back indefinitely in the history of the race; it takes on a mythical, and finally a mystical, quality; it is remembered in the blood. The meeting of the lovers in "Epithalamion" suggests earlier lovers' meetings, when men in gray halted by an Ohio farmhouse; and a still earlier meeting

> Brief by the Frisian coast, when the fair-haired Goths
> Came a-harrying over the path of the whale . . .
> Young was the herald of Goths. The light of his eyes
> Burned in the crowded hall. And the eyes of a girl
> Met his warm through the spears.[19]

Third, there is an unusual talent for narrative verse, a form which has appeared only sporadically since Chaucer. Narrative verse seems to be in critical disfavor at the present time. Not that a modern poem doesn't tell a "story"; but the story must be ferreted out, constructed from the images (as in Warren's "Original Sin: A Short Story"). Davidson is capable of a straightforward narrative remarkable for verve and movement. A short segment of "The Sod of Battle-Fields" will illustrate the quality.

> And there was a tale of Jim Ezell and the Yankees,
> How he licked ten of them—fifty, maybe—
> All by himself. Oh, he was a Forrest scout
> And a Chapel Hill boy, you know. The Yankees
> Heard he was lying wounded and in bed
> At old Dad Smiley's farm up by the creek,
> So they sneaked up, all ten of them (maybe fifty),
> And the first thing he knew he was surrounded.
> Then Jim rared out of bed like a young colt,
> Kicked up his heels, spit bullets in their faces,
> That-a-way, this-a-way, lit in his saddle fighting,

19. *Poems: 1922–1961* (Minneapolis: University of Minnesota Press, 1966), p. 177.

> Bang through the fence and splash in the creek,
> And up the dirt road with his shirt-tail flapping.
> The Yankees yelled and shot their guns. No use!
> None of your butter-fingered Yankee cavalry
> Ever could touch Jim Ezell. It took
> Ten Yankees anyhow to lick a Southerner,
> Even to make him run.[20]

Perhaps the best-sustained narrative is "The Running of Streight," where Bedford Forrest chased Streight and his federal cavalry out of Alabama. The following excerpt gives a real sense of movement through the countryside:

> That running went to the Black Warrior River
> That running went over the rocks and fallen trees,
> By crossroads and by field, by land and water
> They gnawed and nagged and shot and charged him down,
> And soon by country stores and villages
> Came fast and hard, while women and old men
> Waved from porches, whooped at roadside gates.
> Without a rest for the spent fox, without
> A spell to tighten girth or breathe a horse.
> They left him not a shady place to lie in,
> They cut him off from every telegraph,
> They drove him from his oats, his corn, his pasture,
> They harried Streight to hell in Alabama.[21]

Fourth, there is everywhere (in the verse as in the prose, for Davidson is all of a piece) the old agrarian-industrial antinomy. He sees the Civil War as a struggle between the rural and urban economies, and, as a corollary, between local self-government and the rule of the power state. In "The Deserter: A Christmas Eclogue," one of the interlocutors declares:

> Nashville was occupied by Federal troops
> In eighteen sixty-two. *They hold it still!*

20. *Ibid.*, pp. 128–129.
21. *Lee in the Mountains and Other Poems* (New York: Charles Scribner's Sons, 1938), p. 31.

The only difference is, they do not wear
Blue uniforms.[22]

Many of the images throughout Davidson's verse—if they were tagged and classified—would be found to fall in one or the other of the two antinomies. In the poem just quoted from, there is the ever-present smoke: "But soot means money./ More smoke, more trade." Rural scenes have retreated to a remote distance: ". . . down the hollow through the pasture, past/ The big spring."[23] City and farm, of course, are symbols. They symbolize guilt and innocence, respectively. But in Davidson's poetry they are more than symbols: they are facts.

There is, fifth, the religious bias. In "The Breaking Mould," the narrator speaks of himself as one

> Who learned of a gentle mother the Ten Commandments
> And read the Good Book through at the age of twelve,
> Chapter by chapter. The hymns of country choirs
> Haunt my tongue. The words of stately men
> Speaking from ghostly pulpits forbid me still
> From shameful things. And youthful prayers arise
> Unbidden to my lips in hours of dread.
> Woman is sacred still, and wine is a mocker,
> The words of God are written in the Book
> Which I will keep beloved though earth may speak
> A different language unto those who read her.[24]

In the same poem the narrator says that he is "three men": the one just described; another, "with pagan blood"; and a third, "born to weigh the sun." But the reader feels that the old-fashioned Christian is the most real, for the paganism is partly something read about, and the scientism something imposed by the Age of Science. Not that Davidson is a "churchman": he is critical of the clergy's doctrinal softness; of the church's adop-

22. *Ibid.*, p. 21.
23. *Ibid.*, pp. 16, 19.
24. *Poems*, p. 171.

tion of business methods; of the big neon sign "Jesus Saves" in front of an old downtown church. But the religious bias goes deeper than current churchly aberrations. ". . . if I pass you by, O House of God,/ It is not now in scorn. I would not sit/ In the seat of the scornful or walk in the way of sinners." [25]

Two of the better poems, readers will agree, are "Lee in the Mountains" and "Fire on Belmont Street," which can be read as two modes of prophecy.

The image of Lee grows into symbol. It is an accretion of parts which finally glow in a single incandescence. The parallel between his career and his father's is a contributing part; the re-creation of Civil War battles is another; the "acceptance" of the new era of "little men," another. These and other elements are interfused to make the complex symbol that is Lee. Lee's going to the mountains extends the symbolic dimension. He had formerly been identified with the Tidewater, while the more "puritan" Jackson had stood for the Blue Ridge. But now Lee comprehends them both, and other places and times as well. Toward the end he speaks to the young men about the God of their fathers.

> Young men, the God of your fathers is a just
> And merciful God Who in this blood once shed
> On your green altars measures out all days,
> And measures out the grace
> Whereby alone we live;
> And in His might He waits,
> Brooding within the certitude of time,
> To bring this lost forsaken valor
> And the fierce faith undying
> And the love quenchless
> To flower among the hills to which we cleave,
> To fruit upon the mountains whither we flee,
> Never forsaking, never denying

25. *Ibid.*, pp. 170, 171.

His children and His children's children forever
Unto all generations of the faithful heart.[26]

The words have the tone of prophecy. Whatever virtue there was in the lost cause—whatever valor, faith, love—will have a rebirth, when the fullness of time shall have come. The prophecy is quiet, confident, long-range.

"Fire on Belmont Street" is imminent and alarmist. The predicament comes closer home today than the poet could have foreseen when he wrote the poem two decades ago. He asks the contemporary question:

Who can quench
The white-hot fury of the tameless atoms
Bursting the secret jungle of their cells?

One is reminded of Cassandra, who had the prophetic gift but was fated to be disbelieved.

Davidson's more recent poetry is less explicitly partisan, less admonitory. It is as if, with Wordsworth, he "will grieve not, rather find/ Strength in what remains behind." [27]

One source of "strength" is the old friendships. This is expressed with nostalgic beauty in "Lines Written for Allen Tate on His Sixtieth Anniversary."

So, Allen, you have kindled many an evening
When the creed of memory summoned us to your fire.
I remember that blazon, remember firelight blessing
Owsley's uplifted head, Ransom's gray eye,
The Kentucky voice of Warren, until that household's
Oaken being spoke like a plucked lyre. . . .[28]

Another source is nature and religion. "Gradual of the Northern Summer" is a case in point. The "nature" is in Vermont, where the Davidsons have a summer home, near Middle-

26. *Ibid.*, p. 46.
27. "Ode: Intimations of Immortality," ll. 180–181.
28. *Poems*, p. 15.

bury. This is not a new note, for Vermont nature had received
due appreciation in the early essay, "Still Rebels, Still Yankees,"
but the Catholic aura perhaps is, the "gradual" being a portion
of the Mass. The author gives a religious particularization to
certain aspects of nature: ". . . vesper deer come forth to
browse"; and

> The little, naked red fox peers
> With prayerful face and upright ears,
> Then genuflects, with sweep of paw,
> To mark the rigor of God's law. . . .[29]

These are of course not identities, but only analogies; the
poem does not say that God and nature are one; the deer and
fox are fellow creatures, endowed by "pathetic fallacy" with
worshipful attitudes. The road connecting the highway and the
author's house is rough and steep.

> Whoso would turn to our abode
> Must take the narrow, rain-scraped road
> And learn by one-way steeps and grooves
> God loves best where he unimproves.[30]

The old polemic about "improvements" persists.

The disposition of the present world of neo-conformism is to
go along servilely with the prevailing, statistically demonstrated
trends—whether in space exploration, or organization monopoly,
or leveling nationalism, or whatnot. The key word of our age is
"adjust." Ours not to reason why. Davidson (in both poetry and
prose) is one of our few living writers who fixes the responsibility unmistakably and precisely where it belongs—upon each
individual. "I do not surrender . . . to the servile notion," he
says, "that the existence of a powerful 'trend' is a mark of its
'inevitability.' All the works of men result from human choices,

29. *Ibid.*, pp. 8, 9.
30. *Ibid.*, p. 10.

human decisions. There is nothing inevitable about them. We are subject to God's will alone; we are not subject to any theory of mechanical determinism originating in 'social forces.' " [31] Only by such a steadfast position can we hope to maintain a culture worthy of our loyalty and the world's respect.

31. "The Agrarians Today," p. 17.

THE OUTLOOK
FOR SOUTHERN WRITING:
DIAGNOSIS AND PROGNOSIS

THE present paper will deal more with diagnosis than prognosis. Specific prediction, especially when it comes to picking rising young writers, is a risky business. Shortly after World War II one of our leading magazines (one with a very large circulation) ventured to nominate a certain young writer as the one most likely to lead the way and to achieve greatness in the field of the novel. I shall not mention the young novelist's name, and it is quite possible that the prediction by this important magazine may yet come true; but the critical acclaim in recent years seems to have gone in other directions. Refusing to take unnecessary risks, therefore (I am safe enough mentioning the stalwarts included in this article), I prefer to deal here with such general, yet important, matters as the soil and climate, the traditions and habits of mind, the kinds of literary growth which the South has fostered in the past and in the present.

The most striking aspect of the contemporary literary scene in the United States, it now goes without saying, is the Southern renascence. The South has now, and has had for a number of years, an importance in American literature comparable to that of the Middle West in the first quarter of the present century and to that of New England a hundred years ago. The South is bursting with writers today. It is doubtful whether any time and place since Elizabethan England have been so stirred by the creative impulse.

No one knows what brought about the Southern revival, any more than anyone knows what brought about the Shakespearean age, or the flowering of New England, or the Middle Western renascence of the 1910s. There does seem to be, though, one factor in common: the presence of radical change, the twilight of an old order. Shakespeare wrote in the twilight of the feudal age. Hawthorne wrote when New England was changing from farm to factory and from Puritan to Unitarian. Sherwood Anderson (to name the most brilliant of the Middle Western writers) wrote when Chicago was beginning to dominate the upper Mississippi Valley, and countless young people on the farms, responding to the powerful urban attraction, the irresistible magnet of the megalopolis, decided that life on the farm was not for them. By the same token, Southern writers have been confronted by change.

Industrial change, for one thing. A Southern exile returns today to find, to his surprise and perhaps his grief, that the tempo of Atlanta and Birmingham, of Richmond and Nashville, even, is not much slower than that of the great Northern cities. Along with the industrial change, of course, is a vast societal transformation. The South of our time has been moving out of a kind of feudalism into something at once progressive and precarious. Southern writers have dealt seriously with the change.

But economic and social change is not in itself a sufficient cause. Many ages have witnessed great alterations without witnessing the appearance of a Shakespeare or a Hawthorne or a Faulkner. The historians cannot predict a renascence. Still less can the sociologists. The sociological indices in Mississippi, for example, have been for a long while unfavorable, comparatively, to the appearance of literary talent, and yet, as everyone knows, Mississippi now enjoys a splendid eminence in the contemporary literature of the United States. The converse may also be true: the sociological indices in Massachusetts, and in New England generally, are favorable, comparatively, to the appearance of literary talent, but actually one finds it there today rather sparsely. New England today is a region of libraries and museums, institutions dedicated to preserving the creations which have been handed down to them. Scholarly investigation has taken the place of creation in the New England of our time.

These things go in cycles, and it was the South's turn to have a flowering. Allen Tate has put it this way: "With the war of 1914–1918, the South re-entered the world—but it gave a backward glance as it stepped over the border: that backward glance gave us the Southern renascence, a literature conscious of the past in the present." [1] Tate says elsewhere: "After the [first world] war, the South again knew the world, but it had a memory of another war; with us, entering the world once more meant not only the obliteration of the past, but a heightened consciousness of it; so that we had . . . a double focus, a looking two ways, which gave a special dimension to the writing of our school . . . which American writing as a whole seemed to lack." [2] The statement is useful: it suggests change as a factor; at the same time, it leaves to divine Providence, where it properly belongs, the business of supplying persons who are capable of transmuting "a backward glance" and "a looking two ways" into significant literature.

If the historian cannot foresee a renascence, neither can he predict its duration or the course it will take. But he can still reason from analogy and indulge in conjecture. The Southern revival invites comparisons, particularly with the revivals of New England and the Middle West. Such comparisons may prove suggestive.

One particularly distressing characteristic of the Middle West (in its culture generally) has been, it seems to me, a lack of confidence, a painful deference to the modes and judgments of the Eastern states. Chicago was an exciting literary center in the 1910s, but the Middle Western writers were not content to gather there and stay there; they fairly itched to be in New York. Sherwood Anderson wrote from Chicago in 1917 to Waldo Frank, after talking with him in New York: "Your willingness

1. "The New Provincialism," *Collected Essays* (Denver: Alan Swallow, 1959), p. 292.

2. "*The Fugitive* 1922–1925: A Personal Recollection Twenty Years After," *Princeton University Library Chronicle*, III (April 1942), 83.

to listen to my provincial, Western point of view warmed my heart" [3]; and to Van Wyck Brooks in 1919 he wrote under similar circumstances: "I feel like a very small boy in the presence of your mind, and of Waldo's too." [4] The spectacle of the Middle Western genius bowing down before the demigods of New York and almost apologizing for his "provincial, Western point of view" is a pathetic one, and it is all the more regrettable because Anderson was repeating a Middle Western attitude which had been taken before him by Garland and Howells and the great Mark Twain himself. The author of *Winesburg, Ohio,* it seems clear enough now, did not stand to profit much by going to school to the New York critics.

The best writers of the New England flowering—Thoreau, Hawthorne, and Emily Dickinson—were provincial in the best sense and autochthonous to the last degree. They took their stand, and worked out their salvation, which was in New England or nowhere. It was the minor figures (like Longfellow and Lowell) who sought to be cosmopolitan, who deprecated the "provincial," who looked for illumination outside themselves, outside their own place and time. The results are plain enough.

Modern Southern writers seem to appreciate the value of autochthonousness. As a rule, they have been content to stay at home. Or, if the exigencies of their careers have carried them elsewhere, residence outside the South has not diminished their Southernness: they have not given up their Southern accent; they have not sought materials from unfamiliar sources; they have not been softened by alien propaganda. Warren, though a professor at Yale, can still draw upon Kentucky. (It is to be hoped that Faulkner's separation from Yoknapatawpha in *A Fable* is nothing more serious than a passing indiscretion.) Along with the autochthonousness has been a certain intransigence, a certain tough-mindedness, displayed not only in the fiction and

3. *Letters of Sherwood Anderson,* ed. by Howard Mumford Jones (Boston: Little, Brown and Company, 1953), p. 7.
4. *Ibid.,* p. 53.

poetry, but in a work like *I'll Take My Stand*, that brilliant symposium which is now being seen to have an importance not as an economic blueprint (which its early critics took it for), but (somewhat like Thoreau's *Walden*) a philosophy of a way of life. Southern writers, it may be well to recall, did not join to any appreciable extent (I frankly never heard of *any*) the expatriates of the twenties or the fellow travelers of the thirties. Confidence in one's inheritance, belief in one's instinctive knowledge, faithfulness to one's artistic vision—these are qualities which augur well for the continued fruitfulness of the Southern renascence. So long as they are present to a marked degree, the outlook for Southern writing will continue bright.

The case of Mississippi is, or ought to be, particularly instructive. Hodding Carter in an essay entitled "Why We Write in the South" (published in 1954 by George Peabody College as part of a symposium called *Literature in the Modern World*) pictures a delightful state of literary affairs in the town of Greenville—the same town in which, the London *Times* recently informed us, "seventeen authors are in the national print." [5] Writers there apparently work with a will and with joy. They are bards of passion and of mirth. They seem to be a part, too, of that rarity in the modern world—a community life. One recalls in this connection Faulkner's announcement, made at the time of the Nobel award, that he would give the prize money to the public schools of Oxford for the purchase of some much-needed equipment. The statement seemed a bit old-fashioned: it seemed to hark back to an earlier era in our history when local responsibilities were locally assumed, to an era when community life was a vital thing. One gets the impression that it is still a vital thing in Mississippi, and if this is true, the outlook for Mississippi writing is enhanced appreciably.

Another source of strength to the Southern movement is the

5. *Times Literary Supplement* of September 17, 1954, reprinted in *American Writing Today*, ed. by Allan Angoff (New York: New York University Press, 1957), p. 206.

variety of the Southern literary past. Southern literature from the beginning has been more diverse, more varied, than the literature of New England or of the Middle West. There have been greater extremes in Southern literature, and the basic difference is that which separates two traditions, which one may call the "aristocratic" tradition and the "frontier" tradition. There is no such division in New England literature, for the frontier in New England was never very pronounced or articulate; nor in the literature of the Middle West, because that region has been more homogeneously democratic. But in the South, the contrast has been marked indeed. It would be difficult to find writers more different than William Byrd of Westover and George Washington Harris, the author of "Sut Lovingood"; or, to take more recent examples, Ellen Glasgow of Richmond and Jesse Stuart of W-Hollow in the Kentucky mountains. It is a remarkable fact about Southern literature that both traditions have had a great deal of vitality.

In modern times, the aristocratic tradition is represented by the Virginians, Ellen Glasgow and James Branch Cabell; by John Crowe Ransom and Allen Tate of the Nashville school; by Mississippians like Stark Young and Eudora Welty. These writers stem spiritually and culturally from William Byrd's Tidewater: they are courtly, sophisticated, intellectual; they cultivate "wit" (in the older sense) and a fine irony; they address an inner circle; they possess restraint, dignity, a sense of form; they are classicists.

The frontier tradition first found expression in the early nineteenth century. This was a full hundred years after Byrd's *History of the Dividing Line*, but it is extraordinary that the frontier should have been represented in literature at all, let alone so early. The Southern frontiersman—whether in the mountains of East Tennessee or the cane brakes of Arkansas—was a pretty lively fellow, and he has his niche—and a secure one it is turning out to be—in such writings as Longstreet's *Georgia Scenes, The Autobiography of David Crockett,* Harris's *Sut*

Lovingood, Hooper's *Adventures of Captain Simon Suggs,* Baldwin's *Flush Times in Alabama and Mississippi,* Thorpe's "Big Bear of Arkansas." In modern times the tradition is represented by such literary descendants as Erskine Caldwell and Jesse Stuart. Thomas Wolfe, who came from the same mountainous region as George Washington Harris, belongs with the members of this frontier school in some respects, though he lacked their sense of humor and their mastery of the vernacular.

The two schools—aristocratic and frontier—have maintained a good deal of separateness from each other down to our own time. Certain members of one school probably do not have a very high opinion of the writings of certain members of the other. It is interesting and significant, however, that the two traditions are united in the works of the writer who, all agree, is the greatest in the South today, and possibly this is one important reason why he *is* the greatest. For like Shakespeare, Faulkner embraces the high and the low, the aristocratic and the plebeian, the courtly and the uncouth, the educated and the illiterate, the literary and the vernacular, the traditional and the modern. Faulkner's *Bear* is pretty clearly a lineal descendant of Thorpe's "Big Bear," and his "Spotted Horses," which is a part of *The Hamlet,* might almost have come out of the tales of Sut Lovingood. (Faulkner, in fact, is said to admire Harris and Wolfe, too—the two great writers of the Great Smokies.) On the other hand, his sympathetic interest in the Sartorises, the Compsons, and other gentry allies him with the Tidewater. It is the comprehensiveness of Faulkner which sets him apart from the others. It should be added that Robert Penn Warren has something of the same comprehensiveness.

The analogy with sixteenth-century England again suggests itself. It is noteworthy that these two traditions—however we may name them—should have flourished side by side in the South; that they should have achieved a vigorous expression in two schools of literature; and that they should have been combined and fused in the writings of the greatest of all Southern writers, William Faulkner, very much, *mutatis mutandis,* as the classical and native traditions formed separate schools in pre-Elizabethan England and were united in the works of Shakespeare. The relevance of these remarks to the "diagnosis and prognosis" promised in the title of this paper is merely this: the present Southern movement has a long background in Southern writing (a genetic relationship not always recognized or clearly seen), and this fact suggests a growth of some hardihood and durability.

Another characteristic of modern Southern literature which suggests a favorable prognosis is its religious, anti-naturalistic frame of reference. Several observers have recently pointed out the decline of naturalism. They have noted the shift in interest (among the better young writers and readers) from the sociological to the symbolic in fiction and have been inclined to attribute the change, in part at least, to the influence of Faulkner and other Southern writers. If this analysis is correct, younger writers outside the South may be expected to follow the Southern example. Faulkner at the moment certainly seems to be a more potent influence than Dreiser or Farrell.

The fact is that the naturalistic view—which is an amoral, deterministic view of man, and the product of the modern sciences of biology, sociology, and bio-psychology—has never taken a very strong hold in the South. One plausible explanation is that orthodox religious belief has been more vigorous and tenacious in the South than in most other places (in the case of the South, it is chiefly, of course, orthodox Protestant belief), and the teachings of modern science have not been accepted so completely there as elsewhere.

To most Southerners, God and the Devil—especially the Devil —are still pretty real. There is a good deal of deviltry in modern Southern literature. But Southern writers, as a class, do not cloak the deviltry in an amoral disguise, or treat it disinterestedly as an inevitable product of natural forces. Rather, they show it honestly and forthrightly for what it is—namely, deviltry. This is one reason why Faulkner is more closely akin to an older Puritan writer like Hawthorne or Melville than to a modern amoralist like Dos Passos or Farrell. Writers like Faulkner and Warren (whom one feels disposed to bracket with Faulkner for several reasons) have their roots in the Southern fundamentalist tradition of heaven and hell, God and the Devil, sin and salvation. The sense of sin is being rediscovered now in other parts of the world and made to do duty, because it is seen to be essential to man's dignity, but it was hardly necessary for the South to make this rediscovery. A distinguished neo-orthodox New England clergyman, searching recently for something in modern American literature on man's sinfulness to quote in a sermon, hit upon a passage, interestingly enough, in a Southern poem, *Brother to Dragons*. The incident seems worth mentioning for two reasons: one is that Southern literature has never been much quoted in New England, and the other is that the Calvinistic premise of man's sinfulness has not been much insisted upon by New England writers since the death of Nathaniel Hawthorne.

A happy omen for Southern writing is that it is drawing upon the great sources of literary inspiration. Robert Penn Warren, a few years ago, said in an interview with Ralph Morissey of the Nashville *Tennessean:* "All novelists, budding or otherwise, should read and mark their Shakespeare, also their Bible. These are the two greatest founts for writers." It is excellent advice, and Warren's books show that he has marked his Shakespeare and Bible to good purpose.

That perhaps greatest of all American writers, Herman Melville, did the same thing, and a perceptive critic in the recent issue of the London *Times Literary Supplement* devoted to present-day American writing, commenting on certain resemblances between Warren and Melville, observed that "The similarities seem not a matter of influence but a matter of a common view of the human condition." [6] The common view,

6. *Ibid.*, p. 53.

of course, is precisely the view presented in the Bible and in Shakespeare, for it cannot be too often reiterated that these two books were for Melville and Hawthorne, as they are for Warren and Faulkner, the two greatest founts. It was one of the unfortunate aspects of the period between the mid-nineteenth-century renascence and the modern Southern revival that American literature drew upon these founts less and less, and wherever naturalism triumphed drew upon them not at all. The frame of reference of the naturalists was not religious but scientific, or quasi-scientific, and readers today who are acclimated to naturalism, and unacquainted with the Christian tradition, often experience difficulty in understanding Hawthorne's symbols, for example, or Faulkner's. But familiarity with these important matters is more general today, I should suppose, in the South than in the non-South, and this is a distinct advantage and adds brightness to the outlook for Southern writing.

One of the most illuminating commentaries on the Southern revival is an essay by Donald Davidson entitled "Why the Modern South Has a Great Literature." Davidson points out that "the new literature of the South is not a literature of protest but a literature of acceptance which renders its material . . . objectively and seriously." [7] The Southern writer (to summarize Davidson) has been born into a traditional society, and he accepts that society in its wholeness; his knowledge is intuitive and of the heart, not of the head merely; he sees people as complete persons with significant personal histories; he sees the total human situation in its full complexity.

In his recent cogent, important, and much-quoted book, *After the Lost Generation,* John W. Aldridge took a discouraged view of the young writer's situation in America today. The writers of the lost generation—Hemingway, Fitzgerald, Dos

7. *Still Rebels, Still Yankees and Other Essays* (Baton Rouge: Louisiana State University Press, 1957), p. 169.

Passos—had the advantage of the stimulus of disillusion, he reasoned, but the writers who have emerged since World War II have been denied even that resource, for they had no illusions to lose. "What we need today to give us a literature of vitality and significance," Aldridge declares, "is a few writers of genius, men who would be able to go on day in and day out, year in and year out, patiently creating out of their own spiritual resources master works of art." "They would have to be big enough," he continues, "and dedicated enough, to withstand all our efforts to kill them, frighten them, buy them off, or send them to prison." [8]

These are challenging statements and contain much truth. They seem, however, to apply more to the non-South than to the South. They seem indeed to have been written with the author's eyes averted from the entire Southern tradition as well as the modern Southern literary movement. The disillusionment of which so much has been made, and its sequel, the absence of disillusionment and the presence only of what Aldridge calls "the chaos of loss"—all this has been the necessary product of the romantic-scientific progressivism of the nineteenth century, which promulgated the cruel belief that man was approaching perfection (through technology), and that Utopia was within easy reach. But the South never subscribed to this view, and it does not (despite technological advances) subscribe to it today. Southern fundamentalism never made the mistake of supposing that man is innately good (a romantic assumption) or perfectible by machinery (a scientific assumption). The South, on the contrary, has held pretty tenaciously to (a) the view—at once Christian and classical—that man is a limited, imperfect creature, and (b) the view—specifically Christian—that man has sinned and fallen short of the glory of God, and that he may rise to a modicum of virtue and good deeds through faith, through prayer, through discipline, through God's redemptive grace.

8. New York: McGraw Hill Book Company, Inc., 1951, p. 257.

As one contemplates such a view of life, it is not easy to find room for the "disillusionment" or "the chaos of loss" to which historians have attached so much importance in modern literature.

Aldridge, then, it would seem, omitted from his survey of the contemporary literary scene a factor which may turn out to be decisive—namely, the Southern temper. (Possibly this was Andrew Lytle's meaning when he said recently, somewhat cryptically, "The South may well become the salvation of this country yet, both at home and abroad." [9]) For surely when we call the roll (and there is space here for only a partial roll-calling) of the writers who have made (and happily in most instances are still making) the Southern renascence (the order of names is by dates of birth)—Ellen Glasgow, James Branch Cabell, Stark Young, William Alexander Percy, Elizabeth Madox Roberts, John Crowe Ransom, Donald Davidson, Paul Green, Katherine Anne Porter, Caroline Gordon, William Faulkner, Allen Tate, Thomas Wolfe, Andrew Nelson Lytle, Merrill Moore, Erskine Caldwell, Robert Penn Warren, Cleanth Brooks, Jesse Stuart, Eudora Welty, Randall Jarrell, Carson McCullers, Peter Taylor—and when we think of still others who ought to be included in such a list, we are aware of the fact that we are confronted, by and large, with writers who *have* been big enough and dedicated enough to withstand any efforts from whatever source to kill them, frighten them, buy them off, or send them to prison. The Southern renascence looks like much the hardiest we have had in this country since the renascence of New England, which began with Hawthorne's tales in the 1830s and ended with the death of Emily Dickinson some fifty years later. The South's seems likely to last as long as New England's, possibly even longer; and to be as fruitful, possibly even fruitfuller.

9. "How Many Miles to Babylon," *Southern Renascence*, ed. by Louis D. Rubin, Jr., and Robert D. Jacobs (Baltimore: The Johns Hopkins Press, 1953), p. 33.

RANDALL STEWART: A BIBLIOGRAPHY
1929-1966

Editorial Note: This bibliography of Randall Stewart's published work is divided into five sections: books edited, books, textbooks edited, articles (including miscellaneous pieces), and reviews. Each section is arranged chronologically so that the reader can follow the course of Mr. Stewart's scholarship and criticism—and see in part the development of his career.

I. BOOKS EDITED

1932

The American Notebooks by Nathaniel Hawthorne. New Haven: Yale University Press, 1932. Reprinted in 1933.

Contains an introductory essay by Mr. Stewart with these chapters: "Mrs. Hawthorne's Revisions of the American Notebooks," "The Adaptation of Material from the American Notebooks," "The Development of Character Types in Hawthorne's Fiction," and "Recurrent Themes in Hawthorne's Fiction." The complete text of Hawthorne's American Notebooks will be published in the Centenary Edition of the Works of Nathaniel Hawthorne by the Ohio State University Press. It will be largely based upon Mr. Stewart's 1932 edition and will also incorporate additions and changes which Mr. Stewart made with the assistance of Miss Jane Ann Barkau in the preliminary stages of revising the text. Approximate date of publication: 1970.

1941

The English Notebooks by Nathaniel Hawthorne. New York: Modern Language Association of America and London: Oxford University Press, 1941. Reprinted by Russell & Russell, Inc. of New York in 1962.

Contains an introductory essay by Mr. Stewart with these chapters:

"Mrs. Hawthorne's Revisions of the English Notebooks" and "Hawthorne in England."

II. BOOKS

1948

Nathaniel Hawthorne: A Biography. New Haven: Yale University Press, 1948. Reprinted as a Yale paperbound in 1961.

1958

American Literature and Christian Doctrine. Baton Rouge: Louisiana State University Press, 1958. Reprinted in 1963.

1964

American Literature: A Brief History. Chicago: Scott, Foresman and Company, 1964. (With Walter Blair and Theodore Hornberger, co-authors.)

III. TEXTBOOKS EDITED

1946–1947

The Literature of the United States. 2 vols. Chicago: Scott, Foresman and Company, 1946–1947. (With Walter Blair and Theodore Hornberger, co-editors.)

1949

The Literature of the United States. 1 vol. Chicago: Scott, Foresman and Company, 1949. (With Walter Blair and Theodore Hornberger, co-editors.)

1952

The Literature of the South. Chicago: Scott, Foresman and Company, 1952. (General editor with Richmond Croom Beatty, Floyd G. Watkins, and Thomas Daniel Young, co-editors.)
Contains a foreword by Mr. Stewart.

1953

The Literature of the United States. Rev. ed. 2 vols. Chicago: Scott, Foresman and Company, 1953. (With Walter Blair and Theodore Hornberger, co-editors.)

1954

Living Masterpieces of American Literature. Chicago: Scott, Foresman and Company, 1954. (With Dorothy Bethurum, co-editor.)

This anthology was originally published in two forms—as a one-volume edition and as four separate books. Book One is *Concord Idealism: Emerson and Thoreau;* Book Two, *Classic American Fiction: Poe, Hawthorne, Melville, James;* Book Three, *Modern American Narration: Mark Twain, Hemingway, Faulkner;* and Book Four, *American Poetry: Poe, Emerson, Whitman, Dickinson, Frost, Eliot. Concord Idealism* is no longer published as a separate book. *American Poetry* was revised in 1964: see entry below.

Living Masterpieces of English Literature. Chicago: Scott, Foresman and Company, 1954. (With Dorothy Bethurum, co-editor.)

This anthology is published in two forms—as a one-volume edition and as four separate books. Book One is *Classics of the Christian Tradition: The Bible, Milton;* Book Two, *Classics of the Enlightenment: Pope, Swift;* Book Three, *English Lyric Poetry: Donne, Wordsworth, Keats, Yeats;* Book Four, *Chaucer and Shakespeare: The Dramatic Vision.* The single-volume texts of both *Living Masterpieces of American Literature* (see entry above) and *Living Masterpieces of English Literature* contain general introductions which include an essay by Mr. Stewart, "The Free Spirit."

The Literature of the United States. Rev. ed. 1 vol. Chicago: Scott, Foresman and Company, 1957. (With Walter Blair and Theodore Hornberger, co-editors.)

1963

The Literature of the United States. Short ed. Chicago: Scott, Foresman and Company, 1963. (With Walter Blair and Theodore Hornberger, co-editors.)

1964

American Poetry: Poe, Emerson, Whitman, Dickinson, Frost, Eliot. Rev. ed. Chicago: Scott, Foresman and Company, 1964. (With Dorothy Bethurum, co-editor.)

1966

The Literature of the United States. 3rd ed. 2 vols. Chicago: Scott, Foresman and Company, 1966. (With Walter Blair, Theodore Hornberger, and James E. Miller, Jr., co-editors.)

IV. ARTICLES

1929

"Ethan Brand," *Saturday Review of Literature,* V (April 27, 1929), 967. [A note-length letter to the editor which was later entitled "Melville and Hawthorne's 'Ethan Brand' " by Mr. Stewart.]

1932

"Hawthorne and Politics: [Hawthorne's] Unpublished Letters to William B. Pike," *New England Quarterly,* V (April 1932), 237–263.

1933

"Hawthorne and *The Faerie Queene,*" *Philological Quarterly,* XII (April 1933), 196–206.

"Vaughan Kester," *Dictionary of American Biography,* X, 360.

"William Benjamin Basil King," *Dictionary of American Biography,* X, 406.

1934

"Hawthorne's Contributions to *The Salem Advertiser,*" *American Literature,* V (January 1934), 327–341.

"Hawthorne in England: The Patriotic Motive in the Notebooks," *New England Quarterly,* VIII (March 1935), 3–13.

"William Davis Ticknor," *Dictionary of American Biography,* XVIII, 528–529.

"Charles Wentworth Upham," *Dictionary of American Biography,* XIX, 121–122.

1936

"Hawthorne's Speeches at Civic Banquets," *American Literature,* VII (January 1936), 415–423.

"The Concord Group," *Sewanee Review,* XLIV (October 1936), 434–446.

"Two Uncollected Reviews by Hawthorne," *New England Quarterly,* IX (September 1936), 504–509.

1937

"Hawthorne and the Civil War," *Studies in Philology,* XXXIV (January 1937), 91–106.

1941

"Regional Characteristics in the Literature of New England," *College English*, III (November 1941), 129–143.

1943

"The Moral Aspect of Henry James's 'International Situation,' " *University Review*, X (Winter 1943), 109–112.

1944

"The Social School of American Criticism," *South Atlantic Quarterly*, XLIII (January 1944), 22–26. Reprinted in *Fifty Years of "The South Atlantic Quarterly*," ed. by W. B. Hamilton. Durham: Duke University Press, 1952, pp. 244–248.

"Three Views of the Individual as Reflected in American Literature," *College English*, V (March 1944), 297–302.

"Letters to Sophia," *Huntington Library Quarterly*, VII (August 1944), 387–395.

"The Hawthornes at the Wayside, 1860–1864: Selections from Mrs. Hawthorne's Letters to Mr. and Mrs. Fields," *More Books*, XIX (September 1944), 263–279.

" 'Pestiferous Gail Hamilton,' James T. Fields, and the Hawthornes," *New England Quarterly*, XVII (September 1944), 418–423.

"Hawthorne's Last Illness and Death: Selections from Mrs. Hawthorne's Letters to Mr. and Mrs. Fields," *More Books*, XIX (October 1944), 303–313.

1945

"Recollections of Hawthorne by His Sister Elizabeth," *American Literature*, XVI (January 1945), 316–331.

"Editing Hawthorne's Notebooks: Selections from Mrs. Hawthorne's Letters to Mr. and Mrs. Fields, 1864–1868," *More Books*, XX (September 1945), 299–315.

"American Literature between the Wars," *South Atlantic Quarterly*, XLIV (October 1945), 371–383. Reprinted in *The Literature of the United States* and in *American Literature: A Brief History*.

1946

"The Growth of Thoreau's Reputation," *College English*, VII (January 1946), 208–214.

"Mrs. Hawthorne's Financial Difficulties: Selections from Her Letters to James T. Fields, 1865–1868," *More Books*, XXI (February 1946), 43–52.

"Puritan Literature and the Flowering of New England," *William and Mary Quarterly*, Third Series, III (July 1946), 319–342.

"Mrs. Hawthorne's Quarrel with James T. Fields: Selections from Letters to Fields by Mrs. Hawthorne and Elizabeth Peabody," *More Books*, XXI (September 1946), 254–263.

1952

"Melville and Hawthorne," *South Atlantic Quarterly*, LI (July 1952), 436–446. Reprinted in *Moby-Dick Centennial Essays*, ed. by Tyrus Hillway and Luther S. Mansfield. Dallas: Southern Methodist University Press, 1953, pp. 153–164.

1953

"Appreciation of American Literature Finally Arrives in U. S. Universities," Providence *Evening Bulletin*, October 28, 1953.

"Rhode Island Literature," *Rhode Island History*, XII (October 1953), 97–105.

"New Critic and Old Scholar," *College English*, XV (November 1953), 105–111.

1954

"Rhode Island Literature," *Rhode Island History*, XIII (January 1954), 1–10.

"Certain Caveats and Comments," *Brown Alumni Monthly*, LIV (January 1954), 5–7.

"Deviltry is Deviltry," *Vanderbilt Alumnus*, XXXIX (July–August 1954), 8–9, 12. [The Vanderbilt Commencement Address for 1954.]

1955

"American Literature and the Christian Tradition," *Faculty Papers*, Third Series. Christian Perspectives in University Life. New York, 1955. [A pamphlet published by the National Council of the Episcopal Church.]

"Outlook for Southern Writing: Diagnosis and Prognosis," *Virginia Quarterly Review*, XXXI (Spring 1955), 252–263.

"Our Present Opportunity," *The CEA Critic*, XVII (May 1955), 1–2.

Foreword to *The Southern Literary Renascence: A Symposium, Shenandoah*, VI (Summer 1955), 3.

"The Golden Age of Hawthorne Criticism," *University Review*, XXII (October 1955), 44–46.

"The Freshman Course Needs a Current of Ideas," *College English*, XVI (October 1955), 16–19. Reprinted as "Bringing a Current of Ideas to Programs in Reading and Writing" for the Introduction to John F. Butler, *Exercises in Literary Understanding*. Chicago: Scott, Foresman and Company, 1956, pp. 1–11.

1956

"Hawthorne and Faulkner," *College English*, XVII (February 1956), 258–262. Reprinted in *College English*, XXII (November 1960), 128–132.

1957

"Present Trends in the Study and Teaching of American Literature," *College English*, XVIII (January 1957), 207–211.

"The Vision of Evil in Hawthorne and Melville," *The Tragic Vision and the Christian Faith*, ed. by Nathan A. Scott, Jr. New York: Association Press, 1957, pp. 238–263. Reprinted with some changes and additions in Chapter IV of *American Literature and Christian Doctrine*.

"Emerson, Asset or Liability?" *Tennessee Studies in Literature*, II (1957), 33–40. Reprinted in expanded form as part of Chapter III of *American Literature and Christian Doctrine*.

1958

"Dreiser and the Naturalistic Heresy," *Virginia Quarterly Review*, XXXIV (Winter 1958), 100–116. Reprinted in Japanese translation in *Americana*, IV (July 1958), 55–67. Reprinted in slightly altered form as Chapter V of *American Literature and Christian Doctrine*.

"Editing *The American Notebooks*," Essex Institute *Historical Collections*, XCIV (July 1958), 277–281.

"Nathaniel Hawthorne," *Masterplots: Cyclopedia of World Authors*, I, 487–489.

1959

"A Doctrine of Man," *Mississippi Quarterly*, XII (Winter 1959), 4–9.

"Paperbacks," *College English*, XX (April 1959), 365–367.

"Tidewater and Frontier," *Georgia Review*, XIII (Fall 1959), 296–307.

"Moral Crisis as Structural Principle in Fiction: A Few American Examples," *The Christian Scholar*, XLII (December 1959), 284–289.

"On the Meaning of Vanderbilt." Nashville, 1959. [A pamphlet published by Vanderbilt University devoted solely to this address by Mr. Stewart to the Class of 1961.] Reprinted in part by the Vanderbilt Alumni and Development Office as another pamphlet (undated). Reprinted in *Toward Liberal Education*, ed. by Louis G. Locke, William M. Gibson, and George Arms. 4th ed. New York: Holt, Rinehart and Winston, Inc., 1962, pp. 43–46.

1960

"The Importance of Literature at the Present Time," *Shenandoah*, XI (Winter 1960), 3–11.

"The Relation between Fugitives and Agrarians," *Mississippi Quarterly*, XIII (Spring 1960), 55–60.

"Nathaniel Hawthorne," *Encyclopedia Britannica*, 14th ed. (1960), XI, 278–280.

"John Crowe Ransom," *Encyclopedia Britannica*, 14th ed. (1960), XVIII, 979.

"Allen Tate," *Encyclopedia Britannica*, 14th ed. (1960), XXI, 833.

"Robert Penn Warren," *Encyclopedia Britannica*, 14th ed. (1960), XXIII, 370.

1961

"Donald Davidson," *South: Modern Literature in Its Cultural Setting*, ed. by Louis D. Rubin, Jr., and Robert D. Jacobs. Garden City: Doubleday and Co., 1961, pp. 248–259.

"Doctrines of Man in American Literature," *Religious Education*, LVI (March–April 1961), 83–89.

"A Little History, A Little Honesty: A Southern Viewpoint," *Georgia Review*, XV (Spring 1961), 9–19.

" 'Poetically the Most Accurate Man Alive,' " *Modern Age*, VI (Winter 1961–1962), 81–90. Reprinted in Japanese translation in *Nichibei*

Forum, VIII (August 1962), 26–38, under the title "William Faulkner: Poetically the Most Accurate Man Alive."

1962

"[Puritan Humanism *vs.* Romantic Naturalism]," *The Scarlet Letter: An Annotated Text*, ed. by Sculley Bradley, Richmond Croom Beatty, and E. Hudson Long. New York: W. W. Norton & Co., Inc., 1962, pp. 342–349. Reprinted from *American Literature and Christian Doctrine*, pp. 4–17 *passim* and 83–89. The title is supplied by the editors. [Listed here individually because this arrangement does in fact constitute a separate essay which is not otherwise published in this form.]

"Editing Hawthorne," *Mississippi Quarterly*, XV (Summer 1962), 97–99.

1964

With Seymour L. Gross. "The Hawthorne Revival," *Hawthorne Centenary Essays*, ed. by Roy Harvey Pearce. Columbus: Ohio State University Press, 1964, pp. 335–366.

1966

"Human Nature and the American Dream," Ball State University *Forum*, VII (Spring 1966), 3–5.

V. REVIEWS

1929

The Heart of Hawthorne's Journals, ed. by Newton Arvin, *New England Quarterly*, II (July 1929), 517–521.

1931

Hawthorne by Newton Arvin, *American Literature*, II (January 1931), 446–448.

"Hartford Sentimentalist and Knickerbocker Amateur," (*Mrs. Sigourney* by G. S. Haight and *Fitz-Greene Halleck* by N. F. Adkins), *Yale Review*, XX (Spring 1931), 632–633.

A Literary History of the American People by Charles Angoff, *New England Quarterly*, IV (July 1931), 534–537.

Whitman and Burroughs by Clara Barrus, *Saturday Review of Literature*, VIII (August 29, 1931), 87.

1932

Fenimore Cooper: Critic of His Times by Robert E. Spiller, *Saturday Review of Literature*, VIII (February 27, 1932), 553.

I Sit and Look Out: Editorials from "The Brooklyn Daily Times" by Walt Whitman, ed. by Emory Holloway and Vernolian Schwarz, *Saturday Review of Literature*, IX (October 22, 1932), 188.

1934

Emerson, ed. by Frederic I. Carpenter; *Hawthorne*, ed. by Austin Warren; *Longfellow*, ed. by Odell Shepard; and *Whitman*, ed. by Floyd Stovall in the American Writers Series, *New England Quarterly*, VIII (December 1934), 737.

The Flowering of New England by Van Wyck Brooks, Nashville *Banner*, September 13, 1934.

1938-1939

The Memoirs of Julian Hawthorne, ed. by Edith Garrigues Hawthorne, *New England Quarterly*, XI (September 1938), 651-652, and *American Literature*, X (November 1939), 380.

1940

Elizabeth Lloyd and the Whittiers: A Budget of Letters, ed. by T. F. Currier, *New England Quarterly*, XIII (June 1940), 361-362.

Hawthorne's Contemporaneous Reputation by Bertha Faust, *American Literature*, XII (November 1940), 373-374.

1941

Nathaniel Hawthorne, A Modest Man by Edward Mather, *American Literature*, XIII (March 1941), 73-74.

Sylvester Judd by P. J. Brockway, *American Literature*, XIII (November 1941), 272-274.

1943

Jones Very by W. J. Bartlett, *American Literature*, XV (May 1943), 202-203.

The Wind Blew from the East by Ferner Nuhn, *American Literature*, XV (May 1943), 204-205.

1945

Hawthorne the Artist by Leland Schubert, *American Literature,* XVI (January 1945), 352–353.

Hawthorne, Critic of Society by L. S. Hall, *Modern Language Notes,* LX (February 1945), 138–140.

1946

The Journals of Charles King Newcomb, ed. by Judith K. Johnson, *Books at Brown,* VIII (January 1946), 2–3.

1948

The Times of Melville and Whitman by Van Wyck Brooks, *Yale Review,* XXXVII (Spring 1948), 542–544.

American Dreams: A Study of American Utopias by Vernon L. Parrington, Jr., New York *Herald-Tribune Books,* July 18, 1948.

1951–1952

The Hawthornes by Vernon Loggins, Providence *Sunday Journal,* October 7, 1951, and *Modern Language Notes,* LXII (April 1952), 287–288.

The Riddle of Emily Dickinson by Rebecca Patterson, Providence *Sunday Journal,* November 4, 1951.

The Calvacade of the American Novel by Edward Wagenknecht, Providence *Sunday Journal,* May 25, 1952.

"Two Approaches to Melville" (*Melville's Quarrel with God* by Lawrance Thompson and *Melville's "Mardi": A Chartless Voyage* by Merrell Davis), *Virginia Quarterly Review,* XXVIII (Autumn 1952), 606–609.

Charles Stearns Wheeler: Friend of Emerson by J. O. Eidson, *American Literature,* XXIV (November 1952), 414–415.

1953

Frederick Goddard Tuckerman: An American Sonneteer by S. A. Golden, *American Literature,* XXIV (January 1953), 569–570.

Hawthorne's Fiction: The Light and the Dark by Richard Harter Fogle, Providence *Sunday Journal,* February 15, 1953, and *American Literature,* XXV (May 1953), 246–247. Reprinted in *Analyzing*

Literary Works: A Guide for College Students, ed. by Lee Steinmetz. Evanstown: Row, Peterson and Company, 1962, pp. 129–131.

Herman Melville: Cycle and Epicycle by Eleanor Melville Metcalf, Providence *Sunday Journal*, November 8, 1953.

1954

"The Southern Literary Revival" (*Southern Renascence: The Literature of the Modern South*, ed. by Louis D. Rubin, Jr., and Robert D. Jacobs), *Virginia Quarterly Review*, XXX (Winter 1954), 140–143, and Providence *Sunday Journal*, January 31, 1954.

Hawthorne's Faust: A Study of the Devil Archetype by William Bysshe Stein, *American Literature*, XXV (January 1954), 506–507. Reprinted in *Analyzing Literary Works: A Guide for College Students*, ed. by Lee Steinmetz. Evanstown: Row, Peterson and Company, 1962, pp. 131–133.

A Fable by William Faulkner, Providence *Sunday Journal*, August 1, 1954, and *Georgia Review*, XXII (Spring 1968).

1955

The Complex Fate: Hawthorne, James, and Some Other American Writers by Marius Bewley, *American Literature*, XXVI (January 1955), 580–583.

The South in American Literature, 1607–1900 by Jay B. Hubbell, Providence *Sunday Journal*, February 13, 1955, and *New England Quarterly*, XXVIII (March 1955), 113–116.

Hawthorne: A Critical Study by Hyatt Waggoner, *Saturday Review*, XXXVIII (March 26, 1955), 18–19.

Melville's *Journal of a Visit to Europe and the Levant*, ed. by Howard C. Horsford, Providence *Sunday Journal*, August 14, 1955.

The Opposing Self by Lionel Trilling, Providence *Sunday Journal*, September 4, 1955.

Poet and Psychiatrist: Merrill Moore, M.D. by Henry W. Wells, Nashville *Tennessean*, October 2, 1955.

1955-1956

Hawthorne's "Dr. Grimshawe's Secret," ed. by Edward Davidson, Providence *Sunday Journal*, August 14, 1955, and *American Literature*, XXVII (January 1956), 595–596.

1956

"The Exciting, Exotic South" (*A Southern Reader*, ed. by Willard Thorp), *Virginia Quarterly Review*, XXXII (Winter 1956), 150–153.

The Year of My Rebirth by Jesse Stuart, Nashville *Tennessean*, December 2, 1956.

1957

The Man in the Name: Essays on the Experience of Poetry by Leonard Unger, Nashville *Tennessean*, January 27, 1957, and *American Literature*, XXIX (May 1957), 227–228.

Still Rebels, Still Yankees and Other Essays by Donald Davidson, *New England Quarterly*, XXX (June 1957), 260–262.

1958

"Christian Schooling" (*The Christian Idea of Education, A Seminar at Kent School*, ed. by Edmund Fuller), *Modern Age*, II (Spring 1958), 202–204.

Eight American Authors: A Review of Research and Criticism, ed. by Floyd Stovall, *American Literature*, XXX (March 1958), 119–121.

The Social Ideas of Allen Tate by Willard Burnett Arnold, *American Literature*, XXX (May 1958), 260–261.

American Panorama, ed. by Eric Larrabee, *American Quarterly*, X (Summer 1958), 189.

The South In Northern Eyes, 1831–1861 by Howard R. Floan, *South Atlantic Quarterly*, LVII (Autumn 1958), 525–526.

1959

The Prophetic Voice in Modern Fiction by William R. Mueller, *Religious Education*, LIV (November–December 1959), 546.

Religion and American Democracy by Roy F. Nichols, *Mississippi Quarterly*, XII (Summer 1959), 154–155.

1960

Literature and the American Tradition by Leon Howard, *American Quarterly*, XII (Winter 1960), 528.

"The Achievement of Faulkner" (*William Faulkner: From Jefferson to the World* by Hyatt Waggoner), *Modern Age*, IV (Summer 1960), 321–323.

1961

Prodigal Puritan: A Life of Delia Bacon by Vivian C. Hopkins, *American Literature*, XXXII (January 1961), 476–478.

Nathaniel Hawthorne: Man and Writer by Edward Wagenknecht, *American Literature*, XXXIII (November 1961), 380–381.

Symbolism in Religion and Literature, ed. by Rollo May, *Georgia Review*, XV (Winter 1961), 463–464.

1962

Religious Perspectives in American Culture, ed. by James Ward Smith and A. Leland Jamison, *Theology Today*, XVIII (January 1962), 522–523.

The Novelist and the Passion Story by F. W. Dillistone, *Religious Education*, LVII (January–February 1962), 7.

1963

Inward Sky: The Mind and Heart of Nathaniel Hawthorne by Hubert H. Hoeltje, *American Literature*, XXXIV (January 1963), 577–578.

INDEX